T0334581

Automation and Its Macroeconomic Consequences

Theory, Evidence, and Social Impacts

Automation and Its Macroeconomic Consequences

Theory, Evidence, and Social Impacts

Klaus Prettner
University of Hohenheim, Institute of Economics, Stuttgart, Germany

David E. Bloom
Harvard T.H. Chan School of Public Health, Boston, MA, United States

ACADEMIC PRESS
An imprint of Elsevier

ELSEVIER

Academic Press is an imprint of Elsevier
125 London Wall, London EC2Y 5AS, United Kingdom
525 B Street, Suite 1650, San Diego, CA 92101, United States
50 Hampshire Street, 5th Floor, Cambridge, MA 02139, United States
The Boulevard, Langford Lane, Kidlington, Oxford OX5 1GB, United Kingdom

Notices
Knowledge and best practice in this field are constantly changing. As new research and experience broaden our understanding, changes in research methods, professional practices, or medical treatment may become necessary.

Practitioners and researchers must always rely on their own experience and knowledge in evaluating and using any information, methods, compounds, or experiments described herein. In using such information or methods they should be mindful of their own safety and the safety of others, including parties for whom they have a professional responsibility.

To the fullest extent of the law, neither the Publisher nor the authors, contributors, or editors, assume any liability for any injury and/or damage to persons or property as a matter of products liability, negligence or otherwise, or from any use or operation of any methods, products, instructions, or ideas contained in the material herein.

British Library Cataloguing-in-Publication Data
A catalogue record for this book is available from the British Library

Library of Congress Cataloging-in-Publication Data
A catalog record for this book is available from the Library of Congress

ISBN: 978-0-12-818028-0

For Information on all Academic Press publications
visit our website at https://www.elsevier.com/books-and-journals

Publisher: Brian Romer
Editorial Project Manager: Amy Moone
Production Project Manager: Niranjan Bhaskaran
Cover Designer: Mark Rogers

Typeset by MPS Limited, Chennai, India

Working together
to grow libraries in
developing countries

www.elsevier.com • www.bookaid.org

Dedication

The authors dedicate this book to their "very human" families, whose love and support could never be replaced.

Contents

Preface   xi

1. **Introduction**   1

   1.1 Technological progress and its economic consequences   1
   1.2 The economic consequences of automation: could this time be different?   5
   1.3 The social impacts of automation   7
   1.4 The race against, or the race with, the machine?   11
   1.5 Summary   13
   References   14

2. **The stylized facts**   21

   2.1 Adoption of automation technology   21
   2.2 Dynamics of economic growth and welfare   22
   2.3 Dynamics of the labor force and of unemployment   30
   2.4 The evolution of inequality   34
   2.5 Summary   41
   References   42

3. **Empirical evidence on the economic effects of automation**   47

   3.1 Occupations, jobs, and tasks susceptible to automation   47
   3.2 Cross-country evidence on the economic consequences of automation   51
   3.3 Summary   62
   References   63

4. **A simple macroeconomic framework for analyzing automation**   67

   4.1 Preliminaries and definitions   67
     4.1.1 Growth rates in discrete and in continuous time   67
     4.1.2 Representative individuals and representative firms   69
     4.1.3 Aggregate production function   70

4.2 The simplest version of the standard 1956 Solow model in
discrete time   75
4.3 The Solow model in continuous time with technological
progress and with population growth   82
4.4 The Solow model with automation   90
4.5 Endogenization of the share of investment in traditional
physical capital   98
4.6 Automation and wage inequality   101
4.7 The tradeoff between growth and inequality   104
4.8 Summary   107
References   109

5.   Endogenous savings and extensions of the baseline
     model   113

5.1 Introduction   113
5.2 Cookbook procedures for static and dynamic
optimization   114
     5.2.1 The method of Lagrange   115
     5.2.2 The method of Karush–Kuhn–Tucker   123
     5.2.3 Dynamic optimization in discrete time in the case of
            two time periods   124
     5.2.4 Dynamic optimization in continuous time   126
5.3 Endogenous savings in the Ramsey–Cass–Koopmans model   131
5.4 Automation in the Ramsey–Cass–Koopmans model   138
5.5 Endogenous savings in the OLG model   140
5.6 Automation in the OLG model   147
5.7 Discussion of extensions   150
     5.7.1 Endogenous technological progress and automation   150
     5.7.2 Technological unemployment   152
     5.7.3 International trade, foreign direct investment, and
            automation   154
5.8 Summary   156
References   158

6.   Automation as a potential response to the challenges
     of demographic change   163

6.1 Introduction and stylized facts   163
6.2 Demographic change and its economic consequences   168
6.3 How robots can help   172
6.4 Future employment projections based on automation   175
6.5 The reverse channel: could robots affect demography?   176
6.6 Summary   177
References   179

7.	Policy challenges	187
	7.1 The challenges	187
	7.2 Education as a strategy to cope with the negative effects of automation	188
	7.3 Labor market policies	190
	7.4 Taxation in the age of automation	192
	7.5 Social security in the age of automation	197
	7.6 Demand-side policies	201
	7.7 Summary	202
	References	205
8.	Peering into the future: long-run economic and social consequences of automation; with an epilogue on COVID-19	209
	8.1 Joblessness, misery, and deaths of despair or "the happy leisure society"?	210
	8.2 Spatial and regional implications: the future of cities	212
	8.3 The question of how we care for each other	214
	8.4 The meaning of being human	216
	8.5 Epilogue on COVID-19	217
	References	218
Index		223

Preface

News reports abound that robots, three-dimensional (3D) printers, and algorithms based on machine learning are outperforming humans in many different tasks (see, e.g., Davison, 2017; Financial Times, 2019; The Economist, 2014, 2017a, 2019). Industrial robots have long been familiar sights on assembly lines in many businesses—especially in the automotive industry. Recent advances, however, relate to tasks and activities that were seen as being nonautomatable just a few years ago. For example, because driving cars and trucks requires many instinctual moves and reactions to unforeseen events, it has been regarded as an activity that an algorithm cannot perform. Yet driverless cars are now being tested on public roads, and self-driving cars and trucks are widely expected to become increasingly common within the next 10−20 years—and much safer than human drivers (Chen, Kuhn, Prettner, & Bloom, 2019; The Economist, 2018). Producing customized parts, prototypes, and medical implants without any human labor input has become feasible by advances in 3D printing (Abeliansky, Algur, Bloom, & Prettner, 2020; The Economist, 2016, 2017b). Algorithms can diagnose illness—particularly rare diseases—and reliably interpret X-rays based on advances in machine learning, the availability of large datasets to inform the algorithms, and the secular rise in computing power over the preceding decades (Ford, 2015). While programs have written simple reports and straightforward newsflashes for quite some time, more surprising is that computers have surmounted more complex challenges, such as writing novels and conducting experiments to uncover some laws of nature (Barrie, 2014; National Science Foundation, 2009; Schmidt & Lipson, 2009).

These unprecedented technological advances have raised fears that society is unprepared for the attendant—potentially dramatic—economic and social changes that may be looming. The most pressing concern from an economic perspective is that the replacement of labor by automation technologies will lead to high rates of technological unemployment. In addition, because less-educated persons are likely more susceptible to displacement by automation, some fear that wage inequality might rise. Moreover, in contrast to the wages of workers, the revenue that robots and other automation technologies generate flows to the owners of these devices, who are predominantly wealthy. Thus, functional income distribution might change such that capital's share of income rises further and the labor income share correspondingly decreases. Because labor income is much more equally distributed than wealth and the returns thereof, such changes would mechanically lead to a rise in overall inequality.

The fear that new technologies might create technological unemployment and raise inequality—sometimes referred to as "automation anxiety" and a potential source of political resistance—is not a recent phenomenon (LeVine, 2018; see Frey, 2019 for an overview). The emergence of new types of machines that threaten to replace workers has always sparked resistance in different parts of the population (e.g., the Luddite uprisings in the 19th century). Also the economic literature analyzing the effects of technological changes from different angles (Ricardo, 1821; Wicksell, 1906) concedes that the course of technological progress does not only produce winners. However, past dire predictions of mass unemployment and widespread poverty due to the emergence of modern machines did not come to pass.

The crucial question to ask in the age of automation is whether this time will be different (Ford, 2015). Industrial robots, 3D printers, and devices based on machine learning are not only increasing labor productivity and thereby allowing workers to produce more output with less labor input, but are also performing their tasks with full autonomy—i.e., they are replacing workers altogether. For example, while the assembly line raised the productivity of those workers who were still required to staff the lines in factories (and thereby their wages), an industrial robot does not require direct labor input and thus replaces workers without raising their productivity (see Growiec, 2019 for a discussion of the important distinctions among mechanization, automation, and artificial intelligence (AI)). To what extent this difference between machines' historical effects and robots' contemporaneous effects changes the likely outcomes of technological progress in the future remains an open and highly important question.

While the potential economic effects of automation frighten many, other ramifications of an automated future will potentially redefine the patterns and rules by which we live together as a society. For example:

- Driverless cars will likely reduce the expense of commuting in terms of opportunity costs. Easier commuting could lead to changes in settlement patterns as cities are viewed as less attractive spaces to live (as opposed to work), the elimination of public transport systems, and potentially dramatic increases in the relative price of rural homes versus urban homes. The loss of public transportation and the rise in the price of rural homes could in turn reinforce the negative direct effects of automation on inequality discussed previously.
- The implications of living together with robots might be profound for human relations, and many related ethical and legal questions are highly complex. What happens if the robot you own hurts someone or commits

a crime? What is the definition of and what are the limits to ownership when applied to a robot—a device that operates with at least a modicum of its own (artificial) intelligence? Is having sex with a robot marketed for that purpose the same as prostitution?

● Many people are uncomfortable with the superiority of computers over humans when it comes to performing different tasks; some foreboding predictions even speculate that robots will displace humans from the top of the "evolutionary ladder." Massachusetts Institute of Technology physicist Tegmark (2017) shows that this scenario is not as easily dismissed as we might like, speculating that things could go wrong even without the "hostile" AI that we know from movies. All that is required for potentially serious trouble is that the objective function of a superintelligent AI differs from that of humans. Tegmark (2017) describes constructing a dam for electricity generation as an example. If humans flood the valley after the construction of the dam, they are not, in general, hostile toward the ants that populate that valley. However, this lack of hostility does not help the ants. Or, in the words of Elon Musk, "if there is a superintelligence whose utility function is something that's detrimental to humanity, then it will have a very bad effect ... it could be something like getting rid of spam email ... well, the best way to get rid of spam is to get rid of humans."[1]

While some understandable fears accompany the rapidity of automation, automation also has many positive effects that we are already experiencing and that will intensify in the future. For example, industrial robots often substitute for human labor in physically demanding or even unhealthy tasks, such as painting cars and lifting heavy goods and equipment. Thus, workers are often spared these types of drudgery and can focus on more pleasant tasks. In addition, robot-produced goods typically become cheaper, which benefits consumers greatly, and 3D printing enables customized designs that might not have been available before. Yet another example is the benefit many patients receive from improved diagnostic tools and better targeted treatments due to advances in machine learning. From a macroeconomic perspective, rich countries are currently facing population aging and declines in their labor force. Robots could help to alleviate such challenges (Abeliansky & Prettner, 2017; Abeliansky et al., 2020; Acemoglu & Restrepo, 2018).

From a policy perspective, finding ways to cope with the challenges of automation, such as a declining labor income share, will become important because social security systems and pension schemes are predominantly based on worker contributions. In this debate, many favor the introduction of robot taxes. For example, Bill Gates argued in a 2017 interview that "taxation is certainly a better way to handle it than just banning some elements of it" and sketched out

---

1. Quoted from Vanity Fair, 2014, *New establishment summit interview*. Retrieved from https://www.youtube.com/watch?time_continue = 63&v = Ze0_1vczikA.

how such a tax could be levied: "Some of it can come on the profits that are generated by the labor-saving efficiency there. Some of it can come directly in some type of robot tax" (Delaney, 2017). However, in practical terms, problems can emerge with the implementation of such schemes. For example, the tax would have to be introduced in many countries to avoid the relocation of the mobile production factor "capital" to jurisdictions that do not collect the tax (Gasteiger & Prettner, 2020). Furthermore, if both education and technology are endogenous, taxing robots could discourage technological progress and educational investments to the extent that the welfare effects of a robot tax will be negative (Prettner & Strulik, 2020). As another response to automation, some argue that the introduction of an unconditional (universal) basic income will become necessary.

At the time this manuscript went to press, the world was in the grip of the COVID-19 pandemic. Notwithstanding the economic and social challenges posed by robots, we would note that they can also facilitate and support our adaptations to the continued threat of COVID-19 and of other infectious disease risks that lurk ahead. Indeed, robots make social and physical distancing among humans easier, and they can be designed to undertake—safely—a wide range of essential tasks ranging from personal grooming, medical exams, and shopping/delivery to detecting disinformation, physical training, and deep cleaning/sanitization. On the other hand, the success of robots, automation, and AI in slowing disease transmission and cushioning the impacts of communicable diseases on business activities may magnify the economic consequences for workers of actual and expected pandemics.

This volume will not be able to solve—or even address—all of the ethical, legal, and existential dilemmas that emerge in the age of widespread automation or give you useful advice on how to behave when coveting a neighbor's robot. It aims to shed some light on the possible macroeconomic effects and socioeconomic consequences of automation. We also hope to sketch some useful policy initiatives to cope with the negative effects of automation. Given the speed of change we see on a daily basis, some of our references, examples, numbers, and predictions are likely to become outdated quickly. Therefore, we recognize that our endeavor can be only a first step in understanding the far-reaching consequences of automation.

A tour of the book

Chapter 1 provides an overview of historical forms of technological progress and recent developments in automation and AI. In so doing, it also summarizes the public debate on the potential benefits and challenges of these developments and compares historical and current arguments. In this context, we try to identify aspects that still hold true in the debate on the effects of new technologies and those that are either outdated or based on mixing up concepts such as automation, mechanization, robotics, and AI. In addition, we describe potential changes due to automation and AI that go way beyond economic effects, starting from legal questions, to the choices of whether to live in a city or in the countryside, and even to interpersonal relationships.

Chapter 2 provides an overview of the stylized facts of automation, the long-run evolution of per capita income in the United States and other rich countries, the development of employment and hours worked in the United States over the last several decades, the evolution of income inequality, and the share of aggregate income that accrues to labor as a factor of production. In the discussion, we identify theoretical explanations for these stylized facts, focusing on those dynamics in which automation might play a major role.

Chapter 3 is devoted to a survey of recent empirical findings that go beyond mere descriptive analyses. First, we discuss the results of the literature that identify the technological potential of substituting robots for workers, in particular, the prominent works by Frey and Osborne (2013, 2017) and Arntz, Gregory, and Zierahn (2016, 2017). We then argue that economic considerations deserve more scrutiny when discussing the potential substitution of human labor by robots because replacing a cheap and flexible worker with an expensive and inflexible robot might not always pay off (Abeliansky et al., 2020; Bloom, McKenna, & Prettner, 2019). Finally, we discuss the aggregate macroeconomic effects of automation based on several prominent recent studies that, despite many differences, surprisingly all tend to agree that automation will have (1) positive productivity effects; (2) negative employment and wage effects for low-skilled workers in manufacturing, but either insignificant or even positive employment and wage effects for high-skilled workers; (3) a positive effect on job creation in the service sector; and (4) a negative effect on the labor income share. These aspects are those that we model from a theoretical perspective in the two subsequent chapters.

Chapter 4, the core chapter of the book from a theoretical perspective, first introduces the basic model of economic growth (Solow, 1956) as virtually all classes on economic growth teach it. Subsequently, we propose an automation-augmented Solow-like model of economic growth that is capable of generating the main results that the empirical literature finds when discussing the effects of automation (increasing per capita GDP and a declining labor income share). This framework is quite flexible, and relaxing various model assumptions can provide additional insights that the baseline framework cannot, for example, on the automation-driven effects on wage inequality in a model version that allows for skill-specific heterogeneity of workers. Finally, we discuss the potential welfare effects of automation based on the specifications of different social welfare functions.

Chapter 5 is an extension of Chapter 4 that can be used in advanced courses on automation at the bachelor's degree level or in introductory courses at the master's degree level. It begins with a discussion of the main mathematical tools of static and dynamic optimization and describes procedures for solving the corresponding types of problems. We then apply these techniques to endogenize the consumption-savings decision of households and to characterize the two workhorse models of modern macroeconomics: the neoclassical Ramsey−Cass−Koopmans model (Cass, 1965; Koopmans, 1965; Ramsey, 1928) and the Diamond (1965) overlapping generations (OLG) model. Subsequently, we augment these models with automation and show how the results differ (1) between the Ramsey−Cass−Koopmans model and the OLG model and (2) between the baseline automation-augmented Solow (1956) model introduced in Chapter 4 and the models with an endogenous consumption-savings choice in Chapter 5. The chapter ends with a brief overview of the effects of automation in (1) R&D-based economic growth models, (2) search and matching models of the labor market, and (3) models of international trade and offshoring.

Chapter 6 discusses the stylized facts of demographic change from a worldwide perspective and in Organisation for Economic Co-operation and Development (OECD) countries. Then, it delves into the challenges that declining fertility, rising life expectancy, and a declining workforce pose for economic wellbeing and for the sustainability of social security systems and pension schemes. Next, the chapter discusses the extent to which robots can help in mitigating the negative effects of demographic change and presents evidence suggesting that aging economies are indeed investing more in robot adoption than countries that are not aging that rapidly.

Chapter 7 is devoted to discussing potential economic policies that might help to cope with some anticipated negative effects of automation, such as increasing inequality, declining labor income shares, and rising unemployment among some skill groups. First, we discuss rather uncontroversial policy measures such as investments in education and skill upgrading for those who are substituted by robots, but we also argue that these policies might not be a silver bullet to cope with all automation-related challenges (compare with Prettner & Strulik, 2020). We then address the question of whether and how robots should be taxed and which alternatives to labor taxation are available in times when the labor income share declines. Finally, we address issues related to reforming social security and the introduction of conditional and unconditional (universal) basic income schemes.

Finally, Chapter 8 provides an outlook of possible future scenarios of the social and economic implications of automation and related moral issues. In this chapter, we discuss topics such as automated warfare, automation-driven deaths of despair, and human augmentation. This chapter is more speculative than most of the other chapters, which tend to be built on theoretical models and empirical evidence.

Recommended use of the book in teaching

This book is mainly intended as a core textbook for introductory courses at the bachelor's degree level that are related to (1) automation and technological change, (2) economic growth, (3) technology-induced inequality dynamics, and (4) economic policy responses to technological change. For such courses, we recommend Chapters 1−4 and 6−8. A syllabus for such a course could be structured roughly along the following lines:

- Topic 1: Introduction and motivation (Chapter 1).
- Topic 2: The stylized facts of automation, economic growth, and inequality (Chapter 2).
- Topic 3: Empirical results on the effects of automation (Chapter 3).
- Topic 4: Introduction to economic modeling (Section 4.1).
- Topic 5: The Solow (1956) model as the basic framework for the analysis of economic growth (Sections 4.2 and 4.3).
- Topic 6: The automation-augmented Solow (1956) model (Section 4.4).
- Topic 7: Extensions of the automation-augmented Solow (1956) model (Sections 4.5 and 4.6).
- Topic 8: The welfare effects of automation (Section 4.7).
- Topic 9: Automation as a solution to the challenges of population aging (Chapter 6).
- Topic 10: Implications of automation for economic policy (Section 4.7 and Chapter 7).
- Topic 11: A glimpse into the future of automation and AI (Chapter 8).

This book could also be useful for more advanced courses at the bachelor's degree level or for introductory courses at the graduate level on automation and economic growth. In this case, we recommend including the more advanced topics discussed in Chapter 5. A syllabus for such a course could be structured along the following lines:

- Topic 1: Introduction and motivation (Chapter 1).
- Topic 2: The stylized facts of automation, economic growth, and inequality (Chapter 2).
- Topic 3: Empirical results on the effects of automation (Chapter 3).
- Topic 4: Introduction to economic modeling and optimization (Section 4.1 and Sections 5.1 and 5.2).
- Topic 4: The Solow (1956) model as the basic framework for the analysis of economic growth (Sections 4.2 and 4.3).
- Topic 5: The automation-augmented Solow (1956) model and its extensions (Sections 4.4−4.6).
- Topic 6: The welfare effects of automation (Section 4.7).
- Topic 7: Workhorse models of modern macroeconomics I: the representative agent neoclassical growth model (Section 5.3).

xviii Preface

- Topic 8: Workhorse models of modern macroeconomics II: the overlapping generations model (Section 5.5).
- Topic 9: Automation in the workhorse models of modern macroeconomics (Sections 5.4 and 5.6).
- Topic 10: Extensions: automation in the context of endogenous technological progress, search and matching on the labor market, and international trade (Section 5.7).
- Topic 11: Automation as a solution to the challenges of population aging (Chapter 6).
- Topic 12: Implications of automation for economic policy (Section 4.7 and Chapter 7).
- Topic 13: A glimpse into the future of automation and AI (Chapter 8).

In addition, this book can also be used as a supplemental source for other courses at the introductory level, for example, on optimization and its economic applications (Chapter 5); on macroeconomics, particularly when courses deal with the medium and the long run (Chapters 4 and 5); and on technological progress in general. Finally, we hope that the book might be useful to experts in other fields, journalists, and policymakers. For this audience, the more interesting chapters might be Chapters 1−3 and 6−8.

Acknowledgments

Of course, a book like this would not have been possible without many insightful conversations on issues related to automation and without many helpful comments and recommendations from colleagues at universities and research institutes, feedback from students, advice from publishers and editors, and, of course, the great support of our families throughout this endeavor and way beyond. In particular, we would like to thank Ana Abeliansky, Jeff Adams, Eda Algur, Philipp Baudy, Tobias Baur, Thomas Beißinger, Scott J. Bentley, Matthias Beulmann, Niranjan Bhaskaran, Lakshmi Bloom, Sahil Bloom, Sonali Bloom, Julia Bock-Schappelwein, Sebastian Böhm, Dario Cords, Giacomo Corneo, Daniel Dujava, Tora Estep, Michael Evers, Maddalena Ferranna, Inga Freund, Emanuel Gasteiger, Niels Geiger, Volker Grossmann, Harald Hagemann, Yueqing Hao, Franz X. Hof, Karen Horn, Andreas Irmen, Sheela Bernardine Josy, Torben Klarl, Mark Knell, Wolfgang Koller, Vadim Kufenko, Michael Kuhn, Astrid Krenz, Martin Labaj, Clemens Lankisch, Mikulas Luptacik, Bernhard Mahlberg, Inmaculada Martinez-Zarzoso, Anna Matysiak, Pedro Mazeda Gil, Volker Meier, Redding Morse, Graham Nisbet, Catherine Prettner, Alexia Prskawetz, Andreas Pyka, Miguel Sanchez-Romero, Julia Schmid, Johannes Schwarzer, JP Sevilla, Christa Simon, Alfonso Sousa-Poza, Holger Strulik, Paul Tscheuschner, Francesco Venturini, Huang Xu, Alexander Zeuner, Rafaela Zierbus, Oliver Zwiessler, and the participants of research seminars at the University of Bremen, the University of Economics in Bratislava, the University of Hohenheim, the Ludwig Maximilian University of Munich, the University of Porto, the University of Tübingen, the University of Würzburg, and the Austrian Institute of Economic Research for highly valuable discussions, comments on parts of the book or on drafts of some of the research papers on which the book is based, and various helpful suggestions for improvements. Some of the book's materials draw on the lectures "Economic Growth," "Technology and Growth," "Structural Change and Inequality," "Advanced Economic Growth," "Economics of Inequality," and "Advanced Topics in Macroeconomics" taught at the University of Hohenheim; the lecture "Quantitative Solution of Endogenous Growth Models" taught at the University of Aarhus; the lectures "Open Economy Macroeconomics" and "Advanced Macroeconomics" taught at the University of Göttingen; and the lecture "Dynamic Macroeconomics" taught at the Vienna University of Technology. We are indebted to the students in these courses for their valuable feedback and their constructive criticism. Preparation of this book was supported in part by grants from the National Institute on Aging of the National Institutes of Health under Award Number P30AG024409, and from the Carnegie Corporation of New York.

References

Abeliansky, A., Algur, E., Bloom, D. E., & Prettner, K. (2020). The Future of Work: Meeting the Global Challenge of Demographic Change and Automation. *International Labour Review*. (forthcoming).

Abeliansky, A., & Prettner, K. (2017). Automation and demographic change. University of Hohenheim, Discussion Papers in Business, Economics, and Social Sciences 05-2017.

Acemoglu, D., & Restrepo, P. (2018). *Demographics and automation*. Cambridge, MA: National Bureau of Economic Research, NBER Working Paper 24421.

Arntz, M., Gregory, T., & Zierahn, U. (2016). *The risk of automation for jobs in OECD countries. A comparative analysis*. Paris: OECD Publishing, OECD Social, Employment and Migration Working Papers No. 189.

Arntz, M., Gregory, T., & Zierahn, U. (2017). Revisiting the risk of automation. *Economics Letters, 159*, 157−160.

Barrie, J. (2014). Computers are writing novels: Read a few samples here. Retrieved from <http://www.businessinsider.com/novels-written-by-computers-2014-11?IR = T>. Accessed 22.01.17.

Bloom, D., McKenna, M., & Prettner, K. (2019). Global employment and decent jobs, 2010-2030: The forces of demography and automation. *International Social Security Review, 72* (3), 43−78.

Cass, D. (1965). Optimum growth in an aggregate model of capital accumulation. *The Review of Economic Studies, 32*(3), 233−240.

Chen, S., Kuhn, M., Prettner, K., & Bloom, D. (2019). The global macroeconomic burden of road injuries: Estimates and projections for 166 countries. *The Lancet Planetary Health, 3* (9), e390−e398.

Davison, N. (2017). 3D-printed cities: Is this the future? *The Guardian*. Retrieved from <https://www.theguardian.com/cities/2015/feb/26/3d-printed-cities-future-housing-architecture>. Accessed 08.08.18.

Delaney, K. J. (2017). Droid duties: The robot that takes your job should pay taxes, says Bill Gates. Retrieved from <https://qz.com/911968/bill-gates-the-robot-that-takes-your-job-should-pay-taxes/>. Accessed 01.06.17.

Diamond, P. A. (1965). National debt in a neoclassical growth model. *American Economic Review, 55*(5), 1126−1150.

Financial Times (2019). Robots/ageing Japan: I, carebot. Retrieved from <https://www.ft.com/content/314c65a8-8829-11e9-a028-86cea8523dc2>. Accessed 24.11.19.

Ford, M. (2015). *Rise of the robots: Technology and the threat of a jobless future*. New York: Basic Books.

Frey, C. B. (2019). *The technology trap: Capital, labor, and power in the age of automation*. Princeton, NJ: Princeton University Press.

Frey, C. B., & Osborne, M. A. (2013). The future of employment: How susceptible are jobs to computerisation? Retrieved from <https://web.archive.org/web/20150109185039/http://www.oxfordmartin.ox.ac.uk/downloads/academic/The_Future_of_Employment.pdf>. Accessed 15.12.19.

Frey, C. B., & Osborne, M. A. (2017). The future of employment: How susceptible are jobs to computerisation? *Technological Forecasting and Social Change, 114*(C), 254−280.

Gasteiger E., & Prettner K. (2020). Automation, Stagnation, and the Implications of a Robot Tax. Macroeconomic Dynamics. (forthcoming).

Growiec, J. (2019). The hardware-software model: A new conceptual framework of production, R&D, and growth with AI. Warszawa, Poland: Warsaw School of Economics, Working Paper 2019-042.

Koopmans, T. C. (1965). *On the concept of optimal economic growth*. Johansen, J. (Ed). *The econometric approach to development planning*. North Holland: Amsterdam.

LeVine, S. (2018). The anti-robot uprising is coming. Retrieved from <https://www.axios.com/anti-robot-uprising-automation-anxiety-carl-frey-fa8c4441-f7f2-4538-b8a5-8531a1255074.html>. Accessed 11.05.19.

National Science Foundation (2009). Maybe robots dream of electric sheep, but can they do science? Press release. Retrieved from <https://www.nsf.gov/news/news_summ.jsp?cntn_id = 114495>. Accessed 01.01.18.

Prettner, K., & Strulik, H. (2020). Innovation, automation, and inequality: Policy challenges in the race against the machine. *Journal of Monetary Economics*. (forthcoming).

Ramsey, F. P. (1928). A mathematical theory of saving. *The Economic Journal, 38*(152), 543−559.

Ricardo, D. (1821). *On the principles of political economy and taxation* (3rd ed.). London: John Murray.

Schmidt, M., & Lipson, H. (2009). Distilling free-form natural laws from experimental data. *Science, 324*(5923), 81−85.

Solow, R. M. (1956). A contribution to the theory of economic growth. *The Quarterly Journal of Economics, 70*(1), 65−94.

Tegmark, M. (2017). *Life 3.0: Being human in the age of artificial intelligence*. London: Allen Lane−Penguin Random House.

The Economist. (2014). Immigrants from the future. A special report on robots. March 27, 2014.

The Economist. (2016). A printed smile. 3D printing is coming of age as a manufacturing technique. April 30, 2016.

The Economist. (2017a). Adidas's high-tech factory brings production back to Germany. Making trainers with robots and 3D printers. January 14, 2017.

The Economist. (2017b). Ghost in the machine: Rio Tinto puts its faith in driverless trucks, trains and drilling rigs. December 7, 2017.

The Economist. (2018). Reinventing wheels. Special report on autonomous driving. March 1, 2018.

The Economist. (2019). Grandma's little helper. An ageing world needs more resourceful robots. February 14, 2019.

Wicksell, K. (1906). *Lectures on political economy*. London: Routledge & Kegan Paul.

Chapter 1

Introduction

1.1 Technological progress and its economic consequences

The exceptionally rapid pace of technological progress since the Industrial Revolution has allowed many countries and their inhabitants to reach historically unique levels of economic and social prosperity.[1] In the 18th century, global life expectancy hovered around 30 years, almost every other child died before the age of 5 years, average income levels were barely above subsistence level, and close to 90% of the population was illiterate (Maddison, 2010; Roser, 2018). The situation could not be more different a bit more than 200 years later. Global average life expectancy is above 70 years, more than 95% of children survive their fifth birthday, average real incomes have increased by a factor of 11 on a global scale, and illiteracy is below 15% (Maddison, 2010; Roser, 2018). Because these numbers are collective averages, they imply that some richer countries such as Australia, Canada, France, Germany, Japan, the United Kingdom, and the United States have experienced substantially larger gains and more pronounced transformations.

Notwithstanding the positive effects of technological progress on material well-being and quality-of-life in the aggregate, some have expressed fears about the distribution of the gains among different segments of the population—in terms of high unemployment, the impoverishment of workers, and the evolving nature of work in general (see, e.g., Frey, 2019; Scott & Gratton, 2020; Geiger, Prettner, & Schwarzer, 2018;

---

1. For a nonexhaustive list of articles and books showing that technological progress is the central driver of economic growth and well-being and analyzing the extent to which technological progress has profoundly changed our lives over the last few centuries, see Lucas (1988), Adams (1990), Romer (1990), Grossman and Helpman (1991), Aghion and Howitt (1992, 1999, 2009), Jones (1995, 2001, 2002, 2015), Nordhaus (1996, 2007), Jones and Williams (1998, 2000), Kortum (1997), Dinopoulos and Thompson (1998), Landes (1998), Peretto (1998), Segerström (1998), Young (1998), Howitt (1999), Galor and Weil (2000), Dalgaard and Kreiner (2001), Kögel and Prskawetz (2001), Hansen and Prescott (2002), Mokyr (2002, 2005, 2018); Tamura (2002), Barro and Sala-i-Martin (2004), Doepke (2004), Galor (2005, 2011), Acemoglu (2009), Jones and Vollrath (2009), Morris (2010), Weil (2012), Grossmann, Steger, and Trimborn (2013), Peretto and Saeter (2013), Strulik, Prettner, and Prskawetz (2013), Gersbach and Schneider (2015), Kaplan (2015), Wootton (2015), Avent (2016), Brynjolfsson and McAfee (2016), Gordon (2016), Norberg (2016), Prettner and Werner (2016), Ross (2016), Acemoglu and Restrepo (2018b), Gersbach, Sorger, and Amon (2018), and Frey (2019).

Automation and its Macroeconomic Consequences. DOI: https://doi.org/10.1016/B978-0-12-818028-0.00001-6

Prettner, Geiger, & Schwarzer, 2018). As early as 1776, Adam Smith expressed some concerns in his book *An Inquiry into the Nature and Causes of the Wealth of Nations* (1776). While generally optimistic about the quantitative employment effects of technological progress, the accompanying increase in the division of labor could, in his view, result in a greater monotony of work and thus less pleasant working conditions.

The most prominent resistance to new technologies from a historical perspective emerged in the Luddite uprisings, which took place between 1811 and 1816 in England. These violent protests were directed against the introduction of the mechanical loom, which raised weaving productivity by a factor of more than three. The Luddites destroyed weaving machines as their main form of protest in uprisings that the military ultimately suppressed. In response to the riots, David Ricardo revised his previous view that the introduction of a new technology would, without fail, be advantageous to all. In the newly appended chapter "On Machinery" in the third edition of his book *On the Principles of Political Economy and Taxation*, Ricardo (1821) examines the conditions under which technological unemployment can arise in the wake of technological changes. He claims that advances in the form of new machines could lead to higher unemployment over time, given that capitalists spend heavily on the new labor-saving machines and reduce the overall outlays for wages. This in turn could lead to competition among workers, reducing their wages. These changes could even lead to starvation in some parts of the population as the price of food could be put out of reach for some households. Ricardo's analysis, which remains influential to this day, led to significant contributions by well-known economists such as Wicksell (1906), Hicks (1973), and Samuelson (1988).

In contrast to Ricardo (1821), Wicksell (1906) views labor supply as inelastic and wages as elastic, such that reducing wages could avert technological unemployment. Wages only become inelastic when they are at the subsistence level and cannot fall further. Only from that point onward might unemployment rise, in which case Wicksell (1906) recommends a social security system financed by the profits of capital owners—who gain from the introduction of new machines—as a remedy for technological unemployment (see also Hagemann, 1995; Humphrey, 2004). On top of these arguments, Wicksell (1906) questions whether the new technologies introduced in the 19th century are always labor saving and reduce the marginal value product of workers; in fact, he expected the opposite to be true because the advances were at least somewhat complementary to the production factor of labor. This argument, however, cannot be transferred unconditionally to today's technological debate in the area of automation, as we will see later.

This brief discussion already demonstrates that the expected economic effects of technological change in general and of automation in particular depend crucially on the underlying modeling assumptions. Thus, from a theoretical perspective, the likely outcomes of technological changes in terms of employment, inequality, and overall economic growth and well-being are rather sensitive to variations in the underlying framework. Consequently, complementing theoretical considerations with empirical analyses to gauge the total effects of automation is particularly important.

If we depart from theoretical considerations that have shaped historical debates and look more closely at the data, clearly some of the fears regarding the economic effects of technological changes were overblown. As far as technological unemployment is concerned, a record number of persons are employed worldwide today and unemployment rates are comparatively low.[2] Furthermore, at least in industrialized countries, mass starvation has been eradicated.

The negative economic consequences of technological changes that many feared did not materialize primarily for the following three reasons: first, technological developments triggered strong growth in income levels and declines in the relative price of the goods that were produced with the advanced technologies. As a result, aggregate demand increased to such an extent that, despite the increase in labor productivity due to technological progress, the volume of work did not decrease; on the contrary, it often increased. Take, for example, the power loom that raised productivity in weaving (by a bit more than a factor of three). If the overall increase in wages and the relative price decline of textiles due to better technology lead to a rise in demand by a factor of five, then even more workers are needed in the new long-run equilibrium for weaving. Of course, this mechanism only works when labor remains an essential input in operating the looms. In general, the described mechanism is relevant for technologies that are, to some extent, complementary to labor. However, this mechanism might not be operative in the age of automation because—if we take the definition of automation seriously—it implies a perfect and complete substitution of capital for labor (see, e.g., Merriam-Webster, 2017, for the formal definition of automation and Acemoglu & Restrepo, 2018b; Growiec, 2019; Hémous & Olsen, 2018; Prettner, 2019; and Prettner & Strulik, 2020, for the differences in the economic effects of automation versus other forms of technological progress such as mechanization).[3]

The second reason why past technological changes did not result in mass unemployment is the structural transformation of modern industrialized economies (cf. Vermeulen, Kesselhut, Pyka, & Saviotti, 2018; Vermeulen, Pyka,

---

2. This does not necessarily imply that the overall number of labor hours worked are also at an all-time high because average hours worked per employee have been decreasing over the past decades and many jobs are now part time. In addition, the sheer fact of high employment tells us nothing about working conditions, wages, etc. (Bloom, McKenna, & Prettner, 2019).

3. Of course, in reality, the substitutability between robots and workers might not yet be perfect for many tasks and sometimes substituting for human workers might be impossible. However, as we will show later in the book, most effects of automation in the perfect substitutability case carry over to the case in which the substitutability is not yet perfect.

& Saviotti, 2020). Two hundred years ago, most of the population was employed in agriculture producing food. Today, the employment share of agriculture in developed countries is below 5% (see, e.g., Herrendorf, Rogerson, & Valentinyi, 2014). Where did all that labor go? Of course, entirely new employment possibilities emerged in manufacturing due to technological changes. More important, a whole new sector emerged: labor-intensive services. Two factors drove the shift in employment away from agriculture and later from manufacturing:

- The first factor was the increasing demand for services because the income elasticity of many services is well above unity since they often represent a kind of luxury good. By contrast, the income elasticity of agricultural production, in particular of food, is typically well below unity because consumers are subject to satiation. With this structure of nonhomothetic preferences, rising income levels imply a mechanical rise in the demand for services and thus, a rising employment share of the service sector.
- The second factor is that technological progress raised productivity in agriculture and manufacturing such that fewer workers were needed to satisfy the limited demand of goods that exhibit an income elasticity below unity. Thus the higher productivity set workers free and drove them into services, where productivity did not rise that much (cf. Autor & Dorn, 2013; Baumol & Bowen, 1966).

Based on these arguments, Cowen (2013, p. 23) claims that demand will always exist for increasingly more personal services by high-income earners or by the wealthy. The reason is that opportunities always exist "to make them feel better. Better about the world. Better about themselves. Better about what they have achieved." Two hundred years ago, when most people lived close to the subsistence level, the modern labor structure—wherein the majority of the population is employed in the service sector in occupations such as care assistant, nursery school teacher, nutrition adviser, marketing expert, manicurist, and yoga instructor—would have been inconceivable. People would not have been willing or able to spend money on such services when living close to the subsistence level.

The third main reason why employment did not decrease in the face of technological progress is that the production and maintenance of labor-saving machines intrinsically requires human workers. Thus, historically, one possible adjustment effect to reduce the pressure of technological progress on employment was that the producers of machines hired additional workers to create, install, operate, and fix the devices (which we call the "machine production argument"). However, the anticipated increase in automation may also lead to increased automated production of machines, robots, and three-dimensional (3D) printers. Consequently, the positive employment effects regarding the machine production argument might be diminished in the future (see also Hicks, 1973, and Lowe, 1976, for earlier versions of this argument).

1.2 The economic consequences of automation: Could this time be different?

Automation can be performed in various ways. Most frequently, robots and 3D printers are referred to as devices that can fully automate certain tasks. However, automation also comprises algorithms that automate stock trading, search for precedent cases in law firms, scan X-rays, write newsflashes, drive cars, etc. The central question in terms of automation is whether this time will be different (Ford, 2015): will the use of robots, 3D printers, and algorithms based on machine learning that can fully substitute for workers yield another human labor adjustment along the lines described above—or promote its obsolescence? Recent developments in full automation of certain tasks have led to the concern that these latest advances might not imply similar changes and adjustment effects as historical technological advances. The very definition of automation implies that this form of technological change does not increase the productivity of workers, but replaces them (cf. Merriam-Webster, 2017; Prettner, 2019; Prettner & Strulik, 2017, 2020). For example, when autonomous cars are widespread and humans cease to be taxi drivers, increasing the demand for taxi rides will clearly no longer have positive direct employment effects.[4] This disables the adjustment mechanism of increasing demand for labor in the course of falling prices and rising incomes described previously with regards to the power loom. Thus the adjustment effect of increasing demand might vanish in the presence of full automation. At the same time, the new sectors that emerged in the last decade seem to be less labor intensive than services. For example, while Volkswagen, a traditional car manufacturer, employed around 650,000 people in 2017 and generated a revenue of slightly more than US$250 billion, Alphabet, the parent company of Google, had 85,000 employees and generated a revenue of US$110 billion. Another illustrative case is WhatsApp, which Facebook acquired for US$19 billion in 2014 with a staff of about 50 employees. Finally, the production of robots and machines might require less and less labor input in the future due to increased automation such that the corresponding adjustment mechanism also weakens. The landing spot for

---

4. Positive indirect employment effects could still occur, for example, for mechanics, programmers, car washers, road maintenance workers, and insurance company staff as long as these occupations are not fully automated or have not yet become redundant. An example of why these occupations might also become less important is that autonomous driving might reduce accidents such that the demand for insurance company staff and mechanics could decline (cf. Chen, Kuhn, Prettner, & Bloom, 2019).

those workers displaced by automation technologies is therefore an open question.

Apart from employment effects, our preliminary analyses hint at the ways automation could amplify inequality. Recent technological changes have often allowed individual innovators to make enormous profits by servicing larger markets, while the preponderance of the working population has seen no corresponding income gains. This phenomenon is called the economics of superstars (Frank & Cook, 1996; Manasse & Turrini, 2001; Rosen, 1981), the premise being that technological change and globalization have made it easier for the very best of the best in many domains (or simply those who manage to predict the next consumer trend) to flourish because they can access a much larger market today than in the past. As compared with a composer in the 18th century—whose audience was exclusively local—today's pop stars, movie stars, athletes, TV chefs, authors, software developers, and even CEOs have a global audience or customer base. The reason is that technological changes such as the Internet, streaming platforms, and broadcasting in various forms—or, a generation before, storage media such as DVDs—enabled these superstars to serve an exponentially larger population at almost zero marginal cost (Korinek & Ng, 2017). Extending this reach is the explosion of social media, which manufactures demand for the next buzzy product or person when mentioned or "liked" by the right influencers. A composer such as Vivaldi, for example, had to endure arduous travel for weeks to perform in a large city, serving an audience of, at most, a few hundred listeners. Today more than 3 billion people on Earth with Internet access can buy the music of virtually any performer they want instantaneously on a device they carry around in their pocket.

Apart from the economics of superstars, two other factors regarding the spread of inequality are closely connected with automation. First, the fact that robots and 3D printers are more likely to replace low-skilled workers than high-skilled workers implies that the former lose out disproportionately due to advances in automation while the latter might benefit. This leads to an increasing gap between the wages of low-skilled and high-skilled workers (i.e., a rising skill premium) and could even be responsible for the decreasing real wages of low-skilled workers observed in the United States.[5] As such, this increase in the gap between low and high wages is one crucial driving force of the overall rise in income inequality observed since the 1970s (Atkinson, 2015; Atkinson, Piketty, & Saez, 2011; Milanovic, 2016; Piketty, 2014; Piketty & Saez, 2003).

---

5. For theoretical models and empirical evidence analyzing this claim, see Acemoglu (1998, 2002), Krusell, Ohanian, Ríos-Rull, and Violante (2000), Autor (2002, 2014), Goldin and Katz (2008), Acemoglu and Autor (2012), Acemoglu and Restrepo (2018a), Lankisch, Prettner, and Prskawetz (2019), and Prettner and Strulik (2020).

Second, when robots and 3D printers constitute an important competitor for workers on the labor market—and considering that owners actually earn the income these devices generate—downward pressure is exerted on the share of labor income. The labor income share has decreased in many countries over the previous decades (Elsby, Hobijn, & Sahin, 2013; Karabarbounis & Neiman, 2014), while the number of industrial robots has increased from practically zero to 2 million operative units in 2018. Thus, a negative effect of automation on the labor income share is consistent with the stylized facts (though certainly not proof of it). Prettner (2019) uses data from the International Federation of Robotics (2016) to show that about 0.7 percentage points (or 14%) of the reported decline in the labor income share since the 1970s is likely due to the rise in industrial robots. Eden and Gaggl (2018), using the stock of information and communication technologies as a different proxy for automation, find larger effects and attribute half of the decline in the labor income share to automation. Because labor incomes are much more equally distributed than capital incomes, a reduction in the labor income share is mechanically associated with a higher level of income inequality (Krusell & Smith, 2015; Piketty, 2014; Piketty & Zucman, 2014).

Overall, automation seems to promise improved living standards, but the distributional consequences could be highly adverse in terms of technological unemployment, increasing skill premia, rising wage inequality, and a shift in the functional income distribution toward capital. This book illuminates the expectations and fears associated with automation from both theoretical and empirical perspectives. We will see that many of the projected developments depend crucially on the modeling assumptions underlying the theoretical contributions and that, from an empirical point of view, some of the dire predictions do not (yet?) have a foundation in the data.

1.3   The social impacts of automation

Of course, a purely economic perspective on the consequences of automation overlooks some of its crucial effects on other domains of society. In this section, we consider some cases where automation has the potential to instigate deep changes in our daily lives. These scenarios are necessarily speculative and, as noted previously, vulnerable to being instantaneously outdated. Modern technology's astonishing rate of change can render a notion old fashioned as it is being born.

For example, Japan was an early adopter of robots as nurses and caregivers (*The Economist*, 2017). This innovation could profoundly change how older adults are taken care of, which is particularly important in the rapidly aging populations of industrialized countries. As a first step, robots could work alongside nurses in care homes for seniors and hospitals performing physically demanding tasks, such as lifting patients and equipment, or narrative activities, such as giving exercise instructions and reading books aloud

(*The Economist*, 2017; Moro, Lin, Nejat, & Mihailidis, 2019). However, in the long run, more profound changes could occur. Traditionally, older adults were taken care of at home, with women bearing almost all the associated burden. Then, as incomes increased and the labor force participation rates of women rose, the demand for institutionalized care services for older adults skyrocketed. If robots become more and more competent substitutes for care assistants, the way older adults live out their twilight years could transform once again. If robot nurses were able to help with showering, going to the bathroom, preparing meals, and dispensing medication, seniors could age in the familiar environment of home, without putting (physical, emotional, psychological, social, and time-related) burdens of intimate care on close family members. Technological changes might even transform childcare in a similar way, though surrendering one's children to a robot nursery school teacher may be a mental hurdle too high for some.

Although considerable uncertainty surrounds the timing of the adoption of autonomous driving, widespread use of this technology would imply another profound social change. Autonomous driving not only affects the economic prospects of driving instructors and taxi/rideshare and truck drivers,[6] as alluded to previously, but will also affect the process of urbanization and how cities are designed. If the time spent on driving to work could be used for more productive—or more relaxing—tasks than focusing on traffic (e.g., sleeping, going through work e-mails, watching a movie, or reading a book), commuting would become much less expensive in terms of inconvenience and opportunity costs. Consequently, living close to work would become less important, which could lead to urban sprawl, a flattening of the housing price and rent gradient, and a substantial rise in traffic. Autonomous driving could also lead consumers away from public mass transport toward personal transportation by means of driverless cars because of the convenience, solitude, and direct, point-to-point nature of private transport. This trend could be bolstered by those who cannot currently drive for various reasons (such as minors without a driver's license, older people who might not be confident in driving anymore, or those with physical and mental impairments that prohibit driving, etc.) who might switch to autonomous cars instead of public mass transport. On the one hand, these technology-induced changes could crowd roads to the limit of what they can bear. On the other hand, these technologies might also suggest self-regulating management practices, such as implementing congestion-dependent toll systems on highways and improving access to car sharing. In fact, private cars sit idle more than 95% of the time (*The Economist*, 2018a, 2018b), which implies a high demand for parking in

---

6. In the whole process, the status gratification that some derive from owning and driving their cars could all but vanish. Together with emerging environmental concerns, this could imply a drastic shift of consumer preferences away from more polluting large cars toward less polluting small cars based on cleaner technologies, to which the car industry would need to respond.

cities; using shared autonomous cars could reduce the amount of time that cars are parked and thus, reduce the need for dedicated parking spaces.[7] These technological trends could weaken the upward pressure on property prices in urban areas as people move to the countryside and commute to work, while space that is currently reserved for parking becomes available for development as residential areas, office buildings, bicycle lanes, or parks, or generally reduces urban congestion. Of course, in the background, other major forces will continue to drive property prices up, such as population growth, rising incomes, increasing need for office space, and zoning restrictions.

Translation programs and voice recognition represent a further example of the potential for automation/artificial intelligence (AI) to change our lives profoundly. If the past decade's enormous progress in translation programs and voice recognition software is any guide for the future, then another possibility might be that international communication will be less dependent on learning foreign languages or hiring translators. For example, the European Union (EU) has 24 official languages, and all EU citizens have the right to access EU documents in all of those tongues. In addition, EU citizens have the right to correspond with the European Commission and receive a response in their own language. The European Commission, therefore, is one of the world's biggest employers of linguists and interpreters.[8] The possibility of real-time, accurate language translation by algorithms could reduce the demand for translators and lead to greater international economic integration—increases in trade, foreign direct investment, tourism, and working abroad—because language obstacles are often one of the major barriers impeding these activities.

A complex topic in the realm of technological advance is the issue of sex robots. Many news reports over the last several years have debated how sex robots will affect the porn industry and prostitution. However, sex robots could change human interactions altogether, and the legal and ethical challenges of integrating sex robots are not yet understood (see Sharkey, van Wynsberghe, Robbins, & Hancock, 2017). Will buying sex robots be legally analogous to prostitution and therefore be banned in some countries but allowed in others? Could the use of sex robots increase individual social isolation? Could sex robots affect marriage rates and the formation and durability of sexual unions more generally? How would the availability of sex robots change actual and perceived gender roles in society? The property status of robots from a legal perspective will shape these conversations, as will

---

7. Flying autonomous cars/taxis could also reduce road congestion by utilizing another dimension of space (*The Economist*, 2019a). However, many additional concerns come with this technology, such as negative effects on air traffic safety and excessive pollution even when these cars/taxis operate with electric motors.

8. See, for example, http://ec.europa.eu/education/official-languages-eu-0_en.

the possible implementation of certain legal restrictions, such as preventing a robot from being treated in a way that would constitute a serious crime against a human. For example, sex robots can already be programmed to imitate nonconsenting victims—a simulation of sexual assault. The debate on whether this should be banned is in its infancy and ongoing (Danaher, 2014; Sharkey et al., 2017; Sparrow, 2017). Even if a solution were found, where would lawmakers draw the line between virtual reality and sex robots?

Despite the word "robotic" being synonymous with an austere and impersonal disposition, automation has made tremendous strides in psychological counseling. For example, programs have been developed to treat autism and dementia (Vitelli, 2014). A meta-analysis by Costescu, Vanderborght, and David (2014) shows that robot-enhanced therapy has positive overall effects on the outcome of psychotherapy as compared with a control group in which no robot-enhanced therapy is used.

From a governmental perspective, military robots will be a challenge to conventional warfare because in deploying military robots, the decision whether or not to kill, or whom to kill, might be outsourced to an algorithm (Hellström, 2013). Some are afraid that autonomous AI-based weapons could lower the threshold of going to war, lead to new arms races, and, particularly if they get into the hands of terrorists, constitute a highly dangerous threat to society. *The Guardian* (2015) cites a letter signed by more than a thousand experts, including Elon Musk and Stephen Hawking, that claims that "The endpoint of this technological trajectory is obvious: autonomous weapons will become the Kalashnikovs of tomorrow."[9] At an even larger scale, AI-based strategic reasoning in the context of military decisions is currently attracting substantial funding in the United States and in China (*The Economist*, 2019b). While autonomous AI-based decision-making might allow a much faster reaction to potentially deadly threads than human decision-making, it also carries the risk of catastrophic consequences due to misdetermination.[10] The obvious solution to this is to "keep humans in the loop" such that the final strategic decision is always based on human judgment. Doing so, however, implies foregoing the strategic advantage of faster decision-making, and some nations might not be willing to give up this advantage.

Beyond overpowering military technologies, modern economies—in which almost all devices are connected and require stable Internet

---

9. The Avtomat Kalashnikova, or Kalashnikov, is also known as the AK-47, the gas-powered assault rifle developed for the Soviet Union army. Its simple and robust design renders it a cheap weapon that is widely used by guerrillas, terrorists, and criminals (Franko, 2017).
10. See the story of Stanislav Yevgrafovich Petrov, who likely prevented a full-scale nuclear war between the United States and the Soviet Union in 1983 when he did not follow the standard protocol and instead classified an alleged first strike of the United States against the Soviet Union—that was reported automatically by an early warning system—as a false alarm.

connections and reliable power grids to operate properly—are highly vulnerable to blackouts, natural catastrophes, hacking, or the spread of computer viruses. Even now, a longer blackout would prevent supermarkets from selling anything without electronic payment systems, keep electrically powered doors closed (or open and vulnerable to intruders), and disable pumps at gas stations. The stored food in refrigerators and freezers would, of course, spoil quickly without electricity, and people would soon begin to suffer as the vast majority is not self-sufficient in terms of food. As digitalization progresses, the more interconnected societies become and the more vulnerable to such disasters they become. An attack on one reflexively becomes an attack on all. This poses a significant challenge for policymakers to design emergency systems that ensure the continued functioning of society during catastrophes.[11]

1.4 The race against, or the race with, the machine?

How can we prepare for the economic and social challenges of automation and digitalization? One of the standard answers in this context is "preparation through education." This, however, is a convenient answer that has been workshopped to provide comfort, as almost everybody views education as positive and uncontroversial and because it suggests that we will be able to cope with anything if we are just willing and able to spend some time learning something new. Of course, education is a crucial component in the response to the challenges of automation, but it will not be able to solve all of the associated problems. Thinking that we can retrain all truck drivers displaced by automation to become quantum physicists or personal yoga teachers is absurd. That said, in terms of education, learning skills that machines do not naturally, easily, or effectively perform—such as empathy, teamwork, and the ability to interpret verbal and nonverbal signals by others appropriately (although algorithms are getting better at these, too, as we have seen previously)—will become increasingly important. In addition, lifelong learning, a well-known and widespread cliché, will become necessary when robots increasingly handle routine tasks. Finally, at least at the moment, going into STEM (science, technology, engineering, and mathematics) fields provides employment opportunities that appear likely to endure for the immediate future. Investing in these areas could be a worthwhile defense against the encroaching challenges of automation.

---

11. That said, it is also worth noting that the Internet allowed delivery of massive amounts of vital information and enabled the social and economic connectivity that protected physical and mental health and facilitated much economic activity throughout the world during the COVID-19 pandemic. It would be difficult to overstate its value to humanity during the COVID-19 crisis, or its expected value during other pandemics that lurk ahead.

Social security systems are currently (predominantly) financed out of payroll taxes. Insofar as human labor might become less important due to automation, some argue that social security systems will have to be redesigned in response. Proposals for how to finance social security in the future range from robot taxes (or, more generally, capital taxes) to consumption taxes and digital taxes (Delaney, 2017; Geiger et al., 2018; Guerreiro, Rebelo, & Teles, 2018). The idea behind these proposals is that robots will generate a larger part of income in the future, and thus imposing taxes on robots to replace the lost payroll taxes of displaced workers would be fair. One argument against robot and capital taxes is that capital is much more mobile than labor, such that robots could easily be used in other countries or jurisdictions that do not impose a robot tax (Gasteiger & Prettner, 2020; Guerreiro et al., 2018). By contrast, consumption cannot easily move abroad such that a higher taxation of consumption could be feasible and efficient. Of course, in this context, problems arise because consumption taxes are regressive, meaning that households with a lower income level spend a higher proportion of their income on the tax, which has adverse effects on inequality. However, some observers have suggested ways to design consumption taxes in a progressive way (Frank, 2008; Geiger et al., 2018). Apart from these financing issues, the introduction of an unconditional basic income—a universal wage paid to citizens by the government with no conditions—is often floated as a necessary policy measure in response to technological unemployment in the age of automation. Because the unconditional basic income is usually conceived as a full replacement of the traditional social security system, such a policy might, however, even generate economic hardship for those persons who need more than the unconditional basic income to survive. This would apply, for example, to those who are chronically ill. In addition, according to most estimates, the costs of such an unconditional basic income would be rather high, implying the need for higher tax rates or additional taxes along the lines mentioned previously.

From an individual perspective, Cowen (2013) and Brynjolfsson and McAfee (2016) argue that, in the age of smart machines, a successful adaptation strategy is to run with the machine rather than against it. As a case in point, Cowen (2013) refers to "Advanced Chess," where each player can use a prespecified chess program and the computers on which it runs have the same performance in case of both opponents, and "Freestyle Chess," where human teams can use all types of different programs in their games against each other. While the best human players lose against most standard chess programs, a hybrid team of humans and chess programs working together beats even the best standalone chess programs. Thus, even with today's very sophisticated and computationally powerful chess programs, a certain complementarity exists between the computing power of machines and the intuition of humans, which implies only an imperfect substitutability. As a corollary, people need to seek these complementarities if they want to be successful in the age of smart machines; we should avoid trying to compete with machines in areas in which they are good and appropriate substitutes. For example, doctors may find working with a diagnostic robot like "Watson" to be a threat to their jobs. However, patients still get a large additional benefit from having a medical doctor who communicates with and cares for them. In this sense, a strong complementarity remains between the new technologies and personal skills, something that might not be the case for industrial robots and assembly line workers.

A more radical idea in the context of the race against the machine is the burgeoning notion of human augmentation. At one end of the spectrum, human augmentation could comprise smart sunglasses that take videos of the surroundings and place them in the view of the wearer, exoskeletons that strengthen body parts and make physical work easier, or implants in the form of microchips in place of identification cards (Ma, 2018; Young, 2017); at the other end of the spectrum, human augmentation could comprise direct brain–machine interfaces (Velleste, Perel, Spalding, Whitford, & Schwartz, 2008). While people's willingness to undergo surgery to install these types of implants and brain–machine interfaces may seem strange today, items such as contact lenses, pacemakers, and artificial hips might also have been viewed that way upon their introduction. In addition, direct brain–machine interfaces have already been used successfully in clinical trials to allow paralyzed persons to operate tablets (Nuyujukian et al., 2018).

Overall, the most radical prediction in this context is that of the Singularity. This prediction was first offered by Raymond Kurzweil (2005) building upon previous thoughts of John von Neumann, according to which exponential technological progress will lead to a situation in which machine intelligence will become infinitely more powerful than human intelligence. Kurzweil also predicts the eventual merger of human and machine intelligence, that is, the Singularity, at which point human life will transform (see also Nordhaus, 2015, who does not foresee such a Singularity in the near future). Kurzweil's (2005) main prediction is that once the Singularity is reached, human life will transform in such a way we could not now comprehend. After that point, intelligence, which could still be considered human, although it might be nonbiological, will spread throughout the universe.

However, because we do not want to speculate about what is impossible to comprehend, we will focus on the more concrete and immediate, yet still highly transformative, economic effects of automation and AI in this book.

1.5 Summary

This chapter provides an overview of the effects of past forms of technological progress and the extent to which we can draw conclusions about the future effects of automation and AI based on past experience. With respect to the employment effects of technological change, we have seen adjustment mechanisms that ensure that (some) displaced workers find jobs in other sectors of the economy. However, some of these adjustment effects might not work as well as they did in the past when full automation was not yet an issue.

This chapter also touched upon the social and economic consequences of some widely discussed forms of automation: automation in care for older adults, autonomous driving, autonomous weapons, and sex robots. While the developments in these areas are breathtaking, many challenges remain to be solved. For example, how will the legal system develop to cope with the potential arrival of sex robots and how will strategic military decisions be made in an age of automated warfare?

Finally, we discussed the possibilities of future human competition with robots. Exponential technological progress implies that the race against the machine is lost in many areas. However, racing against the machine might not be necessary; a better strategy may be to race with the machine. The extent to which racing with the machine is possible depends on how long humans will have niches in which they have advantages, such as in personal communication, empathy, and intuition. In the case of the "Singularity" predicted by Raymond Kurzweil, the notion of what it means to be human might be transformed. The remainder of this book, however, does not speculate so much about a world in which this happens, but rather emphasizes the immediate consequences of automation and AI on economic and social outcomes.

References

Acemoglu, D. (1998). Why do new technologies complement skills? Directed technical change and wage inequality. *Quarterly Journal of Economics, 113*(4), 1055–1090.

Acemoglu, D. (2002). Directed technical change. *The Review of Economic Studies, 69*(4), 781–809.

Acemoglu, D. (2009). *Introduction to modern economic growth.* Princeton, NJ: Princeton University Press.

Acemoglu, D., & Autor, D. (2012). What does human capital do? A review of Goldin and Katz's the race between education and technology. *Journal of Economic Literature, 50*(2), 426–463.

Acemoglu, D., & Restrepo, P. (2018a). Low-skill and high-skill automation. *Journal of Human Capital, 12*(2), 204–232.

Acemoglu, D., & Restrepo, P. (2018b). The race between man and machine: Implications of technology for growth, factor shares, and employment. *American Economic Review, 108*(6), 1488–1542.

Adams, J. D. (1990). Fundamental stocks of knowledge and productivity growth. *Journal of Political Economy, 98*(4), 673–702.

Aghion, P., & Howitt, P. (1992). A model of growth through creative destruction. *Econometrica, 60*(2), 323–351.

Aghion, P., & Howitt, P. (1999). *Endogenous economic growth.* Cambridge, MA: MIT Press.

Aghion, P., & Howitt, P. (2009). *The economics of growth.* Cambridge, MA: MIT Press.

Atkinson, A. (2015). *Inequality: What can be done.* Cambridge, MA: Harvard University Press.

Atkinson, A., Piketty, T., & Saez, E. (2011). Top incomes in the long run of history. *Journal of Economic Literature, 49*(1), 3−71.

Autor, D. (2002). Skill biased technical change and rising inequality: What is the evidence? What are the alternatives? Available from https://economics.mit.edu/files/558. Accessed 01.03.18.

Autor, D. H. (2014). Skills, education, and the rise of earnings inequality among the "other 99 percent". *Science, 344*(6186), 843−851.

Autor, D. H., & Dorn, D. (2013). The growth of low-skill service jobs and the polarization of the US labor market. *American Economic Review, 103*(5), 1553−1597.

Avent, R. (2016). *The wealth of humans: Work, power, and status in the twenty-first century.* New York: St. Martin's Press.

Barro, R., & Sala-i-Martin, X. (2004). *Economic growth.* Cambridge, MA: MIT Press.

Baumol, W., & Bowen, W. (1966). *Performing arts—the economic dilemma: A study of problems common to theater, opera, music and dance.* New York: Twentieth Century Fund.

Bloom, D. E., McKenna, M., & Prettner, K. (2019). Global employment and decent jobs, 2010−2030: The forces of demography and automation. *International Social Security Review, 72*(3), 43−78.

Brynjolfsson, E., & McAfee, A. (2016). *The second machine age: Work, progress, and prosperity in a time of brilliant technologies.* New York: Norton & Company.

Chen, S., Kuhn, M., Prettner, K., & Bloom, D. (2019). The global macroeconomic burden of road injuries: Estimates and projections for 166 countries. *The Lancet Planetary Health, 3* (9), e390−e398.

Costescu, C., Vanderborght, B., & David, D. (2014). The effects of robot-enhanced psychotherapy: A meta-analysis. *Review of General Psychology, 18*(2), 127−136.

Cowen, T. (2013). *Average is over: Powering America beyond the age of the great stagnation.* New York: Dutton.

Dalgaard, C., & Kreiner, C. (2001). Is declining productivity inevitable? *Journal of Economic Growth, 6*(3), 187−203.

Danaher, J. (2014). Robotic rape and robotic child sexual abuse: Should they be criminalised? *Criminal Law and Philosophy, 11*(1), 71−95.

Delaney, K. J. (2017). Droid duties: The robot that takes your job should pay taxes, says Bill Gates. Available from https://qz.com/911968/bill-gates-the-robot-that-takes-your-job-should-pay-taxes/. Accessed 01.06.17.

Dinopoulos, E., & Thompson, P. (1998). Schumpeterian growth without scale effects. *Journal of Economic Growth, 3*(4), 313−335.

Doepke, M. (2004). Accounting for fertility decline during the transition to growth. *Journal of Economic Growth, 9*(3), 347−383.

Eden, M., & Gaggl, P. (2018). On the welfare implications of automation. *Review of Economic Dynamics, 29*(July), 15−43.

Elsby, M. W. L., Hobijn, B., & Sahin, A. (2013). The decline of the U.S. labor share. *Brookings Papers on Economic Activity, Fall 2013*, 1−63.

Ford, M. (2015). *Rise of the robots: Technology and the threat of a jobless future.* New York: Basic Books.

Frank, R. (2008). Progressive consumption tax. *Democracy: A Journal of Ideas*, Spring 2008 (8). Available from https://democracyjournal.org/magazine/8/progressive-consumption-tax/. Accessed 12.12.19.

Frank, R., & Cook, P. (1996). *The winner-take-all society: Why the few at the top get so much more than the rest of us.* London: Penguin Books.

Franko, B. (2017). The gun that is in almost 100 countries: Why the AK-47 dominates. *The National Interest*. Available from https://nationalinterest.org/blog/the-buzz/75-million-guns-ready-war-why-the-ak-47-dominates-20561. Accessed 11.10.19.

Frey, C. B. (2019). *The technology trap: Capital, labor, and power in the age of automation*. Princeton, NJ: Princeton University Press.

Galor, O. (2005). From stagnation to growth: Unified growth theory. In P. Aghion, & S. Durlauf (Eds.), *Handbook of Economic Growth* (Vol. 1, pp. 171−293). Amsterdam: Elsevier, Chapter 4.

Galor, O. (2011). *Unified growth theory*. Princeton, NJ: Princeton University Press.

Galor, O., & Weil, D. (2000). Population, technology, and growth: From Malthusian stagnation to the demographic transition and beyond. *The American Economic Review*, *90*(4), 806−828.

Gasteiger, E., & Prettner, K. (2020). A note on automation, stagnation, and the implications of a robot tax. *Macroeconomic Dynamics*. (forthcoming).

Geiger, N., Prettner, K., & Schwarzer, J. (2018). Die Auswirkungen der Automatisierung, auf Wachstum, Beschäftigung und Ungleichheit, *Perspektiven der Wirtschaftspolitik*, *19*(2), 59−77.

Gersbach, H., & Schneider, M. T. (2015). On the global supply of basic research. *Journal of Monetary Economics*, *75*(C), 123−137.

Gersbach, H., Sorger, G., & Amon, C. (2018). Hierarchical growth: Basic and applied research. *Journal of Economic Dynamics and Control*, *90*, 434−459.

Goldin, C., & Katz, L. (2008). The race between education and technology: The evolution of U. S. wage differentials, 1890−2005. NBER Working Paper 12984, National Bureau of Economic Research, Cambridge, MA.

Gordon, R. (2016). *Rise and fall of American growth: The U.S. standard of living since the Civil War*. Princeton, NJ: Princeton University Press.

Grossman, G. M., & Helpman, E. (1991). Quality ladders in the theory of economic growth. *Review of Economic Studies*, *58*(1), 43−61.

Grossmann, V., Steger, T. M., & Trimborn, T. (2013). Dynamically optimal R&D subsidization. *Journal of Economic Dynamics and Control*, *37*(3), 516−534.

Growiec, J. (2019). The hardware-software model: A new conceptual framework of production, R&D, and growth with AI. Working Paper 2019-042, Warsaw School of Economics, Collegium of Economic Analysis.

Guerreiro, J., Rebelo, S., & Teles, P. (2018). Should robots be taxed? NBER Working Paper 23806, National Bureau of Economic Research, Cambridge, MA.

Hagemann, H. (1995). Technological unemployment. In P. Arestis, & M. Marshall (Eds.), *The political economy of full employment* (pp. 36−53). Cheltenham, UK: Edward Elgar.

Hansen, G. D., & Prescott, E. C. (2002). Malthus to Solow. *American Economic Review*, *92*(4), 1205−1217.

Hellström, T. (2013). On the moral responsibility of military robots. *Ethics and Information Technology*, *15*(2), 99−107.

Hémous, D., & Olsen, M. (2018). The rise of the machines: Automation, horizontal innovation and income inequality. Available from https://papers.ssrn.com/sol3/papers.cfm?abstract_id = 2328774. Accessed 12.12.19.

Herrendorf, B., Rogerson, R., & Valentinyi, A. (2014). Growth and structural transformation. In P. Aghion, & S. Durlauf (Eds.), *Handbook of economic growth* (Vol. 2B, pp. 855−941). Amsterdam: Elsevier.

Hicks, J. (1973). *Capital and time*. Oxford, UK: Clarendon Press.

Howitt, P. (1999). Steady endogenous growth with population and R&D inputs growing. *Journal of Political Economy*, *107*(4), 715−730.

Humphrey, T. (2004). Ricardo versus Wicksell on job losses and technological change. *Federal Reserve Bank of Richmond Economic Quarterly, 90*(4), 5−24.

International Federation of Robotics. (2016). Survey: 1.3 million industrial robots to enter service by 2018. IRF press release, Frankfurt, 25 February 2016.

Jones, C. I. (1995). R&D-based models of economic growth. *Journal of Political Economy, 103* (4), 759−783.

Jones, C. I. (2001). Was an industrial revolution inevitable? Economic growth over the very long run. *Advances in Macroeconomics, 1*(2), 1−43.

Jones, C. I. (2002). Sources of U.S. economic growth in a world of ideas. *American Economic Review, 92*(1), 220−239.

Jones, C. I. (2015). The facts of economic growth. NBER Working Paper 21142, National Bureau of Economic Research, Cambridge, MA.

Jones, C. I., & Vollrath, D. (2009). *Introduction to economic growth* (3rd ed.). New York: W. W. Norton & Company.

Jones, C. I., & Williams, J. C. (1998). Measuring the social return to R&D. *The Quarterly Journal of Economics, 113*(4), 1119−1135.

Jones, C. I., & Williams, J. C. (2000). Too much of a good thing? The economics of investment in R&D. *Journal of Economic Growth, 5*(1), 65−85.

Kaplan, J. (2015). *Humans need not apply: A guide to wealth and work in the age of artificial intelligence*. New Haven, CT: Yale University Press.

Karabarbounis, L., & Neiman, B. (2014). The global decline of the labor share. *The Quarterly Journal of Economics, 129*(1), 61−103.

Kögel, T., & Prskawetz, A. (2001). Agricultural productivity growth and escape from the Malthusian trap. *Journal of Economic Growth, 6*(4), 337−357.

Korinek, A., & Ng, D. (2017). *The macroeconomics of superstars. MIMEO*. Washington, DC: International Monetary Fund.

Kortum, S. (1997). Research, patenting and technological change. *Econometrica, 65*(6), 1389−1419.

Krusell, P., Ohanian, L., Ríos-Rull, J.-V., & Violante, G. (2000). Capital-skill complementarity and inequality: A macroeconomic analysis. *Econometrica, 68*(5), 1029−1053.

Krusell, P., & Smith, A. (2015). Is Piketty's "second law of capitalism" fundamental? *Journal of Political Economy, 123*(4), 725−748.

Kurzweil, R. (2005). *The singularity is near: When humans transcend biology*. London: Penguin Books.

Landes, D. (1998). *The wealth and poverty of nations: Why some are so rich and some so poor*. New York: WW Norton & Co.

Lankisch, C., Prettner, K., & Prskawetz, A. (2019). How can robots affect wage inequality? *Economic Modelling, 81*, 161−169.

Lowe, A. (1976). *The path of economic growth*. Cambridge, UK: Cambridge University Press.

Lucas, R. E. (1988). On the mechanics of economic development. *Journal of Monetary Economics, 22*(1), 3−42.

Ma, A. (2018). Thousands of people in Sweden are embedding microchips under their skin to replace ID cards. *The Business Insider*, May 2018. Available from https://www.businessinsider.com/swedish-people-embed-microchips-under-skin-to-replace-id-cards-2018-5? r = DE&IR = T?r = US&IR = T. Accessed 12.12.19.

Maddison, A. (2010). Statistics on world population, GDP and per capita GDP, 1−2008 AD. Available from http://ghdx.healthdata.org/record/statistics-world-population-gdp-and-capita-gdp-1-2008-ad. Accessed 26.11.19.

Manasse, P., & Turrini, A. (2001). Trade, wages, and superstars. *Journal of International Economics, 54*(1), 97−117.

Merriam-Webster. (2017). Automation. Available from https://www.merriam-webster.com/dictionary/automation. Accessed 03.03.17.

Milanovic, B. (2016). *Global inequality. A new approach for the age of globalization.* Cambridge, MA: Harvard University Press.

Mokyr, J. (2002). *The gifts of Athena.* Princeton, NJ: Princeton University Press.

Mokyr, J. (2005). Long-term economic growth and the history of technology. In P. Aghion, & S. Durlauf (Eds.), *Handbook of economic growth* (Vol. 1B, pp. 1114−1180) Amsterdam: Elsevier.

Mokyr, J. (2018). *Culture of growth: The origins of the modern economy.* Princeton, NJ: Princeton University Press.

Moro, C., Lin, S., Nejat, G., & Mihailidis, A. (2019). Social robots and seniors: A comparative study on the influence of dynamic social features on human-robot interaction. *International Journal of Social Robotics, 11*(1), 5−24.

Morris, I. (2010). *Why the west rules−for now: The patterns of history, and what they reveal about the future.* New York: Farrar Straus & Giroux.

Norberg, J. (2016). *Progress: Ten reasons to look forward to the future.* London: Oneworld Publications.

Nordhaus, W. (1996). Do real-output and real-wage measures capture reality? The history of lighting suggests not. In T. F. Breshanan, & R. J. Gordon (Eds.), *The economics of new goods* (pp. 27−70). University of Chicago Press.

Nordhaus, W. (2007). Two centuries of productivity growth in computing. *The Journal of Economic History, 67*(1), 128−159.

Nordhaus, W. (2015). Are we approaching an economic singularity? Information technology and the future of economic growth. NBER Working Paper No. 21547, National Bureau of Economic Research, Cambridge, MA.

Nuyujukian, P., Albites Sanabria, J., Saab, J., Pandarinath, C., Jarosiewicz, B., Blabe, C. H., et al. (2018). Cortical control of a tablet computer by people with paralysis. *PLoS One, 13* (11), e0204566.

Peretto, P. F. (1998). Technological change and population growth. *Journal of Economic Growth, 3*(4), 283−311.

Peretto, P. F., & Saeter, J. J. (2013). Factor-eliminating technical change. *Journal of Monetary Economics, 60*(4), 459−473.

Piketty, T. (2014). *Capital in the twenty-first century.* Cambridge, MA: The Belknap Press of Harvard University Press.

Piketty, T., & Saez, E. (2003). Income inequality in the United States 1913−1998. *The Quarterly Journal of Economics, 118*(1), 1−39.

Piketty, T., & Zucman, G. (2014). Capital is back: Wealth-income ratios in rich countries 1700−2010. *The Quarterly Journal of Economics, 129*(3), 1255−1310.

Prettner, K. (2019). A note on the implications of automation for economic growth and the labor share. *Macroeconomic Dynamics, 23*(3), 1294−1301.

Prettner, K., Geiger, N., & Schwarzer, J. (2018). Die wirtschaftlichen Folgen der Automatisierung. In C. Spiel, & R. Neck (Eds.), Automatisierung: Wechselwirkung mit Kunst, Wissenschaft und Gesellschaft. Verlag Wien, Austria: Böhlau.

Prettner, K. & Strulik, H. (2017). The lost race against the machine: Automation, education, and inequality in an R&D-based growth model. Hohenheim Discussion Papers in Business, Economics, and Social Sciences 08-2017.

Prettner, K., & Strulik, H. (2020). Innovation, automation, and inequality: Policy challenges in the race against the machine. *Journal of Monetary Economics*. (forthcoming).

Prettner, K., & Werner, K. (2016). Why it pays off to pay us well: The impact of basic research on economic growth and welfare. *Research Policy*, *45*(5), 1075–1090.

Ricardo, D. (1821). *On the principles of political economy and taxation* (3rd ed.). London: John Murray.

Romer, P. (1990). Endogenous technological change. *Journal of Political Economy*, *98*(5), 71–102.

Rosen, S. (1981). The economics of superstars. *American Economic Review*, *71*(5), 845–858.

Roser, M. (2018). Our world in data. Available from https://ourworldindata.org/. Accessed 12.12.19.

Ross, A. J. (2016). *The industries of the future*. New York: Simon Schuster.

Samuelson, P. (1988). Mathematical vindication of Ricardo on machinery. *The Journal of Political Economy*, *96*(2), 274–282.

Scott, A. J., & Gratton, L. (2020). *The new long life*. London: Bloomsbury Publishing.

Segerström, P. S. (1998). Endogenous growth without scale effects. *American Economic Review*, *88*(5), 1290–1310.

Sharkey, N., van Wynsberghe, A., Robbins, S., & Hancock, E. (2017). Our sexual future with robots: A foundation for responsible robotics consultation report. Available from https://responsiblerobotics.org/2017/07/05/frr-report-our-sexual-future-with-robots/. Accessed 12.12.19.

Smith, A. (1776). *An inquiry into the nature and causes of the wealth of nations*. Cadell: London: W. Strahan and T.

Sparrow, R. (2017). Robots, rape, and representation. *International Journal of Social Robotics*, *9*(4), 465–477.

Strulik, H., Prettner, K., & Prskawetz, A. (2013). The past and future of knowledge-based growth. *Journal of Economic Growth*, *18*(4), 411–437.

Tamura, R. (2002). Human capital and the switch from agriculture to industry. *Journal of Economic Dynamics and Control*, *27*(2), 207–242.

The Economist. (2017). Machine caring: Japan is embracing nursing-care robots. November 23, 2017.

The Economist. (2018a). Reinventing wheels. Special report on autonomous driving. March 1, 2018.

The Economist. (2018b). Selling rides, not cars. Self-driving cars will require new business models. March 1, 2018.

The Economist. (2019a). Battle algorithm. Artificial intelligence is changing every aspect of war. September 7, 2019.

The Economist. (2019b). Urban aviation. Flying taxis are taking off to whisk people around cities. September 12, 2019.

The Guardian. (2015). Musk, Wozniak and Hawking urge ban on warfare AI and autonomous weapons. July 27, 2015.

Velleste, M., Perel, S., Spalding, M., Whitford, A., & Schwartz, A. (2008). Cortical control of a prosthetic arm for self-feeding. *Nature*, *543*, 1098–1101. (June 2008).

Vermeulen, B., Kesselhut, J., Pyka, A., & Saviotti, P. P. (2018). The impact of automation on employment: Just the usual structural change? *Sustainability*, *10*(5), 1–27.

Vermeulen, B., Pyka, A., & Saviotti, P. P. (2020). Structural change perspective on the labour economic impact of robotics: Future scenarios. In K. F. Zimmermann (Ed.), *Handbook of labor, human resources and population economics*. Berlin/Heidelberg, Germany: Springer. (forthcoming).

Vitelli, R. (2014). The rise of the robot therapist. *Psychology Today*, November 17, 2014. Available from https://www.psychologytoday.com/us/blog/media-spotlight/201411/the-rise-the-robot-therapist. Accessed 12.12.19.

Weil, D. N. (2012). *Economic growth* (3rd ed.). London: Taylor & Francis.

Wicksell, K. (1906). *Lectures on political economy*. London: Routledge & Kegan Paul.

Wootton, D. (2015). *The invention of science: A new history of the scientific revolution*. New York: Harper.

Young, A. (1998). Growth without scale effects. *Journal of Political Economy*, *106*(5), 41−63.

Young, L. (2017). A spectrum of human augmentation. *Strategic Business Insights*, April 2017. Available from http://www.strategicbusinessinsights.com/about/featured/2017/2017-04-spectrum-human-augmentation.shtml. Accessed 12.12.19.

Chapter 2

The stylized facts

2.1 Adoption of automation technology

From a historical perspective, full automation is a relatively new phenomenon. George Charles Devol conceived the first industrial robot in 1954. Devol partnered with Joseph Engelberger to develop Unimation (the first company working on industrial robots) in the late 1950s. Unimate was produced and used on a GM assembly line in 1961, becoming the first industrial robot employed in production.[1] Subsequently, the number of industrial robots worldwide remained negligible until the second half of the 1980s, as Fig. 2.1 illustrates with data from the International Federation of Robotics (IFR, 2016, 2017a, 2018a). An initial marked increase in the number of industrial robots produced occurred in 1985−2007. Following the Great Recession, growth in the stock of industrial robots took off, and recent years have been characterized with annual growth rates of up to 15%—substantially higher than the growth rates of output or population in even the fastest-growing countries. This implies that robot density—the number of robots per worker—has been rising markedly over the past decade. Forecasts from the IFR (2018a) indicate that the number of industrial robots could rise to more than 3.5 million units by 2021.

The adoption of robots varies considerably in international and intersectoral terms. While, for example, a relatively large number of industrial robots are used in the production of automobiles and electrical and electronic devices, their use in food production is still significantly lower (IFR, 2017a). Furthermore, the diffusion of industrial robots is already at a more advanced stage in countries such as Germany, Japan, and South Korea, as compared with other large industrialized countries such as France, the United Kingdom, and the United States. This can partly be explained by the differential pace of population aging in these countries because countries in which the population is aging more rapidly have a higher demand for industrial robots to substitute for retiring workers (Abeliansky & Prettner, 2017; Acemoglu & Restrepo, 2018). Many poor countries barely employ any industrial robots at all (IFR, 2018b). Table 2.1 displays the number of

---

1. See, for example, https://web.archive.org/web/20110926213115/http://www.robothalloffame. org/unimate.html and https://www.robots.com/articles/industrial-robot-history.

Automation and its Macroeconomic Consequences. DOI: https://doi.org/10.1016/B978-0-12-818028-0.00002-8

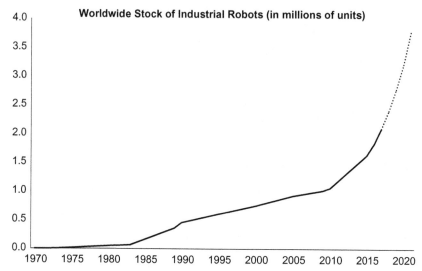

FIGURE 2.1 Worldwide stock of operative industrial robots in millions of units, according to IFR (2016, 2017a, 2018a). The dotted line represents forecasts, whereas the solid line represents actual data.

industrial robots per 10,000 employees in manufacturing (as of 2016) for the leading countries in terms of robot adoption, according to IFR (2018b) data. This table shows, for example, that robot density in Germany is 63% higher than robot density in the United States (see also Dauth, Findeisen, Suedekum, & Woessner, 2017), while South Korea decisively tops the list with twice the robot density of even the other leading countries like Germany and Japan. China has a significantly lower robot density than other countries, despite the fact that it is the largest market for newly delivered robots in absolute terms, as Table 2.2 illustrates (IFR, 2017b). This is due to the large number of available employees in China and the comparatively lower wages that reduce the incentives to invest in automation. China's enormous population lowers the robot density ratio while simultaneously providing an abundance of cheap labor that reduces robot demand (Abeliansky & Prettner, 2017; Acemoglu & Restrepo, 2018).

2.2 Dynamics of economic growth and welfare

Turning to the stylized facts of the evolution of income over time, this section examines historic and recent trends in the development of worldwide income levels. The average global income level before the Industrial Revolution hovered around the subsistence level, a condition that was consistent throughout different regions of the world (Galor, 2011; Malthus, 1798). Fig. 2.2 (data from Maddison, 2010) shows the stunning, skyrocketing

TABLE 2.1 Robots per 10,000 employees in manufacturing as of 2016, according to IFR (2018b).

Country	Robots per 10,000 employees in manufacturing
South Korea	631
Singapore	488
Germany	309
Japan	303
Sweden	223
Denmark	211
United States	189
Italy	185
Belgium	184
Taiwan	177
Spain	160
Netherlands	153
Canada	145
Austria	144
Finland	138
Slovenia	137
Slovakia	135
France	132
Switzerland	128
Czech Republic	101
Australia	83
United Kingdom	71
China	68
Portugal	58
Hungary	57
Norway	51
New Zealand	49
Thailand	45

(Continued)

TABLE 2.1 (Continued)

Country	Robots per 10,000 employees in manufacturing
Malaysia	34
Poland	32
Mexico	31
Israel	31
South Africa	28
Turkey	23
Argentina	18
Greece	17
Romania	15
Estonia	11
Brazil	10
Croatia	6
Indonesia	5
Russia	3
Philippines	3
India	3
World average	74

economic growth—a previously unknown phenomenon—ushered in by the Industrial Revolution. Analyzing this trend by region, we observe in Fig. 2.3 (data from Maddison, 2010) that some areas, such as Western Europe and the Western Offshoots (consisting of Australia, Canada, New Zealand, and the United States) experienced income growth earlier, whereas other regions, such as Africa, still struggle today.

The differential timing of sustained long-run economic growth among the different regions of the world is largely responsible for a strong increase in cross-country income inequality after the Industrial Revolution. Around the year 1000 AD, the richest region in terms of per capita gross domestic product (GDP) was, on average, 10% richer than the poorest region. This difference rose to a factor of 3 in 1820 and, ultimately, to a factor of 18 by the end of the 20th century (Maddison, 2010). More recently, income inequality *between countries* has been decreasing slightly. This is mainly due to the fast growth of China and India, which still have income levels below the

TABLE 2.2 Largest markets for robots in 2016, according to IFR (2017b).

Country	Annual deployment of industrial robots (in thousands)
China	87.0
South Korea	41.4
Japan	38.6
United States	31.4
Germany	20.0
Taiwan	7.6
Italy	6.5
Mexico	5.9
France	4.2
Spain	3.9
Thailand	2.6
India	2.6
Singapore	2.6
Canada	2.3
Czech Republic	2.0

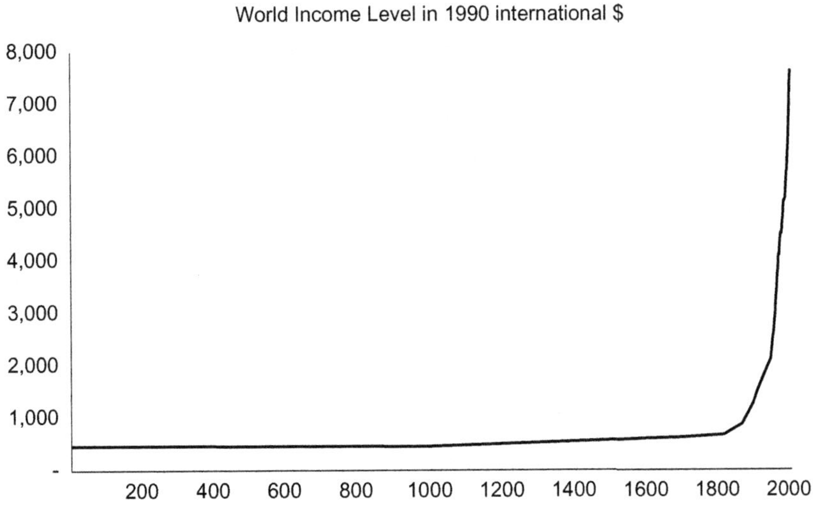

World Income Level in 1990 international $

FIGURE 2.2 Evolution of the world income level per capita from 1 AD to 2008, according to Maddison (2010) 1990 International $.

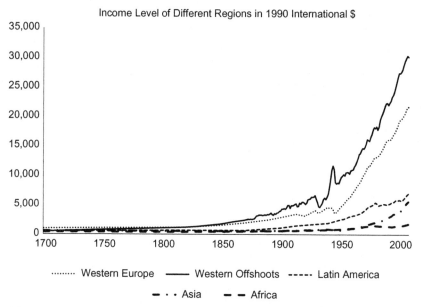

FIGURE 2.3 Evolution of the income level per capita in different regions from 1700 to 2008, according to Maddison (2010) in 1990 International $.

global average (Kufenko, Prettner, & Geloso, 2020; Milanovic, 2016; Sala-i-Martin, 2006). Of course, if and when these countries surpass that global average, their continued fast growth would contribute to the rise in cross-country income inequality.

The reason for long-run stagnation before the Industrial Revolution was the following Malthusian force: if people live close to subsistence, they cannot afford to have many children because the additional mouths to feed would compete for an unchanged amount of food. If food production and average income increase due to technological progress, families choose to raise the fertility rate above the replacement rate, giving rise to population growth and a positive relationship between higher income and fertility. However, in the long run, that additional population growth eliminates the income gains that technological progress brought about in the first place, and the economy converges to a new equilibrium in which income is again at the subsistence level, but the population size and, thus, population density are higher than they were initially (Galor & Weil, 2000; Malthus, 1798). Ongoing technological progress makes investing in children's education increasingly worthwhile because new technologies are naturally complementary with well-educated workers, and corresponding improvements in health and longevity further raise the incentive to invest in education. Investment in education is, of course, costly. Overall, this cost implies a quality-quantity tradeoff in the decision to have children: investing more in the education of each child requires households to reduce the number of children. This reverses the positive relationship between higher incomes and fertility once that education starts to increase (Becker & Lewis, 1973; Galor & Weil, 2000; Strulik, Prettner, & Prskawetz, 2013). From that point onward, higher incomes are negatively related with fertility, the Malthusian forces that sustained economic stagnation break down, countries undergo the demographic transition, and sustained long-run economic growth becomes possible. For the baseline arguments in the so-called Unified Growth Theory that explain the endogenous takeoff from Malthusian stagnation to the Industrial Revolution and sustained long-run growth, see, for example, Galor (2005, 2011), Galor and Weil (2000), Lagerlöf (2006), and Strulik et al. (2013).[2]

While the historical and economic literature explains the mechanisms giving rise to the Industrial Revolution well, this book focuses more on the effects of modern technological changes, specifically the effects of automation, on economic growth and inequality. Because automation is a rather new phenomenon that, so far, affects mainly industrialized countries, we focus on the phase of sustained growth driven by technological progress post-Industrial Revolution. In addition, we narrow our cross-country perspective to those countries that already exhibit a substantial industrial robot density.

To this end, Fig. 2.4 presents the logarithm of per capita GDP of Germany and the United States from 1850 to 2015. The United States and Germany are currently the largest and fourth-largest industrialized countries, respectively. They have a comparatively high stock of industrial robots; can reasonably be expected to have a cache of cutting-edge technological knowledge; and have available, pertinent data over long time periods. Fig. 2.4 reveals some of the main stylized facts that macroeconomic models are designed to explain and that we also aim to capture with our theoretical models (see Chapter 4 and Chapter 5). First, we observe that both countries' incomes have been growing at remarkably similar and approximately constant rates (close to 2%) over the last century and a half. This is, in and of itself, interesting because it shows that the long-run trend dwarfs short-run fluctuations and implies that the

---

2. This is only the basic outline of the story, and many forces complemented the quality−quantity tradeoff in instigating the takeoff to sustained long-run growth. For example, (1) female empowerment leads to an earlier fertility reduction and an earlier demographic transition (Bloom, Kuhn, & Prettner, 2020; Diebolt & Perrin, 2013a, 2013b; Galor & Weil, 1996; Lagerlöf, 2003; Prettner & Strulik, 2017a); (2) cultural forces can be an impediment to fertility control and the demographic transition (Baudin, 2010; Bhattacharya & Chakraborty, 2012; Prettner & Strulik, 2017b); (3) declining mortality leads to an additional incentive to invest in education because it prolongs the time period over which the benefits of education accrue (Cervellati & Sunde, 2005, 2011, 2013); (4) structural change from agriculture to manufacturing fosters overall productivity growth (Kögel & Prskawetz, 2001; Strulik & Weisdorf, 2008); and (5) public compulsory education reinforces the development process by complementing parental investments in the education of their children (Galor, 2011).

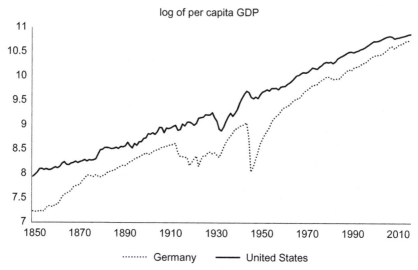

FIGURE 2.4 Logarithm of real GDP per capita for Germany (dotted line) and for the United States (solid line), according to the Maddison Project Database (2018).

knowledge of how to change trend growth rates (even slightly) is of utmost importance for generating long-run economic prosperity. Second, we observe strong deviations from the long-run trend during World War II in Germany and fast convergence growth afterward. Following World War II, nobody imagined that Germany would be able to rebound so quickly, which again hints at the strong gravitational forces of the long-run growth trend. Thus, the rapid recovery and return to strong growth in Germany became known as "The Economic Miracle." Third, a quite persistent long-run gap exists between the United States and Germany that needs to be explained separately from the determinants of trend growth rates and convergence phases. As Chapter 4 shows, the Solow (1956) model can explain all three stylized facts fairly well from a qualitative point of view.[3] Because this model has been quite successful in analyzing long-run growth phenomena in the past, it will also be our starting point for the theoretical analysis of the macroeconomic effects of automation.

We mainly focus herein on the case of the United States, and to a lesser degree on Germany, because of data availability and the fact that the most prominent empirical studies on the effects of automation focus on these two countries. However, many of the theoretical and empirical results in this

---

3. From a quantitative point of view, the Solow (1956) model has difficulties explaining the speed of convergence and the differences in income levels among countries. This book is not much concerned with these aspects, but see the excellent treatment of this topic in Acemoglu (2009); Barro and Sala-i-Martin (2004); Caselli (2005); Mankiw, Romer, and Weil (1992); and Weil (2012).

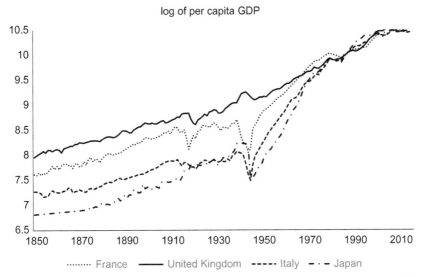

FIGURE 2.5 Logarithm of GDP per capita for France (dotted line), the United Kingdom (solid line), Italy (dashed line), and Japan (dash-dotted line), according to the Maddison Project Database (2018).

book are generalizable to other countries: Fig. 2.5, which displays the evolution of income levels for France, Italy, Japan, and the United Kingdom from 1850 to 2015, supports this notion. Again, we observe persistent long-run growth of per capita GDP in these countries. Similar to Germany, the war-torn nations of France, Italy, and Japan faced a strong decline of their income levels following World War II and fast convergence to the income levels of richer countries afterward (Barro, 1991, 1997; Islam, 1995; Sala-i-Martin, 1997; Sala-i-Martin, Doppelhofer, & Miller, 2004). In 2015, all four economies had reached comparable income levels.

While per capita GDP is an imperfect measure of overall economic well-being (Bloom, Fan, et al., 2020; Fan, Bloom, Ogbuoji, Prettner, & Yamey, 2018; Stiglitz, Sen, & Fitoussi, 2008), it correlates strongly with other indicators of welfare such as health, life expectancy, education, and leisure. Jones and Klenow (2016) build a comprehensive welfare indicator that includes the effects of consumption, leisure, mortality, and inequality based on a social welfare function. They show that while deviations exist between their welfare indicator and per capita GDP across countries, the correlation between the two indicators is 0.98. Bloom, Fan, et al. (2020) propose a new indicator that is the product of purchasing power parity (ppp)-adjusted[4] per capita

---

4. The rationale for the adjustment of purchasing power between countries is that a certain amount of money can be used to buy fewer goods and services in an economy with a high price level such as Switzerland as compared with an economy with a low price level such as Nepal.

GDP, healthy life expectancy, and the inverse of the Gini coefficient. This indicator represents inequality-adjusted lifetime income in good health. While this indicator allows for more nuanced comparisons of well-being across countries that better account for the dimensions of health and inequality, the country rankings based on this indicator and country rankings based on per capita GDP or the human development index are again highly correlated. Finally, Stevenson and Wolfers (2008) show that happiness is strongly related to per capita GDP across countries and over time. Given such demonstrated correlations, we believe the per capita GDP figures presented previously reflect the evolution of welfare reasonably well for the main purposes of the book.

2.3 Dynamics of the labor force and of unemployment

As mentioned in Chapter 1, the number of people employed has never been as high as it is today in most countries. Fig. 2.6 shows the level of nonfarm employment in the United States from 1939 to 2016. Irrespective of the fast pace of technological progress over this time span—which raised labor productivity substantially—and notwithstanding the diffusion of industrial robots since the 1970s, employment increased steadily from about 30 million persons in 1939 to about 145 million persons in 2016, an almost fivefold increase. The overall rise has not abated following the two recessions after the burst of the dotcom bubble in early 2000 and after the burst of the

FIGURE 2.6 Employment levels in the United States outside of agriculture (in thousands of persons), according to the Federal Reserve Bank of St. Louis (2018).

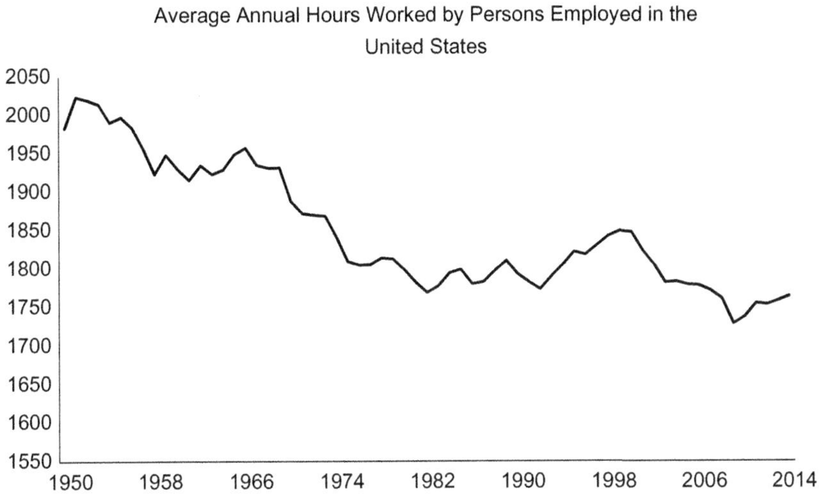

Average Annual Hours Worked by Persons Employed in the
United States

FIGURE 2.7   Average annual hours worked by persons employed in the United States, according to the Federal Reserve Bank of St. Louis (2018).

housing bubble in the mid-2000s. In the wake of these recessions, however, the pace of job creation seems to have decreased.

While these employment numbers seem to indicate that the fear of technological unemployment in the wake of automation is overblown, Fig. 2.7 displays average hours worked per year for employees in the United States. This indicator reveals a strongly decreasing secular trend. The number of hours worked per person decreased from around 1984 hours per year in 1950 to 1765 hours per year in 2016, a decrease of more than 11%. Thus, the focus solely on employment levels might be too narrow to judge the effects of technological progress on the overall amount of work. In general, the goal of almost any technological advance is to make a job easier (and thereby to lower unit cost while holding quality constant). The trend of decreasing (individual) person-hours worked may demonstrate that automation is succeeding in that regard, literally reducing the overall amount of work required, or at least reducing the pace of growth in the overall volume of work below that of the number of persons entering the workforce. Perhaps in the United States, automation is having a more nuanced effect on job trends, leading to underemployment rather than wholesale unemployment.[5]

To show the evolution of the overall amount of work, we calculate the product of employment and average hours worked and display the results in

5. Of course, other reasons than technological change might also play a certain role in explaining the downward trend, for example, household preferences for more leisure, an increase in labor-force participation of groups that pursue part-time work instead of full employment, and changes in labor market institutions and regulation.

FIGURE 2.8 Volume of work calculated as the product of the number of nonfarm employees and average hours worked (in million person-hours), according to the Federal Reserve Bank of St. Louis (2018).

Fig. 2.8. As expected, the volume of work measured by person-hours per year has increased much less than employment due to the secular decline in hours worked by each individual. However, the volume of work did not decline. At the end of the data series in 2014, the number of person-hours worked per year remained at an all-time high from a historical perspective. With a level slightly above 245 million person-hours per year, it stood higher than its previous peak in 2007 of 244.5 million person-hours per year. Irrespective of the overall increase in the volume of work, the fact that total person-hours worked per year in 2007 stood only slightly below the figure in 2014 (despite a higher GDP and a larger population) shows that technology is impacting labor in quantifiably significant ways.

Employment levels are only one part of the bigger picture reflecting how labor markets react to changes in technology. To complete the tableau, knowing how wages and incomes have changed over time is necessary. Switching attention from employment to wages, Fig. 2.9 displays the index of the average real hourly wages of production and nonsupervisory employees in manufacturing in the United States, according to the Federal Reserve Bank of St. Louis (2018). A 25% increase occurred from 1959 to 1979, but since then hourly real wages have declined slightly. The overall increase from 1959 to 2017 is close to 20%. The fact that employment did not decrease in response to the fast pace of automation might be due to the rather sluggish development of wages since the 1990s. Thus, higher employment levels may have been bargained for by accepting lower wages and/or by reducing working hours per week (cf. Lordan & Neumark, 2018).

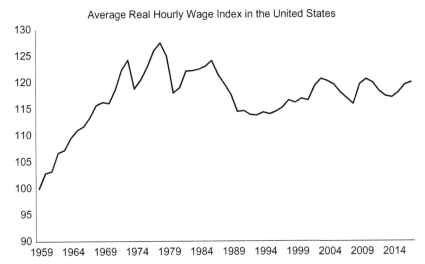

FIGURE 2.9   Average real hourly wage index of production and nonsupervisory employees in manufacturing in the United States, according to the Federal Reserve Bank of St. Louis (2018) (1959 = 100).

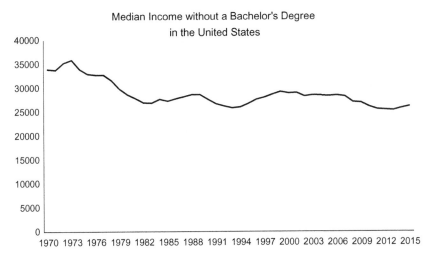

FIGURE 2.10   Real income of persons without a bachelor's degree in the United States, according to the United States Census Bureau (2017).

Unsurprisingly, because most production and nonsupervisory employees are low-skilled workers, a similar picture emerges when we focus on the incomes of all low-skilled workers in the general population. Fig. 2.10 displays the real median annual income of employees without a bachelor's degree in the United States from 1970 to 2015. Despite the overall increase in per capita GDP, the incomes of low-skilled workers have fallen from about US$34,000 in 1970 to about US$26,000 in 2015. This corresponds to a decline of almost 23%. At the same time, incomes of highly educated people have soared, and the skill premium has been rising (see, for example, Acemoglu & Autor, 2012; Goldin & Katz, 2008). Thus, in terms of wages, the data do not contradict the idea that low-skilled workers are suffering from automation, although the sluggish development and even decline of real wages as displayed in Figs. 2.9 and 2.10 could have many explanations (such as globalization and offshoring putting downward pressure on wages of low-skilled workers and other forces discussed in more detail later in this chapter).

Altogether, the diminished incomes of low-skilled workers and the rise in incomes of high-skilled workers are primary contributors to an overall rise in inequality, the topic to which we turn next.

2.4 The evolution of inequality

The fact that an 800-page book that mainly describes time series data on inequality and that includes technical descriptions and even mathematical formulae could become a bestseller underscores the importance of inequality in the public debate. With the publication of *Capital in the 21st Century* (Piketty, 2014), the analysis of inequality has undergone a revival in academia and has also started to attract significant interest from policymakers. Following the book's release, the prestigious international journal *Science* published a special issue on inequality, and *The Journal of Economic Perspectives* dedicated a symposium to the topic of "wealth and inequality." In addition, many commercially successful popular science books on inequality were published in the following years, for example, Atkinson (2015), Bourguignon (2015), Milanovic (2016), and Scheidl (2017).

Thomas Piketty and his co-authors started to analyze the evolution of inequality years before the topic's recent rise to the forefront of popular discourse (cf. Piketty, 2003; Piketty & Saez, 2003). Prior to their contributions, the notion that inequality first rises and then declines in the course of economic development was widespread. This so-called Kuznets Curve relationship (after Kuznets, 1955) was indeed observed in most developed countries until the 1960s and 1970s, with the prime example being the rise of inequality before the Great Depression and its decline afterward. The Kuznets Curve relationship was not only observable over time but also among countries: inequality and development were positively related up to a certain point of income, above which the relationship reversed (see, for example, Galor & Moav, 2004; Galor & Zeira, 1993; Greenwood & Jovanovic, 1990; Perotti, 1996). In the 1970s, however, inequality started to rise again in most countries (Atkinson, Piketty, & Saez, 2011; Bönke, Corneo, & Lüthen, 2015; Piketty & Saez, 2003), invalidating the modern support for the Kuznets

FIGURE 2.11 Income share of the top 1% of income earners in the United States and Germany, according to Piketty (2014) and Alvaredo, Garbiniti, and Piketty (2017).

Curve. Milanovic (2016) argues instead for "Kuznets Waves," with the level of inequality displaying oscillations in the long run. This means that inequality is perpetually rising and falling, either due to benign forces designed to counteract the imbalance, such as public policies that foster equality, or due to nefarious forces, such as the collateral economic impact of wars, which hit the wealthier harder than the poor. Some authors, like Scheidl (2017), even argue that only wars and other catastrophic events have the potential to reduce inequality substantially.

Figs. 2.11 and 2.12 illustrate the evolution of inequality over time by plotting the share of total income earned by the top 1% (Fig. 2.11) and the top 10% (Fig. 2.12) of incomes in the United States and Germany. While these top income shares are an imperfect measure for inequality (e.g., because they do not capture inequality in all parts of the distribution), they nevertheless capture inequality involving the top of the distribution quite accurately. They are also highly correlated with other inequality measures, such as the Gini coefficient.[6] We observe that inequality, according to top income shares, increased until the Great Depression in the United States. The share of total income going to the top 10% surged from 40% in 1910 to almost 50% in 1929, while the share of the top 1% expanded from about

---

6. The Gini coefficient is one of the most prominent measures to assess inequality (predominantly—but not exclusively—in terms of wealth or in terms of income). The Gini coefficient is 1 (or 100%) if one person earns all the income (or possesses all the wealth) and 0 if all persons earn the same income (or possess the same amount of wealth). For the advantages and disadvantages of the different inequality measures, see, for example, Cowell (2011).

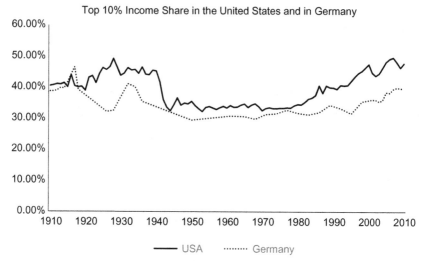

FIGURE 2.12 Income share of the top 10% of income earners in the United States and Germany, according to Piketty (2014) and Alvaredo et al. (2017).

17.5% of total income to 24% in 1929. By the 1970s, the top 10% income share decreased to a range of 32%–34% and the top 1% income share decreased to below 9%. Since then, the top income shares in the United States have been rising significantly and have reached levels unseen since the Great Depression.

In Germany, the evolution of inequality looks a bit different because the decline of the top income shares started earlier, at around the time of World War I. Germany, unlike the United States, was close to the battleground front of the conflict and suffered directly from the war in multiple ways, which was compounded by serious economic problems like the hyperinflation of 1918–1923 and required reparations. All of these problems hit the wealthier parts of the population particularly hard because (1) they owned more assets that were destroyed or damaged directly in the war or that lost parts of their value due to high inflation together with financial repression,[7] and (2) they were disproportionately affected by steeply progressive taxes to finance governmental expenditures, including reparations. Another difference in comparison with the United States is that the increase in inequality since the 1970s has been less pronounced in Germany. Potential reasons for this include stronger labor unions in Germany than in the United States, more redistribution via the tax and transfer system in Germany, and a predominantly governmentally funded education system in Germany versus a stronger private component in the United States. The extent to which these forces influence

---

7. See, for example, https://www.investopedia.com/terms/f/financial-repression.asp. Accessed on October 13, 2019.

the difference between inequality in Germany and in the United States remains, however, a topic of debate (see, for example, Battisti, Felbermayr, & Lehwald, 2016; Fratzscher, 2018).

Unlike market incomes, incomes after taxes and transfers are less unevenly distributed because tax systems are typically progressive, and redistribution via the social security system is designed to benefit those who are less well off. In many countries, the tax and transfer system substantially reduces overall inequality in terms of the Gini coefficient. In Germany, the redistributive effect of the tax and transfer system is relatively high, whereas it is comparatively low in the United States (Battisti et al., 2016; Brandolini & Smeeding, 2006, 2011; Fratzscher, 2018; Smeeding, 2005). Smeeding (2005) calculates that the reduction in the Gini coefficient between gross market incomes and net disposable incomes for the year 2000 amounted to 42% due to taxes and transfers in Germany but only to 18% in the United States. The main redistributive effect in Germany is due to the social security system, which is responsible for half of the reduction of the Gini coefficient between gross market incomes and net disposable incomes (Bach, Grabka, & Tomasch, 2015).

Figs. 2.13 and 2.14 provide insight on the evolution of wealth inequality in the United States and Europe from 1910 to 2010, according to data from Piketty (2014). Unfortunately, detailed long-run data series are not yet available for Germany, which is why we focus on Europe instead. Wealth is usually much more unequally distributed than wage income (Cowell, 2011; Piketty, 2014), which is consistent with the patterns revealed in the two figures here. The richest 1% held 64% of all assets in Europe on the eve of

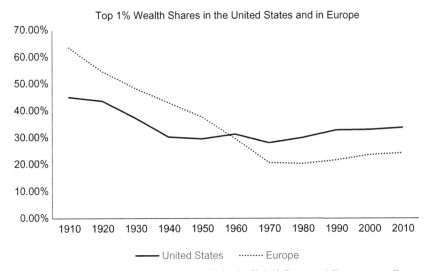

FIGURE 2.13 Wealth share of the richest 1% in the United States and Europe, according to Piketty (2014).

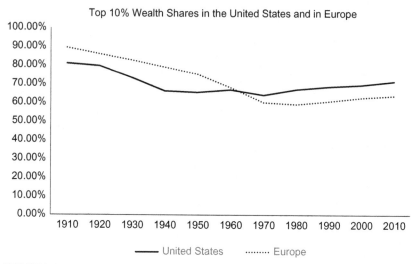

FIGURE 2.14   Wealth share of the richest 10% in the United States and Europe, according to Piketty (2014).

World War I, compared with 45% in the United States. The richest 10% in Europe owned almost all the wealth (close to 90%) in 1910, compared with just over 81% in the United States, an indication that wealth was distributed more equally in the United States than in Europe at that time. In both the United States and in Europe, the top wealth shares fell substantially during World Wars I and II and over the course of the Great Depression. However, the wealth shares declined much more dramatically in Europe following these events, leaving the United States with a more unequal wealth distribution by 2010. Wealth inequality hit new lows in the United States and Europe in the 1970s, with the top 1% wealth share hovering around 30% in the United States and 20% in Europe, while the top 10% wealth share dropped to the range of 65%–70% in the United States and 55%–60% in Europe throughout the era. Since then, the top wealth shares have increased slightly in Europe and in the United States. The strong reduction in wealth inequality preceding the 1960s is again mainly due to the fact that the wealthier parts of the population suffered disproportionately from the destruction of assets during the wars and from comparatively high wealth taxes, coupled with financial repression, to finance the high debt burden after the wars (Piketty, 2014).

Finally, Fig. 2.15 shows another important development in functional income distribution with repercussions for personal income distribution.[8]

---

8. The functional income distribution refers to the distribution of incomes between production factors such as capital, labor, and land, whereas the personal income distribution refers to the distribution of incomes among individuals (see, for example, Cowell, 2011).

FIGURE 2.15   Labor income share of total GDP for the United States, according to the Federal Reserve Bank of St. Louis (2018).

This figure displays the labor income share of total GDP for the United States from 1950 to 2014, according to the Federal Reserve Bank of St. Louis (2018). The labor income share had been rather constant—around 65%−67%—in the decades before the 1970s. This constant labor income share even came to be known as one of "Kaldor's stylized facts" for which every reasonable economic growth model that aims to explain the dynamics of aggregate output of rich countries throughout the 20th century should be able to account (cf. Acemoglu, 2009; Barro & Sala-i-Martin, 2004; Kaldor, 1957). Since the 1970s, however, the labor income share has trended downward, dropping to around 60% in 2014 (cf. Elsby, Hobijn, & Sahin, 2013; Karabarbounis & Neiman, 2014). The reduction in labor's share of total income has implications for the overall income distribution, as wages tend to be more equally distributed than wealth, such that an increase in the share of total income that accrues to capital raises income inequality in a mechanical way (cf. Krusell & Smith, 2015; Piketty, 2014; Piketty & Zucman, 2014).

The literature has offered many explanations for the observed evolution of inequality, for example,

- Globalization tends to exert downward pressure on the wages of low-skilled workers because the goods that they produce can be manufactured more cheaply abroad. At the same time, globalization raises the incomes of high-skilled workers because the demand for the goods that they produce increases with declining tariffs and quotas (cf, Bloom, & Freeman 1990, 1991; and Blackburn & Bloom, 1995; Autor, Dorn, & Hanson, 2016).

- Demographic factors, such as the trend of assortative mating (individuals choosing a partner with similar characteristics, including sociodemographic traits) and the trend toward single households, concentrate higher household incomes at the top while simultaneously increasing the number of poorer households consisting of single parents (see, for example, Blackburn & Bloom, 1995; Burkhauser, Larrimore, & Kosali, 2012; Greenwood, Guner, Korcharkov, & Santos, 2014; Kufenko, Geloso, & Prettner, 2018). At the same time, low birth rates and rising life expectancy lead to a concentration of inherited wealth (Alvaredo et al., 2017).
- Skill-biased technological change[9] raises the return to labor of high-skilled workers by more than the return to labor of low-skilled workers, which thereby increases the skill premium and widens wage gaps (Acemoglu & Autor, 2012; Goldin & Katz, 2008).
- The decline in the membership in, and associated power of, labor unions to negotiate wages affects low-skilled workers more than high-skilled workers. Moreover, a diminished bargaining power of unions implies that a smaller share of firms' revenues needs to be paid out to workers, such that the share of profits increases. This, in turn, benefits the typically wealthier owners of firms, though additional profits may also trickle down to management (as higher bonuses), who already earn comparably higher wages (Piketty, 2014).
- A declining real value of the nominal minimum wage through inflation facilitates decreasing wages of low-income workers.
- The economics of superstars leads to a burgeoning concentration of incomes at the top (Frank & Cook, 1996; Manasse & Turrini, 2001; Rosen, 1981).
- Differential human capital accumulation of children living in richer and in poorer households leads to dynastic wealth accumulation on one end of the scale and a manifestation of poverty across generations on the other (Chetty, Hendren, Kline, Saez, & Turner, 2014; Corak, 2013; Galor & Moav, 2004; Galor & Zeira, 1993; Prettner & Schaefer, 2020).
- Reductions in top marginal income tax rates have made the tax system less progressive since the 1980s, particularly in the United Kingdom and in the United States. Such reductions not only tend to increase inequality in net disposable incomes but also can escalate inequality in gross incomes. The reason is that the incentives to bargain for higher salaries increase with lower marginal top income tax rates, and granting large bonuses to management only makes sense if these bonuses are not taxed at high rates (Piketty, 2014; Piketty, Saez, & Stantcheva, 2014).

---

9. Skill-biased technological progress raises the productivity of high-skilled workers by more than the productivity of low-skilled workers. As long as the productivity level is a crucial determinant of wages (as, for example, in a perfectly competitive economy), this drives a wedge between the wages of high-skilled workers and low-skilled workers.

This book emphasizes the potential contribution of automation to the described changes in inequality. In this context, it is interesting to observe that automation in terms of industrial robots became feasible in the 1960s and that the first substantial increase in the number of industrial robots used in production occurred in the 1980s with both dates falling broadly into the period in which inequality in the United States and Germany was lowest. Since then we have seen both the number of industrial robots used and inequality rise enough to conjecture that these two trends might be causally linked. This does not mean, of course, that other explanations put forward previously would not matter. Quite the contrary, all these aspects play a crucial role in the evolution of inequality, and they might even reinforce each other.

2.5 Summary

This chapter first summarizes data on the adoption of industrial robots over time and in a cross section of countries. The main takeaway is that the stock of industrial robots started to increase significantly in the 1990s, and another boost occurred after the Great Recession of the late 2000s. The countries in which industrial robots have already diffused significantly include most large industrialized nations but also smaller, technologically advanced ones like Singapore and South Korea.

This chapter also provides a glimpse of the evolution of per capita income in the long run. We see that income growth took off for the countries that participated in the Industrial Revolution. These nations have seen relatively stable long-run income growth over the last 150 years mainly due to technological progress. Those of the nowadays rich countries that were poorer in 1850 managed to grow faster over the following 150 years, which led to a convergence in living standards. Furthermore, we see that major wars have the potential to dent the long-run trend in the short term, but that convergence forces are quite strong and seem to steer most economies back toward the long-run trend fairly quickly.

As far as the employment figures are concerned, the fears that automation might lead to mass unemployment thus far seem overstated. A record number of persons were employed in 2018 worldwide, including in the wealthier countries that are adopting robots most quickly. However, when looking at the overall volume of work (employment multiplied by average hours worked per person), a slowdown in the upward trend is clearly evident after the Great Recession. In addition, the fact that employment has not decreased might be due to the rather sluggish trajectory of wages, which might imply that automation-induced adjustments in the labor market run mainly through the wage channel. In particular, we see that low-skilled workers have suffered quite pronounced cuts to their real wages since the 1970s.

With respect to the evolution of inequality, we see mainly the following trends: falling inequality in the aftermath of World War II until around the 1970s, followed by a subsequent and continuing rise in inequality. The fall in inequality is particularly pronounced with respect to wealth inequality, mainly because the wealthier parts of the population suffered more from the destruction of assets during World Wars I and II and from the high taxes afterward. Because this fall in asset inequality implies a similar fall in capital income inequality, it mechanically reduces overall income inequality. By contrast, the fall in the labor income share observed since the 1970s has contributed to the rise in overall income inequality because wage income is more evenly distributed than capital income and wealth.

This book mainly concerns those parts of income growth, changes in employment and the wage structure, and the dynamics of inequality that can be ascribed to automation. In the following chapters, we will first discuss the empirical findings regarding the macroeconomic effects of automation before we explore theoretical frameworks to explain the stylized facts. Then we will sketch out what policymakers can do to mitigate the negative consequences of automation without reducing its positive effects or stifling economic growth. Finally, we will attempt to glimpse the possible future paths of macroeconomic outcomes in the age of automation.

References

Abeliansky, A., & Prettner, K. (2017). Automation and demographic change. Hohenheim Discussion Papers in Business, Economics, and Social Sciences 05-2017.

Acemoglu, D. (2009). *Introduction to modern economic growth*. Princeton, NJ: Princeton University Press.

Acemoglu, D., & Autor, D. (2012). What does human capital do? A review of Goldin and Katz's the race between education and technology. *Journal of Economic Literature, 50*(2), 426−463.

Acemoglu, D. & Restrepo, P. (2018). Demographics and automation NBER Working Paper 24421. National Bureau of Economic Research, Cambridge, MA.

Alvaredo, F., Garbiniti, B., & Piketty, T. (2017). On the share of inheritance in aggregate wealth: Europe and the USA, 1900−2010. *Economica, 84*(34), 239−260.

Atkinson, A. (2015). *Inequality: What can be done*. Cambridge, MA: Harvard University Press.

Atkinson, A., Piketty, T., & Saez, E. (2011). Top incomes in the long run of history. *Journal of Economic Literature, 49*(1), 3−71.

Autor, D. H., Dorn, D., & Hanson, G. H. (2016). The China shock: Learning from labor-market adjustment to large changes in trade. *Annual Review of Economics, 8*, 205−240.

Bach, S., Grabka, M., & Tomasch, E. (2015). Tax and transfer system: Considerable redistribution mainly via social insurance. *DIW Economic Bulletin, 8*. Retrieved from https://www.diw.de/documents/publikationen/73/diw_01.c.497266.de/diw_econ_bull_2015-08.pdf. Accessed 13.10.19.

Barro, R. J. (1991). Economic growth in a cross section of countries. *The Quarterly Journal of Economics, 106*(2), 407−443.

Barro, R. J. (1997). *Determinants of economic growth: A cross-country empirical study.* Cambridge, MA: MIT Press.

Barro, R., & Sala-i-Martin, X. (2004). *Economic growth.* Cambridge, MA: MIT Press.

Battisti, M., Felbermayr, G., & Lehwald, S. (2016). Inequality in Germany: Myths, facts, and policy implications Ifo Working Paper No. 217. Institute for Economic Research, Munich.

Baudin, T. (2010). A role for cultural transmission in fertility transitions. *Macroeconomic Dynamics, 14*(4), 454−481.

Becker, G. S., & Lewis, H. G. (1973). On the interaction between the quantity and quality of children. *Journal of Political Economy, 81*(2), 279−288.

Bhattacharya, J., & Chakraborty, S. (2012). Fertility choice under child mortality and social norms. *Economics Letters, 115*(3), 338−341.

Blackburn, M., & Bloom, D. E. (1995). Changes in the structure of family income inequality in the United States and other industrialized nations during the 1980s, *Research in Labor Economics, vol. 14* (pp. 141−170). Greenwich, Conn., JAI Press.

Blackburn, M. Bloom, D. E., & Freeman, R. B. (1990). The declining economic position of less skilled American men. In: Gary Burtless (Ed.), *A Future of Lousy Jobs?* (pp. 31−67). The Brookings Institution, Washington, D.C.

Blackburn, M., Bloom, D. E,. & Freeman, R. B. (1991). An era of falling earnings and rising inequality? *Brookings Review 9*(1, winter) 1990/91, 38−43.

Bloom, D. E., Fan, V. Y., Kufenko, V., Ogbuoji, O., Prettner, K., & Yamey, G. (2020). Going beyond GDP with a parsimonious indicator: -inequality-adjusted healthy lifetime income. IZA Discussion Papers 12963, Institute of Labor Economics (IZA).

Bloom, D. E., Kuhn, M., & Prettner, K. (2020). The contribution of female health to economic development, *The Economic Journal* (forthcoming).

Bönke, T., Corneo, G., & Lüthen, H. (2015). Lifetime earnings inequality in Germany. *Journal of Labor Economics, 33*(1), 171−208.

Bourguignon, F. (2015). *The globalization of inequality.* Princeton, NJ: Princeton University Press.

Brandolini, A., & Smeeding, T. (2006). Patterns of economic inequality in Western democracies: Some facts on levels and trends. *PS: Political Science and Politics, 39*(1), 21−26.

Brandolini, A., & Smeeding, T. (2011). Income inequality in richer and OECD countries. In W. Nolan, B. Selverda, & T. Smeeding (Eds.), *The Oxford handbook of economic inequality.* Oxford, UK: Oxford University Press.

Burkhauser, R., Larrimore, J., & Kosali, S. (2012). A second opinion on the economic health of the American middle class. *National Tax Journal, 65*(1), 7−35.

Caselli, F. (2005). Accounting for cross-country income differences. In: P. Aghion, & S. Durlauf (Eds.), *Handbook of economic growth* (Vol. 1, pp. 679−741). Amsterdam: Elsevier.

Cervellati, M., & Sunde, U. (2005). Human capital formation, life expectancy, and the process of development. *American Economic Review, 95*(5), 1653−1672.

Cervellati, M., & Sunde, U. (2011). Life expectancy and economic growth: The role of the demographic transition. *Journal of Economic Growth, 16*(2), 99−133.

Cervellati, M., & Sunde, U. (2013). Life expectancy, schooling, and lifetime labor supply: Theory and evidence revisited. *Econometrica: Journal of the Econometric Society, 81*(5), 2055−2086.

Chetty, R., Hendren, N., Kline, P., Saez, E., & Turner, N. (2014). Is the United States still a land of opportunity? Recent trends in intergenerational mobility. *American Economic Review, 105*(5), 141−147.

Corak, M. (2013). Income inequality, equality of opportunity, and intergenerational mobility. *Journal of Economic Perspectives, 27*(3), 79−102.

Cowell,, F. E. (2011). *Measuring inequality.* Oxford, UK: Oxford University Press.

Dauth, W., Findeisen, S., Suedekum, J., & Woessner, N. (2017). German robots—The impact of industrial robots on workers CEPR Discussion Paper 12306. Centre for Economic Policy Research, London.

Diebolt, C., & Perrin, F. (2013a). From stagnation to sustained growth: The role of female empowerment. *American Economic Review, 103*(3), 545−549.

Diebolt, C. & Perrin, F. (2013b). From stagnation to sustained growth: The role of female empowerment AFC Working Paper 4. Association Française de Cliométrie, Restinclières, France.

Elsby, M. W. L., Hobijn, B., & Sahin, A. (2013). The decline of the U.S. labor share. *Brookings Papers on Economic Activity,* 1−63.

Fan, V. Y., Bloom, D. E., Ogbuoji, O., Prettner, K., & Yamey, G. (2018). Valuing health as development: Going beyond gross domestic product. *The BMJ, 363,* k4371.

Federal Reserve Bank of St. Louis. 2018. Economic data. Retrieved from https://fred.stlouisfed. org/. Accessed 01.07.19.

Frank, R., & Cook, P. (1996). *The winner-take-all society: Why the few at the top get so much more than the rest of us.* London: Penguin Books.

Fratzscher, M. (2018). *The Germany illusion. Between economic euphoria and despair.* Oxford, UK: Oxford University Press.

Galor, O. (2005). From stagnation to growth: Unified growth theory. In: P. Aghion, & S. Durlauf (Eds.), *Handbook of economic growth* (Vol. 1, pp. 171−293). Amsterdam: Elsevier, chapter 4.

Galor, O. (2011). *Unified growth theory.* Princeton, NJ: Princeton University Press.

Galor, O., & Moav, O. (2004). From physical to human capital accumulation: Inequality and the process of development. *The Review of Economic Studies, 71*(4), 1001−1026.

Galor, O., & Weil, D. N. (1996). The gender gap, fertility, and growth. *The American Economic Review, 86*(3), 374−387.

Galor, O., & Weil, D. N. (2000). Population, technology, and growth: From Malthusian stagnation to the demographic transition and beyond. *The American Economic Review, 90*(4), 806−828.

Galor, O., & Zeira, J. (1993). Income distribution and macroeconomics. *The Review of Economic Studies, 60*(1), 35−52.

Goldin, C. & Katz, L. (2008). The race between education and technology: The evolution of U.S. wage differentials, 1890−2005 NBER Working Paper 12984. National Bureau of Economic Research, Cambridge, MA.

Greenwood, J., Guner, N., Korcharkov, G., & Santos, X. (2014). Marry your like: Assortative mating and income inequality. *American Economic Review, 104*(5), 348−353.

Greenwood, J., & Jovanovic, B. (1990). Financial development, growth and the distribution of income. *Journal of Political Economy, 98*(5), 1076−1107.

International Federation of Robotics (IFR). 2016. Executive summary world robotics 2016 industrial robots. Retrieved from https://ifr.org/news/world-robotics-report-2016. Accessed 01.08.18.

International Federation of Robotics (IFR). 2017a. Executive summary world robotics 2017 industrial robots. Retrieved from https://ifr.org/downloads/press/Executive_Summary_WR_2017_Industrial_Robots.pdf. Accessed 01.08.18.

International Federation of Robotics (IFR). 2017b. IFR press release September 27th 2017. Retrieved from https://ifr.org/ifr-press-releases/news/ifr-forecast-1.7-million-new-robots-to-transform-the-worlds-factories-by-20. Accessed 09.08.18.

International Federation of Robotics (IFR). 2018a. Executive summary world robotics 2018 industrial robots. Retrieved from https://ifr.org/downloads/press2018/Executive_Summary_WR_2018_Industrial_Robots.pdf. Accessed 10.02.19.

International Federation of Robotics (IFR). 2018b. IFR press release, February 7th 2017. Retrieved from https://ifr.org/ifr-press-releases/news/robot-density-rises-globally. Accessed 10.02.19.

Islam, N. (1995). Growth empirics: A panel data approach. *The Quarterly Journal of Economics*, *110*(4), 1127−1170.

Jones, C., & Klenow, P. (2016). Beyond GDP? Welfare across countries and time. *American Economic Review*, *106*(9), 2426−2457.

Kaldor, N. (1957). A model of economic growth. *The Economic Journal*, *67*(268), 591−624.

Karabarbounis, L., & Neiman, B. (2014). The global decline of the labor share. *The Quarterly Journal of Economics*, *129*(1), 61−103.

Kögel, T., & Prskawetz, A. (2001). Agricultural productivity growth and escape from the Malthusian trap. *Journal of Economic Growth*, *6*(4), 337−357.

Krusell, P., & Smith, A. (2015). Is Piketty's "second law of capitalism" fundamental? *Journal of Political Economy*, *123*(4), 725−748.

Kufenko, V., Geloso, V., & Prettner, K. (2018). Does size matter? Implications of household size for economic growth and convergence. *Scottish Journal of Political Economy*, *65*(4), 437−443.

Kufenko, V., Prettner, K., & Geloso, V. 2020. Divergence, convergence, and the history-augmented Solow model. *Structural Change and Economic Dynamics 53*, 2020, 62−76.

Kuznets, S. (1955). Economic growth and income inequality. *The American Economic Review*, *44*(1), 1−28.

Lagerlöf, N.-P. (2003). Gender equality and long-run growth. *Journal of Economic Growth*, 8 (4), 403−426.

Lagerlöf, N.-P. (2006). The Galor−Weil model revisited: A quantitative exercise. *Review of Economic Dynamics*, *9*(1), 116−142.

Lordan, G., & Neumark, D. (2018). People versus machines: The impact of minimum wages on automatable jobs. *Labour Economics*, *52*(C), 40−53.

Maddison, A. 2010. Statistics on world population, GDP and per capita GDP, 1−2008 AD. Retrieved from http://ghdx.healthdata.org/record/statistics-world-population-gdp-and-capita-gdp-1-2008-ad. Accessed 26.11.19.

Maddison Project Database. 2018. Maddison historical statistics 2018 version. Retrieved from https://www.rug.nl/ggdc/historicaldevelopment/maddison/releases/maddison-project-database-2018. Accessed 26.11.19.

Malthus, T. R. (1798). *An essay on the principle of population*. London: St. Paul's Church-Yard.

Manasse, P., & Turrini, A. (2001). Trade, wages, and superstars. *Journal of International Economics*, *54*(1), 97−117.

Mankiw, N. G., Romer, D., & Weil, D. N. (1992). A contribution to the empirics of economic growth. *Quarterly Journal of Economics*, *107*(2), 407−437.

Milanovic, B. (2016). *Global inequality. A new approach for the age of globalization*. Cambridge, MA: Harvard University Press.

Perotti, R. (1996). Growth, income distribution, and democracy: What the data say. *Journal of Economic Growth*, *1*(2), 149−187.

Piketty, T. (2003). Income inequality in France, 1901−1998. *Journal of Political Economy, 111* (5), 1004−1042.

Piketty, T. (2014). *Capital in the twenty-first century*. Cambridge, MA: The Belknap Press of Harvard University Press.

Piketty, T., & Saez, E. (2003). Income inequality in the United States 1913−1998. *The Quarterly Journal of Economics, 118*(1), 1−39.

Piketty, T., Saez, E., & Stantcheva, S. (2014). Optimal taxation of top labor incomes: A tale of three elasticities. *American Economic Journal: Economic Policy, 6*(1), 230−271.

Piketty, T., & Zucman, G. (2014). Capital is back: Wealth-income ratios in rich countries 1700−2010. *The Quarterly Journal of Economics, 129*(3), 1255−1310.

Prettner, K. & Schaefer, A. (2020). The U-shape of income inequality over the 20th century: the role of education, *The Scandinavian Journal of Economics* (forthcoming).

Prettner, K., & Strulik, H. (2017a). Gender equity and the escape from poverty. *Oxford Economic Papers, 69*(1), 55−74.

Prettner, K., & Strulik, H. (2017b). It's a sin—contraceptive use, religious beliefs, and long-run economic development. *Review of Development Economics, 21*(3), 543−566.

Rosen, S. (1981). The economics of superstars. *American Economic Review, 71*(5), 845−858.

Sala-i-Martin, X. (1997). I just ran two million regressions. *American Economic Review, 87*(2), 178−183.

Sala-i-Martin, X. (2006). The world distribution of income: Falling poverty and... convergence, period. *The Quarterly Journal of Economics, 121*(2), 351−397.

Sala-i-Martin, X., Doppelhofer, G., & Miller, R. (2004). Determinants of long-term growth: A Bayesian averaging of classical estimates (BACE) approach. *American Economic Review, 94*(4), 813−835.

Scheidl, W. (2017). *The great leveler: Violence and the history of inequality from the stone age to the twenty-first century*. Princeton, NJ: Princeton University Press.

Smeeding, T. (2005). Public policy, economic inequality, and poverty: The United States in comparative perspective. *Social Science Quarterly, 86*(s1), 955−983.

Solow, R. M. (1956). A contribution to the theory of economic growth. *The Quarterly Journal of Economics, 70*(1), 65−94.

Stevenson, B. & Wolfers, J. (2008, Spring). Economic growth and subjective well-being: Reassessing the Easterlin paradox. *Brookings Papers on Economic Activity*, 1−102.

Stiglitz, J., Sen, A., & Fitoussi, J. P. (2008). Report by the Commission on the Measurement of Economic Performance and Social Progress. Retrieved from https://ec.europa.eu/eurostat/documents/118025/118123/Fitoussi + Commission + report. Accessed 10.12.19.

Strulik, H., Prettner, K., & Prskawetz, A. (2013). The past and future of knowledge-based growth. *Journal of Economic Growth, 18*(4), 411−437.

Strulik, H., & Weisdorf, J. (2008). Population, food, and knowledge: A simple unified growth theory. *Journal of Economic Growth, 13*(3), 195−216.

United States Census Bureau. 2017. Historical income tables. Retrieved from https://www.census.gov/data/tables/time-series/demo/income-poverty/historical-income-people.html. Accessed 14.08.17.

Weil, D. N. (2012). *Economic growth* (3rd edition), London: Taylor & Francis.

Chapter 3

Empirical evidence on the economic effects of automation

3.1 Occupations, jobs, and tasks susceptible to automation

One of the central concerns regarding the effects of automation surrounds its potentially negative employment effects. A familiar narrative in this context is that increasing robot density will diminish the predominance of human labor and increase unemployment substantially as entire occupations are rendered obsolete. An early warning that received much attention in the public debate was the working paper version of the contribution by Frey and Osborne (2013, 2017) that claimed that 47% of all the jobs in the United States are highly susceptible to automation over the coming two decades. Frey and Osborne classify an occupation as being highly susceptible to automation if it exhibits a 70% probability (or higher) of becoming automated, based on a Gaussian process classifier developed by Rasmussen and Williams (2006) and Rasmussen and Nickisch (2010). The method is based on a machine-learning algorithm to categorize various jobs and their potential for automation. To train the algorithm, Frey and Osborne (2013, 2017) use a subset of 70 occupations that they and a group of experts classified based on subjective evaluation. Ever since the publication of their working paper, widespread concerns about mass unemployment in the age of automation and artificial intelligence have abounded (see, e.g., LeVine, 2017; Sawhney, 2018).

Using the same method as Frey and Osborne (2013), subsequent publications that focus on countries other than the United States have also found a high susceptibility of different jobs to automation. For example, Brzeski and Burk (2015) conclude that 59% of all jobs are at a high risk of automation in Germany and Pajarinen and Rouvinen (2014) and Pajarinen, Rouvinen, and Ekeland (2015) calculate that the corresponding figure amounts to one third in both Finland and Norway, respectively.

In the economic literature, however, the methodology by which these startling numbers are calculated is controversial. According to Autor (2015), many studies overestimate the extent to which different activities that humans perform can be automated and, at the same time, underestimate the complementary, productivity-enhancing effects of automation. Thus, some market

Automation and its Macroeconomic Consequences. DOI: https://doi.org/10.1016/B978-0-12-818028-0.00003-X

reactions might offset the predicted obsolescence of human labor and may augur more of a labor transition than outright replacement.

In a study resembling the basic structure of Frey and Osborne's (2013, 2017) work, Arntz, Gregory, and Zierahn (2016, 2017) emphasize the individual tasks that have to be performed within different occupations and the potential of those tasks to be automated. Their thesis is that tasks vary across workplaces within the same occupation and that the task composition evolves with technological progress (Autor & Handel, 2013; Spitz-Oener, 2006). For example, workers in occupations that are classified as highly susceptible to automation may nevertheless perform tasks that robots cannot easily substitute, such as human interaction and problem solving. While Frey and Osborne (2013, 2017) assign an occupation's probability of being susceptible to automation without considering the task variations across different workplaces within the same occupation, Arntz et al. (2016, 2017) link expert-based assessments of automation risk to individual job tasks.

Assuming homogenous tasks, Arntz et al. (2016, 2017) obtain automation risks that are consistent with the high values calculated by Frey and Osborne (2013, 2017). Allowing the tasks to differ within occupations, however, reduces the automation risk substantially. In the latter scenario Arntz et al. (2016, 2017) find that only about 9% of all jobs in the United States are at a high risk of becoming automated. Arntz et al. (2016, 2017) also apply their method to 20 additional Organisation for Economic Co-operation and Development (OECD) countries[1] and compute the associated automation risks (Table 3.1). They find the lowest share of workers who are at a high risk of being substituted by automation technologies in Estonia and South Korea (6%) and the highest share in Austria, Germany, and Spain (12%). These figures for Germany—which are considerably lower than those determined by Frey and Osborne (2013, 2017)—are largely consistent with the findings of Dengler and Matthes (2015), and the predictions for Austria are largely consistent with the findings of Peneder, Bock-Schappelwein, Firgo, Fritz, and Streicher (2016) and Nagl, Titelbach, and Valkanova (2017). The average automation risk of the 21 OECD countries considered by Arntz et al. (2016) amounts to 9%, the same value found for the United States. Even the highest risk cases of Austria, Germany, and Spain produced by this analysis are still only a quarter of the value that Frey and Osborne (2013, 2017) calculate for the United States. In terms of the average risk of being automated

---

1. The OECD is a club of rich countries that was established in 1961 "to promote policies that will improve the economic and social well-being of people around the world." The 36 member states as of 2019 are Australia, Austria, Belgium, Canada, Chile, Czech Republic, Denmark, Estonia, Finland, France, Germany, Greece, Hungary, Iceland, Ireland, Israel, Italy, Japan, Latvia, Lithuania, Luxembourg, Mexico, Netherlands, New Zealand, Norway, Poland, Portugal, Republic of Korea, Slovak Republic, Slovenia, Spain, Sweden, Switzerland, Turkey, United Kingdom, and the United States (http://www.oecd.org/about/).

TABLE 3.1 Share of workers in 21 OECD countries who face a high risk of automation and average risk of being automated across all occupations in the country according to Arntz et al. (2016).

Country	Share of workers at high risk of automation (%)	Average risk of being automated across all occupations in the country (%)
Austria	12	43
Germany	12	43
Spain	12	38
Slovak Republic	11	44
Czech Republic	10	44
Italy	10	43
Netherlands	10	40
United Kingdom	10	39
Norway	10	37
Canada	9	39
Denmark	9	38
France	9	38
United States	9	38
Ireland	8	36
Poland	7	40
Belgium	7	38
Japan	7	37
Sweden	7	36
Finland	7	35
Estonia	6	36
South Korea	6	35

across all occupations in the country, the Czech Republic and the Slovak Republic exhibit the highest values with 44%, whereas Finland and South Korea exhibit the lowest values with 35%. By and large, the higher the share of people with a high risk of automation, the higher is the average risk of being automated across all occupations in the country.

Another recent OECD study by Nedelkoska and Quintini (2018) finds that 14% of jobs across 32 countries are highly susceptible to automation. While this is higher than the 9% average obtained by Arntz et al. (2016, 2017), it is still much lower than the 47% of Frey and Osborne (2013, 2017). Somewhat in between the results of Arntz et al. (2016, 2017) and Nedelkoska and Quintini (2018), on the one hand, and Frey and Osborne (2013, 2017), on the other hand, lie the results of the McKinsey Global Institute (2017), which finds that automatable tasks make up at least 70% of job-related activities for 26% of all occupations. Overall, the McKinsey Global Institute (2017) finds that 50% of the time spent on work activities globally could be automated using currently available technologies.

Putting aside the wide disparities in the estimates of the automation potential for the workforce as a whole, forecasting which jobs are most susceptible to this fate is a hot topic in a burgeoning field. The literature seems to be in widespread agreement that routine tasks involving rather monotonous activities are the easiest to substitute with robots, whereas nonroutine tasks and those that involve human interactions and empathy are the most difficult (Acemoglu & Autor, 2011; Arntz et al., 2016, 2017; Autor, 2013; Brynjolfsson & McAfee, 2016; Ford, 2015; Frey & Osborne, 2013, 2017; McKinsey Global Institute, 2017). In addition, the results of Frey and Osborne (2013, 2017) and Arntz et al. (2016, 2017) show that more educated workers face a much lower risk of automation than workers with lower education levels and that higher-paying jobs are less vulnerable to automation than lower-paying jobs. Of course, a strong reverse causality could exist with respect to the last finding. The reason is that a high probability of an occupation being automated implies a high competition by robots, which would keep wages down. This could even hold when no actual competition by robots is present but is used as a threat in the wage bargaining process to deter workers from demanding higher pay rises (Arnoud, 2018).

A recent study by Lordan and Neumark (2018) is highly instructive in this context. They analyze the extent to which increases in the minimum wage affected the employability of workers in jobs that are classified as automatable (by Autor & Dorn, 2013). Focusing on the United States from 1980 to 2015, Lordan and Neumark's results imply that increases in the minimum wage reduce the share of automatable employment that low-skilled workers hold, with the effects being particularly strong for older workers in manufacturing (cf. Chu, Cozzi, Furukawa, & Liao, 2019). The result that rising wages lead to automation suggests that workers might apply wage restraint to escape the risk of being substituted by robots. This study therefore demonstrates that automation has the potential of stifling the wage growth of low-skilled workers even if the actual substitution by robots does not yet occur.

To illustrate how automation is likely to affect different types of labor, Tables 3.2–3.6 list different occupations and their attendant vulnerability. The tables are based upon the studies of Frey and Osborne (2017) and Nedelkoska and Quintini (2018), which calculate quite different overall figures for susceptibility, such that considering both results together might provide a more accurate overall picture than considering only one alone.

Tables 3.2 and 3.3 display the 25 occupations that are least and most susceptible to automation in the United States, according to Frey and Osborne (2017). In addition, the tables contain the corresponding employment numbers in May 2017, according to the U.S. Bureau of Labor Statistics (2018). Overall, the tables confirm that occupations generally associated with routine tasks are more susceptible to substitution by automation technologies, whereas occupations that involve a considerable amount of human interaction are less susceptible. In particular, jobs requiring managerial skills tend to be difficult to automate.

Table 3.4 contains the mean probability of automation by occupation, according to Nedelkoska and Quintini (2018), while Tables 3.5 and 3.6 exhibit the mean probability of automation by industry, split into the 20 most (Table 3.5) and 20 least (Table 3.6) susceptible industries. Again, this exercise confirms that education level, managerial skills, and the amount of interaction with humans play an important role in reducing the risk of automation for different jobs.

The foregoing section provides an overview of the potential for replacing different tasks and jobs. However, the technological susceptibility to automation does not tell us much about the actual economic effects of automation. The most dire predictions on the economic consequences of automation may not come to pass because (1) not all jobs that *can* be automated *will* be automated, as the fixed costs of installing a robot and its operating cost might be so high that robots would not pay off as prudent substitutions for labor at the lowest wage levels; (2) adjustment mechanisms, such as higher aggregate demand due to productivity increases in the wake of automation or the structural change from manufacturing to services, might imply the creation of a substantial number of new jobs (sometimes in as-yet-unimaginable occupations); and (3) economic policies have the potential to alter the impact of technological changes quite strongly. As far as the last item is concerned, Chapter 7 discusses different policy measures, such as retraining programs for displaced workers, robot taxes, and public investment programs. In the following section, we focus on empirical evidence that considers the overall equilibrium impact of automation in more detail.

3.2 Cross-country evidence on the economic consequences of automation

Empirical studies of automation effects mostly rely on the annual data reports of the International Federation of Robotics (IFR, 2018). Since 1993,

TABLE 3.2 Twenty-five occupations that are least susceptible to automation, according to Frey and Osborne (2017), and the corresponding employment levels in May 2017 in the United States, according to the U.S. Bureau of Labor Statistics (2018).

Occupation	Probability of automation (%)	Employment
Recreational therapists	0.28	18,490
First-line supervisors of mechanics, installers, and repairers	0.30	460,370
Emergency management directors	0.30	9560
Mental health and substance abuse social workers	0.31	112,040
Audiologists	0.33	12,020
Occupational therapists	0.35	126,050
Orthotists and prosthetists	0.35	7840
Healthcare social workers	0.35	167,730
Oral and maxillofacial surgeons	0.36	4800
First-line supervisors of firefighting and prevention workers	0.36	58,690
Dietitians and nutritionists	0.39	62,980
Lodging managers	0.39	36,610
Choreographers	0.40	5310
Sales engineers	0.41	70,820
Physicians and surgeons (with exceptions, see U.S. Bureau of Labor Statistics, 2018)	0.42	355,460
Instructional coordinators	0.42	157,490
Psychologists (with exceptions, see U.S. Bureau of Labor Statistics, 2018)	0.43	12,880
First-line supervisors of police and detectives	0.44	104,860
Dentists, general	0.44	110,400
Elementary school teachers, except special education	0.44	1,409,140
Medical scientists, except epidemiologists	0.45	111,690
Education administrators (elementary and secondary schools)	0.46	250,280
Podiatrists	0.46	9670

(Continued)

TABLE 3.2 (Continued)

Occupation	Probability of automation (%)	Employment
Clinical, counseling, and school psychologists	0.47	108,060
Mental health counselors	0.48	139,820

the IFR has provided detailed information on the number of operative industrial robots in approximately 60 countries across the world. The stock of industrial robots worldwide is calculated by using sales figures together with estimates of the depreciation of existing robots.

Using IFR data, Graetz and Michaels (2015, 2018) analyze the effects of automation in 14 industries across 17 economies. They conclude that robot use increased productivity growth in the studied countries by 15% between 1993 and 2007. Graetz and Michaels (2015, 2018) estimate that while the diffusion of robots reduced the volume of work for lower and intermediate levels of qualifications, automation had a positive effect on average wages for those working. These findings are consistent with the direct substitution of low-skilled manufacturing workers by robots, according to the technological potential for substitution as described by Arntz et al. (2017), Frey and Osborne (2017), and Nedelkoska and Quintini (2018), together with the contemporaneous presence of adjustment mechanisms like higher aggregate demand and structural change that would *ceteris paribus* lead aggregate employment numbers to increase.

Another recent study, by Acemoglu and Restrepo (2017, 2020), also bases its analysis on IFR data but focuses solely on the United States. As already mentioned, the diffusion of industrial robots has been relatively slow in the United States as compared with other large industrialized countries (especially Germany and Japan). At the heart of Acemoglu and Restrepo's (2017, 2020) work are the causal effects of the diffusion of industrial robots on wages and employment, differentiated by sectors and regions. In almost all areas of activity, with a few exceptions (such as management), a greater robot density has a causal negative impact on both employment and wages (see Acemoglu & Restrepo, 2017, p. 33). Even among negatively affected occupational groups, a higher robot density affects different types of workers in different ways: routine tasks are particularly vulnerable to automation, while higher education levels reduce the risks of negative effects. For individuals with a college degree, the employment effects are only slightly negative, while they are insignificant for individuals with even higher educational attainment. This indicates that Acemoglu and Restrepo (2017) do not find any positive employment effects for well-educated workers. They estimate

TABLE 3.3 Twenty-five occupations that are most susceptible to automation, according to Frey and Osborne (2017), and the corresponding employment levels in May 2017 in the United States, according to the U.S. Bureau of Labor Statistics (2018).

Occupation	Probability of automation (%)	Employment
Telemarketers	99	189,670
Title examiners, abstractors, and searchers	99	53,040
Sewers (by hand)	99	6190
Mathematical technicians[a]	99	510
Insurance underwriters	99	89,910
Watch repairers	99	2130
Cargo and freight agents	99	89,920
Tax preparers	99	68,720
Photographic process workers and processing machine operators	99	22,450
New accounts clerks	99	41,680
Library technicians	99	90,030
Data entry keyers	99	180,100
Timing device assemblers and adjusters	98	680
Insurance claims and policy processing clerks	98	277,130
Brokerage clerks	98	58,930
Order clerks	98	169,120
Loan officers	98	307,240
Insurance appraisers, auto damage	98	16,150
Umpires, referees, and other sports officials	98	18,610
Tellers	98	491,150
Etchers and engravers	98	8620
Shipping, receiving, and traffic clerks	98	671,780
Packaging and filling machine operators and tenders	98	392,910
Procurement clerks	98	70,510
Milling and planing machine setters, operators, and tenders (metal and plastic)	98	17,820

[a]The employment figure for "mathematical technicians" refers to May 2016.

TABLE 3.4 Mean probability of automation by occupation, according to Nedelkoska and Quintini (2018).

Occupation	Mean probability of automation (%)
Food preparation assistants	64
Cleaners and helpers	59
Laborers in mining, construction, manufacturing, transport	59
Assemblers	59
Drivers and mobile plant operators	58
Refuse workers and other elementary workers	58
Agricultural, forestry, and fishery laborers	57
Stationary plant and machine operators	57
Food processing, wood working, garment workers	56
Market-oriented skilled forestry, fishery workers	55
Market-oriented skilled agricultural workers	55
Personal service workers	54
Metal, machinery, and related trades workers	53
General and keyboard clerks	53
Handicraft and printing workers	53
Building and related trades workers	52
Sales workers	52
Electrical and electronic trades workers	52
Numerical and material recording clerks	50
Customer service clerks	49
Other clerical support workers	48
Health-associated professionals	45
Information and communications technicians	44
Protective services workers	44
Business and administration-associated professionals	43
Personal care workers	42
Science and engineering professionals	41
Information and communication technology (ICT) professionals	41

(Continued)

TABLE 3.4 (Continued)

Occupation	Mean probability of automation (%)
Business and administration professionals	41
Science, engineering-associated professionals	40
Legal, social, cultural-associated professionals	39
Legal, social, and cultural professionals	38
Health professionals	35
Hospitality, retail, other services managers	34
Administrative and commercial managers	32
Chief executives, senior officials, legislators	30
Production, specialized services managers	30
Teaching professionals	28

that the number of jobs supplanted by industrial robots ranges from 360,000 to 670,000, with one additional industrial robot substituting for about six workers in the manufacturing sector. While the results are again consistent with the direct substitution of low-skilled manufacturing workers by robots (as described by Arntz et al., 2017; Frey & Osborne, 2017; Nedelkoska & Quintini, 2018), the adjustment mechanisms of additional jobs that are created in producing robots, new tasks that are created in other sectors, and structural changes that raise employment in services seem to be insufficient in the United States. Worth mentioning is that Acemoglu and Restrepo (2017) find that unlike the effects of investment in industrial robots, investments in other capital goods (even computers) are positively related to labor demand and job creation.

Dauth, Findeisen, Suedekum, and Woessner (2017) apply the methods Acemoglu and Restrepo (2017) use to Germany, a country with a substantially higher robot density than the United States. Dauth et al. (2017) show that—as in the United States—an increasing robot density has a negative effect on workers in the manufacturing sector. This holds true in terms of both wage losses and employment losses. However, the negative effect on manufacturing employment in Germany is smaller than it is in the United States, with one industrial robot substituting for only two manufacturing jobs (as compared with six in the United States). Furthermore, Dauth et al. (2017) show that robots do not directly replace workers in Germany, who instead continue to be employed for other tasks until they retire or choose to leave

TABLE 3.5 Mean probability of automation by industry for the 20 industries with the highest probability of automation, according to Nedelkoska and Quintini (2018).

Occupation	Mean probability of automation (%)
Agriculture, hunting	57
Manufacture of clothing apparel	56
Postal and courier activities	56
Food and beverage service activities	55
Fishing and aquaculture	55
Other mining and quarrying	54
Land transport and transport via pipelines	54
Manufacture of wood	54
Manufacture of food products	54
Services to buildings and landscape	53
Printing and reproduction of recorded media	53
Manufacture of textiles	53
Waste collection, treatment	53
Manufacture of other nonmetallic mineral products	52
Manufacture of paper	52
Manufacture of tobacco products	52
Forestry and logging	51
Manufacture of motor vehicles, trailers, and semi-trailers	51
Manufacture of electrical equipment	51

the firm for other reasons. Thus, the overall employment losses are due to the fact that the positions of workers whose previous tasks have been automated are not filled again once these workers leave the firm but that the workers are not immediately fired. One of the main reasons for the less drastic effects of automation in Germany could be more flexible labor market institutions, embodied by unions that are willing to accept alternative wage-setting arrangements in exchange for job security (cf. Dustmann, Fitzenberger, Schoenberg, & Spitz-Oener, 2014). As a consequence, the

TABLE 3.6 Mean probability of automation by industry for the 20 industries with the lowest probability of automation, according to Nedelkoska and Quintini (2018).

Occupation	Mean probability of automation (%)
Residential care	43
Extraction of crude petroleum and natural gas	43
Real estate	43
Employment activities	43
Architectural and engineering, technical testing	43
Public administration and defense, social security	42
Mining support service activities	42
Air transport	42
Advertising and market research	42
Telecommunications	42
Human health	42
Legal and accounting	41
Computer programming, consultancy	41
Travel agency, tour operators	41
Information service activities	40
Programming and broadcasting activities	40
Social work without accommodation	40
Remediation, other waste management	38
Head offices, management consultancy	34
Education	33

labor market adjustment effects might materialize in terms of lower wages rather than in job losses. Furthermore, the German labor market includes many skilled engineers, whose jobs might be less susceptible to displacement via automation.

In contrast to the findings of Acemoglu and Restrepo (2017), who show that workers with the highest skill levels do not tend to benefit from robot use, Dauth et al. (2017) estimate positive effects for this group in Germany. In particular, skilled workers with university degrees experience wage increases not only in management but also in technological and scientific occupations related to automation. Altogether, Dauth et al. (2017) calculate that the increased robot density between 1994 and 2014 is responsible for a direct loss of about 250,000 jobs in the German manufacturing sector. However, a corresponding increase in unemployment, or a decline in the number of persons in employment, did not occur because job creation in the service sector compensated for these job losses in manufacturing.

As far as the adjustment mechanisms by which workers find jobs in other occupations are concerned, Acemoglu and Restrepo (2017) state that this process requires a substantial amount of time. The main reason for this time lag is that the most important adjustment mechanism they identify is the creation of new tasks—essentially a variant of adjustment through product innovation. However, these new tasks often require not only different but also more advanced, qualification levels than the previous jobs and obtaining the requisite training takes a considerable amount of time (and often costs a considerable amount of money). With respect to another adjustment mechanism mentioned in the introduction, the "machine production argument," Dauth et al. (2017) explicitly refer to the fact that labor intensity in the process of robot production is low. Thus, no comprehensive adjustment in the sense of the machine production argument can be observed in Germany. However, the finding that the service sector provides employment for many of the displaced workers suggests that the adjustment mechanism of structural change seems to be quite strong in Germany.

Gregory, Salomons, and Zierahn (2016) examine a task-based framework of regional labor demand in 27 European Union countries from 1999 to 2010. Their structural estimations are based upon the task-based framework of Autor and Dorn (2013) and Goos, Manning, and Salomons (2014). The production of tradeables requires capital and labor, whereas the production of nontradeable services only requires labor. Gregory et al. (2016) distinguish among channels by which automation affects labor demand and show that, overall, labor demand has been increasing at the aggregate level due to routine-replacing technological change—that is, the replacement of jobs consisting of routine tasks by automation. According to their estimates, this form of technological progress has increased labor demand by approximately 11.6 million jobs across Europe, fully half of the total employment growth of 23 million in the same countries over the observed time period. Gregory et al. (2016) show that this overall increase happens against the backdrop of routine-replacing technical change directly decreasing labor demand by 9.6 million jobs; however, additional labor demand emerged in the nontradeable sector by a bit more than 21 million jobs. Thus, the additional labor demand of the nontradeable sector has overcompensated the new technologies' direct labor substitution effects. This overall finding is consistent with recent findings that analyze the extent of job creation and destruction within search-and-matching frameworks[2] of the labor market (Cords & Prettner, 2019; Guimarães & Mazeda Gil, 2019).

Further empirical work by Autor and Salomons (2017, 2018) corroborates these findings for 18 OECD countries since the 1970s. They show that the use of robots in manufacturing increases productivity but lowers employment. At the same time, aggregate adjustment effects work to the extent that new employment opportunities are created in other sectors, such that overall employment actually increases. This is akin to the effect of Baumol's cost disease, according to which productivity in the service sector does not increase by the same amount as in manufacturing, leading to a shift in the overall employment shares toward services (Baumol & Bowen, 1966).

Apart from adjustment mechanisms that ensure that not all of the workers who are displaced by automation will be unemployed in the long run, another important argument exists against disruptive effects from automation in the short to medium run. As mentioned previously, replacing all jobs that could be automated from a technical perspective by even more expensive robots might not pay off from a cost perspective. In addition, building and supplying the robots to replace workers takes quite some time. Based on Acemoglu and Restrepo's (2017) empirical result that one industrial robot replaces about six workers and on the extrapolation of data from the IFR (2018), Bloom, McKenna, and Prettner (2018, 2019), and Abeliansky, Algur, Bloom, and Prettner (2020) calculate a direct substitution of approximately 38−64 million workers worldwide by industrial robots by the year 2030. This is less than the technically possible substitution mentioned in Frey and Osborne (2013, 2017), Brzeski and Burk (2015), and Arntz et al. (2016, 2017). If the extrapolations of Bloom et al. (2018, 2019) and Abeliansky et al. (2020) were instead based on the result obtained for Germany by Dauth et al. (2017) that one industrial robot only substitutes for two workers, then the number of direct job losses due to automation by the year 2030 would amount to approximately 12−20 million workers worldwide. These calculations do not consider any adjustment effects, which would reduce the estimated job losses further. However, IFR (2018) does not keep track of all machines/devices that are capable of automating production, such as smaller personal devices and service sector robots. Thus, from this perspective, the results of Bloom et al. (2018, 2019) and Abeliansky et al. (2020) might underestimate true job losses due to automation.

Eden and Gaggl (2018) show that the adoption of information and communication technology can explain about half of the decline in the labor income share since the 1950s. While based on a different interpretation of automation, this result is qualitatively in line with the results of Prettner (2019), who explicitly shows the mechanism by which automation reduces the labor income share in a simple economic growth model that we discuss

---

2. These models were developed by Mortensen and Pissarides (1994) to analyze the extent to which frictions in the labor market can explain the emergence of equilibrium unemployment.

in detail in Chapter 4. In his calibrations of the model, Prettner (2019) focuses on the role of industrial robots and not on information and communication technologies. He finds that only around 14% of the decline in the labor income share in the United States since the 1970s can be explained by the adoption of industrial robots. Eden and Gaggl's (2018) results are also consistent with a reallocation of labor income, transitioning from those workers who can be easily substituted by information and communication technologies to those who are complementary to these technologies. The authors show that the former tend to be workers performing routine tasks, while the latter tend to be workers performing nonroutine tasks. Overall, Eden and Gaggl (2018) show that declining prices of information and communication technologies have led to overall welfare gains of 4% in terms of the amount of consumption that would be necessary to compensate the representative household for remaining in the counterfactual scenario of no price decline. This calculation refers to the cohort that is born in the year 1980.

DeCanio (2016) focuses on the implications of the elasticity of substitution between human labor and robotic labor. Based on a constant elasticity of substitution (CES) production function[3] with human labor, capital, and robotic labor, he demonstrates that—for a high elasticity of substitution—wages decline with robot adoption, while the reverse holds true for a low elasticity of substitution. Calibrating the production function framework with data for productivity changes in the United States, DeCanio (2016) shows that the corresponding threshold level for the elasticity of substitution is 1.9. Thus, given the results of other authors described previously, the actual elasticity of substitution between low-skilled workers and automation technologies is arguably rather high and lies above this threshold, while the elasticity of substitution between high-skilled workers and automation technologies is still comparatively low and likely to be below this threshold.

Finally, at the firm level, Jäger, Moll, and Lerch (2016) analyze a poll that was regularly conducted among approximately 3000 companies in seven European countries (Austria, France, Germany, the Netherlands, Spain, Sweden, and Switzerland) between 2001 and 2012. They conclude that companies that use robots have higher labor productivity, which is consistent with the effects found in the empirical literature as described previously. However, Jäger et al. (2016) find neither negative nor positive employment effects of automation among the firms considered.

---

3. In a CES production function, the possibility to substitute different production factors with each other in the production process is independent of the employment level of a particular production factor. The easier substituting two production factors is, the higher will be the elasticity of substitution between them. If two production factors are perfect substitutes, their elasticity of substitution tends to infinity. If two production factors are perfect complements (both production factors are necessary inputs in production), then their elasticity of substitution is zero. A widely used production function is the Cobb–Douglas production function with an elasticity of substitution that is equal to unity.

Overall, the studies described in this section point to the following effects of automation: (1) positive labor productivity effects; (2) negative employment and wage effects for low-skilled workers in manufacturing, but either insignificant or even positive employment and wage effects for high-skilled workers; (3) job creation in the service sector; and (4) a decline in the labor income share. We will see in the next chapter that many of these findings can be explained well by simple economic growth models that are augmented by automation.

3.3 Summary

This chapter shows that the estimates regarding the technological potential for automation vary widely. The values range from about 6% of all jobs being deemed highly susceptible to automation in some countries (like Estonia), up to 59% in other countries (like Germany) over two decades. The main reason for the large differences is methodological. The studies that do not account for changes in the heterogeneity of tasks within the same occupation conclude that more jobs are highly susceptible to automation, whereas the studies that do account for variations in the heterogeneity of tasks arrive at substantially lower values.

Apart from these differences, however, the literature by and large agrees that the following characteristics are negatively correlated with the susceptibility of a job to automation: (1) the job requires a higher education level, (2) the job requires managerial and supervisory skills, (3) the job requires human interaction and empathy, (4) the job is associated with a higher salary, and (5) the job consists of many nonroutine tasks.

Altogether, a job's technological susceptibility to automation does not necessarily indicate how many jobs will ultimately be automated. The reason is that simple cost−benefit considerations might lead to the conclusion that employing human labor is cheaper than robots for certain tasks and in certain contexts. Furthermore, as far as aggregate labor market effects are concerned, adjustment mechanisms exist such as higher aggregate demand due to productivity increases in the wake of automation, or structural changes in the economy such that workers displaced in manufacturing find employment in the service sector. These adjustment effects must be considered when assessing the overall labor market effects of automation. Empirical evidence for Europe, and Germany in particular, suggests that these adjustment mechanisms are quite strong and are responsible for the finding that overall employment has actually increased in the wake of automation. In addition, as Chapter 7 will show, economic policies, such as retraining programs for displaced workers, robot taxes, and public investment programs, have some potential to dampen the negative direct impact of technological changes on labor demand.

As far as the aggregate macroeconomic effects of automation are concerned, almost all studies find (1) positive labor productivity effects; (2) negative employment and wage effects for low-skilled workers in manufacturing, but either insignificant or even positive employment and wage effects for high-skilled workers; (3) job creation in the service sector; and (4) a decline in the labor income share. These are the central empirical findings that we aim to explore from a theoretical perspective in the following chapters.

References

Abeliansky, A., Algur, E., Bloom, D.E., & Prettner, K. (2020). The future of work: meeting the global challenge of demographic change and automation. *International Labour Review* (forthcoming).

Acemoglu, D., & Autor, D. (2011). Skills, tasks and technologies: Implications for employment and earnings. In O. C. Ashenfelter, & D. Card (Eds.), *Handbook of labor economics* (Vol. 4, pp. 1043−1171). Amsterdam: Elsevier.

Acemoglu, D., & Restrepo, P. (2017). Robots and jobs: Evidence from US labor markets. NBER Working Paper No. 23285, National Bureau of Economic Research, Cambridge, MA.

Acemoglu, D., & Restrepo, P. (2020). Robots and jobs: Evidence from US labor markets. *Journal of Political Economy*. (forthcoming).

Arnoud, A. (2018). Automation threat and wage bargaining. Available from https://antoinearnoud.github.io/files/jmp.pdf. Accessed 02.01.2019.

Arntz, M., Gregory, T., & Zierahn, U. (2016). The risk of automation for jobs in OECD countries. A comparative analysis. OECD Social, Employment and Migration Working Papers, No. 189, OECD Publishing, Paris.

Arntz, M., Gregory, T., & Zierahn, U. (2017). Revisiting the risk of automation. *Economics Letters*, *159*(C), 157−160.

Autor, D. (2013). The "task approach" to labor markets: An overview. *Journal for Labour Market Research*, *46*(3), 185−199.

Autor, D. (2015). Why are there still so many jobs? The history and future of workplace automation. *The Journal of Economic Perspectives*, *29*(3), 3−30.

Autor, D. H., & Dorn, D. (2013). The growth of low-skill service jobs and the polarization of the US labor market. *American Economic Review*, *103*(5), 1553−1597.

Autor, D., & Handel, M. (2013). Putting tasks to the test: Human capital, job tasks, and wages. *Journal of Labor Economists*, *31*(S1), S59−S96.

Autor, D. & Salomons, A. (2017). Robocalypse now—Does productivity growth threaten employment? European Central Bank Conference Proceedings. Available from http://conference.nber.org/confer/2017/AIf17/Autor.pdf. Accessed 19.12.2019.

Autor, D., & Salomons, A. (2018). Is automation labor-displacing? Productivity growth, employment, and the labor share. *Brookings Papers on Economic Activity, Spring*, 1−63.

Baumol, W., & Bowen, W. (1966). *Performing arts—The economic dilemma: A study of problems common to theater, opera, music and dance*. New York: Twentieth Century Fund.

Bloom, D., McKenna, M., & Prettner, K. (2018). Demography, unemployment, automation, and digitalization: Implications for the creation of (decent) jobs, 2010−2030. NBER Working Paper 24835, National Bureau of Economic Research, Cambridge, MA.

Bloom, D., McKenna, M., & Prettner, K. (2019). Global employment and decent jobs, 2010−2030: The forces of demography and automation. *International Social Security Review*, *72*(3), 43−78.

Brynjolfsson, E., & McAfee, A. (2016). *The second machine age: Work, progress, and prosperity in a time of brilliant technologies*. New York: Norton & Company.

Brzeski, C., & Burk, I. (2015). Die Roboter kommen. ING DiBa Economic Research, April 30, 2015.

Chu, A.C., Cozzi, G., Furukawa, Y., & Liao, C.-H. (2019). Effects of minimum wage on automation and innovation in a schumpeterian economy. MPRA Paper 95824, University Library of Munich, Germany.

Cords, D., & Prettner, K. (2019). Technological unemployment revisited: Automation in a search and matching framework. GLO Discussion Paper Series 308, Global Labor Organization, Essen, Germany.

Dauth, W., Findeisen, S., Suedekum, J., & Woessner, N. (2017). German robots—The impact of industrial robots on workers. CEPR Discussion Paper 12306. Centre for Economic Policy Research, London.

DeCanio, S. (2016). Robots and humans—complements or substitutes? *Journal of Macroeconomics*, *49*, 280−291.

Dengler, K., & Matthes, B. (2015). Folgen der Digitalisierung für die Arbeitswelt. Substituierbarkeitspotentiale von Berufen in Deutschland. IAB Forschungsbericht 11/2015. Institut für Arbeitsmarkt- und Berufsforschung, Nürnberg.

Dustmann, C., Fitzenberger, B., Schoenberg, U., & Spitz-Oener, A. (2014). From sick man of Europe to economic superstar: Germany's resurgent economy. *Journal of Economic Perspectives*, *28*(1), 167−188.

Eden, M., & Gaggl, P. (2018). On the welfare implications of automation. *Review of Economic Dynamics*, *29*, 15−43.

Ford, M. (2015). *Rise of the robots: Technology and the threat of a jobless future*. New York: Basic Books.

Frey, C. B., & Osborne, M. A. (2013). The future of employment: How susceptible are jobs to computerisation? Available from https://web.archive.org/web/20150109185039/http://www.oxford-martin.ox.ac.uk/downloads/academic/The_Future_of_Employment.pdf. Accessed 10.12.2019.

Frey, C. B., & Osborne, M. A. (2017). The future of employment: How susceptible are jobs to computerisation? *Technological Forecasting and Social Change*, *114*(C), 254−280.

Goos, M., Manning, A., & Salomons, A. (2014). Explaining job polarization: Routine-biased technological change and offshoring. *American Economic Review*, *104*(8), 2509−2526.

Graetz, G., & Michaels, G. (2015). Robots at work. CEPR Discussion Paper 10477. Centre for Economic Policy Research, London.

Graetz, G., & Michaels, G. (2018). Robots at work. *Rev Econ Stat*, *100*(5), 753−768.

Gregory, G., Salomons, A., & Zierahn, U. (2016). Racing with or against the machine? Evidence from Europe. ZEW Discussion Paper No. 16-053. Leibniz-Zentrum für Europäische Wirtschaftsforschung, Mannheim.

Guimarães, L., & Mazeda Gil, P. (2019). Explaining the labor share: Automation vs labor market institutions. Economics Working Papers 19-01, Queen's Management School, Queen's University Belfast, UK.

IFR (International Federation of Robotics). (2018). World robotics industrial robots and service robots. Available from https://ifr.org/worldrobotics/. Accessed 10.07.2018.

Jäger, A., Moll, C., & Lerch, C. (2016). *Analysis of the impact of robotic systems on employment in the European Union—Update*. Luxemburg: Publications Office of the European Union.

LeVine, S. (2017). Expert doubles down: Robots still threaten 47% of U.S. jobs. Available from https://www.axios.com/expert-doubles-down-robots-still-threaten-47-of-us-jobs-1513305167-efa6857d-d45f-4810-8d1a-ca018fe1dfb3.html. Accessed 21.08.2018.

Lordan, G., & Neumark, D. (2018). People versus machines: The impact of minimum wages on automatable jobs. *Labour Economics*, *52*(C), 40−53.

McKinsey Global Institute. (2017). Jobs lost, jobs gained: Workforce transitions in a time of automation. Available from https://www.mckinsey.com/~/media/mckinsey/featured%20insights/Future%20of%20Organizations/What%20the%20future%20of%20work%20will%20mean%20for%20jobs%20skills%20and%20wages/MGI-Jobs-Lost-Jobs-Gained-Report-December-6-2017.ashx. Accessed 19.12.2019.

Mortensen, D. T., & Pissarides, C. A. (1994). Job creation and job destruction in the theory of unemployment. *The Review of Economic Studies*, *61*(3), 397−415.

Nagl, W., Titelbach, G., & Valkanova, K. (2017). Digitalisierung der arbeit: Substituierbarkeit von berufen im zuge der automatisierung durch industrie 4.0. IHS Projektbericht, Institut für Höhere Studien, Wien. Available from http://irihs.ihs.ac.at/4231/1/200800.pdf. Accessed 10.07.2018.

Nedelkoska, L., & Quintini, G. (2018). Automation, skill use and training. OECD Social, Employment and Migration Working Paper No. 202. Paris.

Pajarinen, M., & Rouvinen, P. (2014). Computerization threatens one third of Finnish employment. Muistio Brief, ETLA, The Research Institute of the Finnish Economy. Available from https://www.etla.fi/wp-content/uploads/ETLA-Muistio-Brief-22.pdf. Accessed 10.07.2018.

Pajarinen, M., Rouvinen, P., & Ekeland, A. (2015). Computerization threatens one-third of Finnish and Norwegian employment. Muistio Brief, ETLA, The Research Institute of the Finnish Economy. Available from https://www.etla.fi/wp-content/uploads/ETLA-Muistio-Brief-34.pdf. Accessed 10.07.2018.

Peneder, M., Bock-Schappelwein, J., Firgo, M., Fritz, O., & Streicher, G. (2016). Österreich im Wandel der Digitalisierung. Österreichisches Institut für Wirtschaftsforschung, Wien. Available from https://www.wifo.ac.at/jart/prj3/wifo/resources/person_dokument/person_dokument.jart?publikationsid = 58979&mime_type = application/pdf. Accessed 10.07.2018.

Prettner, K. (2019). A note on the implications of automation for economic growth and the labor share. *Macroeconomic Dynamics*, *23*(3), 1294−1301.

Rasmussen, C., & Nickisch, H. (2010). Gaussian processes for machine learning (GPML) toolbox. *Journal of Machine Learning Research*, *11*, 3011−3015.

Rasmussen, C., & Williams, C. (2006). *Gaussian processes for machine learning*. Cambridge, MA: MIT Press.

Sawhney, M. (2018). As robots threaten more jobs, human skills will save us. Available from https://www.forbes.com/sites/mohanbirsawhney/2018/03/10/as-robots-threaten-more-jobs-human-skills-will-save-us/#4ab9b1a13fce. Accessed 21.09.2018.

Spitz-Oener, A. (2006). Technical change, job tasks, and rising educational demands: Looking outside the wage structure. *Journal of Labor Economics*, *24*(2), 235−270.

U.S. Bureau of Labor Statistics. (2018). Occupational employment and wages. Available from https://www.bls.gov/oes/current/oes514035.htm. Accessed 10.08.2018.

Chapter 4

A simple macroeconomic framework for analyzing automation

4.1 Preliminaries and definitions

4.1.1 Growth rates in discrete and in continuous time

In the first section of this chapter, we provide the necessary basic tools for the analysis of phenomena related to long-run economic growth. For more details see, for example, the excellent textbooks by Acemoglu (2009) and Barro and Sala-i-Martin (2003). In our notation, we follow the standard convention of denoting the time index by t, writing it as a subscript to a variable if the variable is measured in discrete time and within parentheses after the variable if the corresponding variable is measured in continuous time. Furthermore, we use uppercase letters to refer to economic aggregates and lowercase letters to refer to variables measured per capita or per worker.

Let Y denote a country's aggregate output, that is, its gross domestic product (GDP), and let N be the population size. Then, according to our notation, per capita output is $y = Y/N$. Denoting the growth rate of a variable x by g_x, the growth rate of per capita GDP is given by

$$g_y = \frac{y_t - y_{t-1}}{y_{t-1}} = \frac{y_t}{y_{t-1}} - 1 \tag{4.1}$$

in discrete time and by

$$g_y = \frac{\dot{y}(t)}{y(t)} = \frac{d\log[y(t)]}{dt} \tag{4.2}$$

in continuous time, where a dot over a variable refers to the derivative of that variable with respect to time. Because the derivative of a variable with respect to time is the instantaneous change of the corresponding variable, its growth rate is given by $g_x = \dot{x}(t)/x(t)$, which is analogous to the discrete time case.

The expression after the second equal sign in Eq. (4.2) shows that the derivative of the logarithm of a time-dependent variable $x(t)$ with respect to

Automation and its Macroeconomic Consequences. DOI: https://doi.org/10.1016/B978-0-12-818028-0.00004-1
67

time t is equivalent to the growth rate of the variable $x(t)$. This can be seen by applying the chain rule when differentiating the expression $\log[x(t)]$ with respect to time, the result of which is $[1/x(t)] \cdot \dot{x}(t)$. Note that the derivative of a variable $x(t)$ with respect to time only exists if time evolves continuously; otherwise the function $x(t)$ would be discontinuous and hence nondifferentiable. In the following analyses, we suppress time arguments whenever we refer to a variable in general, such that it does not matter whether time evolves discretely or continuously in the given context, or when suppressing the time argument increases the exposition's clarity.

We denote the size of the workforce by L and follow the common assumption in the basic economic growth literature that the total population is employed, which renders per capita GDP and per worker GDP equivalent. The reason for this assumption is that economic growth models abstract from short-run fluctuations in unemployment rates and do not distinguish between workers and retirees, or between men and women who might have different labor force participation rates.

The central aim of a formal economic model, which is to simplify as much as possible by abstracting from aspects that are not the focus of interest in analyzing a given question, justifies this abstraction. In the words of Albert Einstein: "Everything should be made as simple as possible, but no simpler." An economic model and the map of a city are strongly analogous in this context. A city map with a scale of 1:1 would be *realistic* but completely useless for the task of helping to find a given location. Therefore, a city map needs to abstract from items that are not necessary for finding the given location (e.g., trees), while capturing those aspects of reality that are useful for finding the location (e.g., streets). When performing such abstractions, the central question to ask is always whether a given simplification is justifiable for the purpose at hand and not so much whether it is realistic per se.

Chapter 5 discusses more general models that allow for unemployment and for retirement such that the population size and the workforce could differ. These models are more complicated but better suited to analyze the effects of automation on employment. However, in this chapter, we are predominantly concerned with aspects of economic growth and distribution that do not necessarily require details of how unemployment is determined.

In Example 1, we provide some simple rules for calculating growth rates.

Example 1

Assume that aggregate output Y grows at rate g_Y and the population N grows at rate $g_N = n$. Calculate the growth rates of per capita GDP in discrete and in continuous time.

Solution

In discrete time, we use Eq. (4.1) to get

$$g_y = \frac{y_t}{y_{t-1}} - 1 = \frac{\frac{Y_t}{N_t}}{\frac{Y_{t-1}}{N_{t-1}}} - 1 = \frac{\frac{Y_t}{Y_{t-1}}}{\frac{N_t}{N_{t-1}}} - 1 = \frac{1+g_Y}{1+n} - 1.$$

In continuous time, we use Eq. (4.2) to get

$$g_y = \frac{d\log[y(t)]}{dt} = \frac{d\log\left[\frac{Y(t)}{N(t)}\right]}{dt} = \frac{d\{\log[Y(t)] - \log[N(t)]\}}{dt} = \frac{\dot{Y}(t)}{Y(t)} - \frac{\dot{N}(t)}{N(t)} = g_Y - n.$$

Example 1 shows that the growth rate of a variable (defined as the fraction of two other variables) is the ratio of the *growth factors* of these two variables minus 1 in discrete time and simply the difference between the *growth rates* of these two variables in continuous time. These relationships come in handy for many of the calculations and adjustments that are required when describing the long-run evolution of different variables.

4.1.2 Representative individuals and representative firms

In reality, all individuals differ from each other at least to some extent, just as all businesses do. In modeling an economy from a "birds-eye view", however, abstracting from this heterogeneity as much as possible is necessary for tractability. A common assumption made in the literature is that the consumption side of an economy consists of one single *representative* individual (or household) who decides upon the optimal consumption path over time and is infinitely lived, while the production side (the firm sector) consists of one single *representative* firm that solves the given profit maximization problem. If this assumption is imposed, aggregation rules are not necessary to calculate economy-wide variables.[1] Instead, per capita variables and economy-wide aggregate variables coincide. In most of the models described in this book, the assumption of representative agents is a very useful simplification that does not invalidate the results.

Again, important to consider is whether an assumption is helpful for analyzing a certain research question and whether it can distort the results rather than whether the assumption is realistic (even economists know that a single representative individual does not exist). When analyzing the effects of technological progress on long-run economic growth, abstracting from heterogenuous agents is usually justifiable. When analyzing the implications of demographic changes or of inequality, by contrast, departing from the single representative agent assumption is usually necessary. In overlapping

---

1. For a more detailed discussion of this assumption and its limitations, see Acemoglu (2009, pp. 149–159).

generations models, for example, heterogeneity of individuals exists with respect to age, wealth, and consumption, such that these models are often better suited to analyzing demographic and distributional issues. In so doing, aggregation rules must be applied to derive expressions for aggregate consumption and aggregate savings from individually optimal decisions. Thus, per capita variables and aggregate variables will generally not coincide in the literature that does not feature representative agents.

4.1.3 Aggregate production function

The aggregate production function describes how the production inputs in an economy combine to produce aggregate output Y. The production inputs are typically the stock of physical capital (K), which comprises production halls, machines, tools, assembly lines, office buildings, and so on; the workforce (L); and the productivity level (A), by which the production inputs capital and labor combine to yield aggregate output.[2] The productivity term A consists of two parts: (1) an economy's state of technology, which determines the location and shape of the *production possibility frontier*, and (2) an economy's efficiency, assessed via its market structure, its organization, its institutions, etc., which determines whether an economy produces at the production possibility frontier (is efficient) or below the production possibility frontier (is inefficient). The general expression of the production function is as follows:

$$Y = F(K, L, A), \qquad (4.3)$$

where $F(\cdot)$ is the functional form by which inputs are transformed into output. Output is usually interpreted as being a single good that households want to buy and consume (the consumption aggregate). Assuming that this final good is the numéraire allows us to normalize its price to unity. While Eq. (4.3) does not impose any structure on the production function, the standard function used in the literature is the *neoclassical* production function, which has the following properties:

1. The neoclassical production function is *homogeneous of degree one* in the accumulable production factors capital and labor. In other words, *constant returns to scale* prevail with respect to capital and labor: if both of these production factors increase by a factor $\lambda > 1$, then aggregate output also increases by this factor. Formally, this property is described by

$$F(\lambda K, \lambda L, A) = \lambda Y. \qquad (4.4)$$

---

2. This basic structure can be extended in many different directions, for example, to include natural resources, land, different skill levels of workers, and so on.

The intuitive interpretation for constant returns to scale is best illustrated by considering the thought experiment of doubling all inputs and considering what happens to output. For this purpose assume that a firm produces output in a production facility with a given number of workers and machines. Then, the firm replicates the exact same production facility again at a place nearby. Under standard conditions, this should lead to twice the output, which implies constant returns to scale.

2. The neoclassical production function has positive but diminishing marginal products with respect to the input factors capital and labor. If one input (capital or labor) increases, while the other input stays constant, output also increases. However, the rate of increase is diminishing in the level of the rising input factor. Formally, this property is described by

$$F_K(K,L,A) > 0, \ F_L(K,L,A) > 0, \tag{4.5}$$

$$F_{KK}(K,L,A) < 0, \ F_{LL}(K,L,A) < 0, \tag{4.6}$$

where F_x denotes the first partial derivative of $F(\cdot)$ with respect to the variable x and F_{xx} denotes the second partial derivative of $F(\cdot)$ with respect to the variable x. These expressions imply that the production function is strictly concave, that is, it has a steeper slope for a low level of a particular factor input and a flatter slope for a higher level of the particular factor input.

The intuition is that if a firm increases only one production factor, say labor, then this leads to more output because, for example, the firm could introduce an additional shift or make sure that workers get enough rest to stay productive. However, squeezing more output out of the given capital stock by employing only additional workers becomes increasingly difficult because only a limited number of shifts are possible per day and worker productivity might not increase that much with the increasing time for rest when the working hours are already comparatively low. Thus, the additional output for additional labor input should *ceteris paribus* decrease.

3. The neoclassical production function fulfills the *Inada conditions*:

$$\lim_{K \to 0} F_K(K,L,A) = \infty, \ \lim_{K \to \infty} F_K(K,L,A) = 0, \tag{4.7}$$

$$\lim_{L \to 0} F_L(K,L,A) = \infty, \ \lim_{L \to \infty} F_L(K,L,A) = 0. \tag{4.8}$$

These conditions imply that the first marginal units of capital and labor are infinitely productive, while the marginal productivity approaches zero if one production factor becomes highly abundant while the other stays constant. The intuition is that if a firm only employs machines, nothing can be produced. The first worker that the firm employs can start to operate the machines and output becomes positive so that the production function is infinitely steep at the origin for the first marginal unit of labor. Because the additional output that can be produced by hiring more workers diminishes, at some point the workplace becomes so crowded that additional workers just step on each others' toes and do not lead to much additional output.

The intuitive explanations show that these assumptions are not unrealistic, and such production functions approximate many production processes well.[3] Most macroeconomic models impose the following specific Cobb–Douglas form on the production function (4.3).

$$Y = K^{\alpha}(AL)^{1-\alpha}, \tag{4.9}$$

where $\alpha \in (0, 1)$ is the elasticity of output with respect to capital input and labor is multiplied by the productivity term A. In this formulation, technological progress that raises productivity is *labor augmenting* (termed "Harrod neutral"). This type of technological progress is most frequently assumed because it allows for the derivation of a balanced growth path, along which the growth rates of output per capita, consumption per capita, investment per capita, and so on, are constant (Jones & Scrimgeour, 2008; Uzawa, 1961). This property is desirable because, as the stylized facts of economic development show, the long-run evolution of per capita GDP has been remarkably constant in rich countries over the past century. Furthermore, Jones (2005) shows that the Cobb–Douglas form of the production function with labor-augmenting technological progress follows directly from microfoundations if new ideas are Pareto distributed.

Other types of technological progress that are frequently mentioned in the literature but usually not applied when modeling long-run economic growth are *capital-augmenting* ("Solow-neutral") technological progress, where the production function has the form $Y = (AK)^{\alpha}L^{1-\alpha}$, and "Hicks-neutral" technological progress, where the production function has the form $Y = A(K^{\alpha}L^{1-\alpha})$. Hicks-neutral technological progress is often assumed in the growth accounting literature to derive the part of output growth that cannot be attributed to the accumulation of physical capital (K) or growth of the workforce (L). For more details on these types of technological progress, see, for example, the books by Acemoglu (2009) and Barro and Sala-i-Martin (2003).

In the following discussion, we restrict our attention to the Cobb–Douglas production function with labor-augmenting technology and use it as the default specification. Example 2 shows that this production function fulfills the properties of a neoclassical production function.

---

3. Other production functions have increasing returns to scale, for example, in the presence of learning-by-doing effects, or decreasing returns to scale, for example, in the presence of quality differences in the production factors such that a firm might hire more productive workers first. In this case, if the firm hires additional workers, they are less productive than those already employed and, therefore, contribute less to output.

Example 2
Show that the Cobb–Douglas production function Eq. (4.9) fulfills the properties of a neoclassical production function.

Solution
For positive A, K, and L, we proceed as follows.

1. We multiply the accumulable production factors capital K and labor L by λ such that

$$(\lambda K)^\alpha (A\lambda L)^{1-\alpha} = \lambda^\alpha \lambda^{1-\alpha} K^\alpha (AL)^{1-\alpha} = \lambda K^\alpha (AL)^{1-\alpha} = \lambda Y.$$

Consequently, the Cobb–Douglas production function with labor-augmenting technology is homogeneous of degree one (has constant returns to scale with respect to the accumulable production factors).

2. To analyze the property of diminishing marginal productivities, we calculate the partial derivatives of the production function with respect to the factor inputs and assess their sign given the parameter restriction $\alpha \in (0,1)$:

$$F_K(K,L,A) = \alpha \left(\frac{AL}{K}\right)^{1-\alpha} > 0,$$

$$F_L(K,L,A) = (1-\alpha)A^{1-\alpha} \left(\frac{K}{L}\right)^\alpha > 0,$$

$$F_{KK}(K,L,A) = \alpha(\alpha-1)K^{\alpha-2}(AL)^{1-\alpha} < 0,$$

$$F_{LL}(K,L,A) = -(1-\alpha)\alpha K^\alpha A^{1-\alpha}(L)^{-\alpha-1} < 0.$$

Consequently, the Cobb–Douglas production function with labor-augmenting technology fulfills the properties of positive but diminishing marginal productivity of the accumulable production factors.

3. To analyze whether the Inada conditions are fulfilled, we calculate the limit of the partial derivatives for the cases in which the employment levels of the corresponding production factor converge either to zero or to infinity:

$$\lim_{L \to 0} F_K(K,L,A) = \lim_{K \to 0} \alpha \left(\frac{AL}{K}\right)^{1-\alpha} = \infty,$$

$$\lim_{L \to \infty} F_K(K,L,A) = \lim_{K \to \infty} \alpha \left(\frac{AL}{K}\right)^{1-\alpha} = 0,$$

$$\lim_{L \to 0} F_L(K,L,A) = \lim_{L \to 0}(1-\alpha)A^{1-\alpha} \left(\frac{K}{L}\right)^\alpha = \infty,$$

$$\lim_{L \to \infty} F_L(K,L,A) = \lim_{L \to \infty}(1-\alpha)A^{1-\alpha} \left(\frac{K}{L}\right)^\alpha = 0.$$

This implies that all four Inada conditions are fulfilled. Altogether, the Cobb–Douglas production function (4.9) fulfills the properties of a neoclassical production function.

Next we derive the factor rewards that firms pay under perfect competition. In so doing, the standard assumption the literature employs is that firms rent physical capital from the representative individual who owns the capital stock. As a consequence, firms pay the capital rental rate to households at each point in time. This assumption is helpful because it allows the static statement of the firm's optimization problem instead of the more complicated dynamic optimization problem that a firm faces when it owns the capital itself. With our particular specification of the Cobb–Douglas production function, the profit maximization problem of the representative firm is given by

$$\max_{K,L} \pi = K^{\alpha}(AL)^{1-\alpha} - wL - RK, \tag{4.10}$$

where π refers to profits, w to the wage rate, R to the capital rental rate, and the choice variables are capital K and labor L. The first term on the right-hand side represents total revenues, the second term represents the wage bill, and the third term represents outlays for the rented capital. The revenues are equal to the firm's output because the final good is used as the numeráire and its price is normalized to unity.

Solving the profit maximization problem yields inverse demand functions for capital and labor. These functions are the demand of firms for the factor inputs capital and labor, but expressed in the price of these factor inputs (hence the term "inverse"). The inverse demand functions imply that firms employ additional capital and additional labor up to the point where the additional costs generated by greater use of the particular production factor starts to exceed the corresponding additional revenue. As is intuitive, from that point onward, employing more of the particular production factor would reduce the profits. Consequently, in the competitive equilibrium, the production factors are paid their marginal value products such that[4]

$$R = \frac{\partial Y}{\partial K} = \alpha \left(\frac{AL}{K}\right)^{1-\alpha}, \tag{4.11}$$

$$w = \frac{\partial Y}{\partial L} = (1 - \alpha)\left(\frac{K}{L}\right)^{\alpha} A^{1-\alpha}. \tag{4.12}$$

We observe that the capital rental rate R rises with the employment of labor L and falls with the employment of capital K, while the reverse holds true for the wage rate w. In addition, capital depreciates because of wear and tear at the rate δ. Thus, the interest rate earned by the representative individual is given by the capital rental rate net of depreciation as follows:

$$r = R - \delta.$$

---

4. Due to the fact that the price of the final output is unity, the marginal product and the marginal value product coincide.

Intuitively, the wedge between the capital rental rate that firms pay and the real interest rate that the representative household receives increases with the rate at which capital depreciates.

Example 3 shows that the share of total income that the production factor labor earns is always constant with this type of production function under the assumption of perfect competition.

Example 3
Derive the share of labor income in the economy with perfect competition.

Solution
Under perfect competition, Eq. (4.12) refers to the wage rate such that the total wage bill in the economy is given by

$$w \cdot L = (1 - \alpha)(K)^{\alpha}(AL)^{1-\alpha}.$$

Hence, the share of total income Y that the production factor labor earns amounts to

$$\frac{w \cdot L}{Y} = \frac{(1 - \alpha)(K)^{\alpha}(AL)^{1-\alpha}}{K^{\alpha}(AL)^{1-\alpha}} = 1 - \alpha. \tag{4.13}$$

Obviously, this share does not depend on any of the variables K, L, or A, such that it is always constant.

Example 3 shows that the standard Solow (1956) growth model that assumes a Cobb–Douglas production function predicts that the share of total income that the production factor labor earns is always constant and given by $1 - \alpha$. This has long been considered an advantage of the model because it is consistent with the stylized facts of economic development presented by Kaldor (1957). Indeed, the labor share in the United States was remarkably constant throughout the 20th century until the late 1970s, with around two thirds of aggregate income going to the production factor labor and one third to the production factor capital. Based on this, estimates suggest that $\alpha = 1/3$ is a good long-run approximation for the United States (see, for example, the studies by Acemoglu, 2009; Jones, 1995).

However, Chapter 2 shows that the US labor income share has been declining since the 1980s. Later, when we augment the Solow model with automation, we will see that the automation-augmented Solow model can account for this decline *and* for a constant labor income share until the 1970s.

4.2   The simplest version of the standard 1956 Solow model in discrete time

To explain the stylized facts outlined in Chapter 2 we start with the simplest version of the Solow (1956) model without population growth and without technological progress.[5] This model was the first to seriously address the question of why economies are able to grow over time. Because economic growth goes hand in hand with an increase in the stock of production capital (such as production halls, machines, assembly lines, office buildings, etc.), capital accumulation could be surmised to be the main explanation for increasing economic prosperity. As we will see, however, this basic Solow model without technological progress can explain convergence and cross-country income differences, but not sustained long-run growth. Later, we will generalize the model to allow for population growth and technological change, the last of which leads to a balanced growth path along which sustained per capita output growth occurs at the rate of technological progress. Thus, the more general model can account for convergence phases, cross-country income differences, and sustained long-run growth. Finally, we will introduce automation into this setting. The introduction of automation will allow the explanation of empirically observable phenomena that the basic Solow (1956) model cannot describe.

Equation (4.14) below describes the evolution of capital over time, relating the capital stock at time $t + 1$ (i.e., K_{t+1}) to

1. The capital stock that is carried over from time t as given by K_t,
2. The gross investments that are made in new capital denoted by $I(t)$, and
3. The depreciation of capital at rate δ.

This difference equation reads

$$K_{t+1} = K_t + I_t - \delta K_t = (1 - \delta)K_t + I_t, \qquad (4.14)$$

where the term $(1 - \delta)K_t$ refers to the part of the capital stock that remains usable in period $t + 1$, that is, the capital stock of period t net of the depreciated capital due to wear and tear. If new gross investments I_t are higher than depreciation δK_t, the capital stock clearly increases over time: from the first two parts of Eq. (4.14) we then have that $K_{t+1} > K_t$, such that the capital stock is rising as time passes (i.e., as t grows larger).

Next, we need to know how investment is determined. From introductory macroeconomics courses (as based, e.g., on the books by Blanchard, 2016; Mankiw, 2015), we already know that a country's GDP—that is, the total value of goods and services produced within a country within a given time period t—can be used for several purposes.[6] The standard national accounts identity posits that $Y_t = C_t + I_t + G_t + NX_t$, where Y_t refers to aggregate output, C_t

---

5. Intuitive introductory textbooks on economic growth with a basic treatment of the Solow (1956) model without automation include Aghion and Howitt (2008), Jones and Vollrath (2009), and Weil (2012). Barro and Sala-i-Martin (2003), Acemoglu (2009), Romer (2011), and Heijdra (2017) provide a more advanced treatment.
6. GDP can be calculated via three methods: (1) the expenditure approach (summing up all expenditures in an economy), (2) the factor income approach (summing up all factor incomes in an economy), and (3) the production approach (summing up all value added created in an economy).

refers to aggregate consumption, I_t denotes gross investment, G_t are governmental expenditures, and NX_t are net exports given by $IM_t - X_t$ with IM_t being the value of imports and X_t being the value of exports. Because a model should avoid unnecessary complications, the basic version of the Solow (1956) model assumes no government role $(G_t = 0)$ and a closed economy $(NX_t = IM_t - X_t = 0)$. Thus, the simplified national accounts identity is given by

$$Y_t = C_t + I_t. \tag{4.15}$$

Rearranging this identity to express investment in terms of the difference between output and consumption, that is, $I_t = Y_t - C_t$, and then substituting the production function (4.9) for Y_t into this expression, we can use the result to rewrite the evolution of physical capital given in Eq. (4.14) as follows:

$$K_{t+1} = K_t^\alpha L^{1-\alpha} + (1 - \delta)K_t - C_t. \tag{4.16}$$

When substituting the production function into the expression for investment, we assume that labor is constant and we normalize the stock of technology to unity. Furthermore, we know that in a closed economy without a government, aggregate savings (S_t) equal aggregate investment, that is, $S_t = I_t$. Assuming that individuals save an exogenously given fraction of their income, denoted by s, aggregate savings and aggregate consumption can be expressed as follows:

$$S_t = sY_t = K_t^\alpha L^{1-\alpha} - C_t = sK_t^\alpha L^{1-\alpha}, \tag{4.17}$$

$$\Leftrightarrow C_t = (1 - s)Y_t = (1 - s)K_t^\alpha L^{1-\alpha}, \tag{4.18}$$

where the second line follows because income can only be consumed or saved. Using Eq. (4.17) in Eq. (4.16) yields the fundamental equation of the Solow (1956) model without technological progress and without population growth as follows:

$$K_{t+1} = sK_t^\alpha L^{1-\alpha} + (1 - \delta)K_t. \tag{4.19}$$

The interpretation of this equation is straightforward. Aggregate investment is the part of total income $Y_t = K_t^\alpha L^{1-\alpha}$ that is not consumed, which is given by the first term on the right-hand side of the fundamental equation (4.19). Clearly, the higher the saving rate s or aggregate income Y_t are, the higher is aggregate gross investment. The second term on the right-hand side refers to the capital stock that is carried over from time t and that remains usable (i.e., it is adjusted for depreciation δK_t). As long as gross investment is higher than depreciation, the capital stock accumulates and $K_{t+1} > K_t$ holds. Eq. (4.19) shows that achieving higher gross investment becomes increasingly difficult with a larger capital stock. This follows directly from the fact that the marginal product of capital in the production function is diminishing (i.e., the exponent of physical capital in the production function is smaller than one), while depreciation is linear at rate δ. Thus, as capital increases, the additional output that this added capital can produce and, hence, the additional future gross investment that accompanies this increase diminish, whereas depreciation of capital rises linearly with the capital stock.

The central prediction of the Solow (1956) model without technological progress is, therefore, that capital accumulation ceases at the point at which $K_{t+1} = K_t = K^*$. This is defined as the *steady-state equilibrium*, wherein capital no longer grows and, consequently, output stagnates. The argument can be easily illustrated formally when recalling the expression of aggregate output:

$$Y_t = K_t^\alpha L_t^{1-\alpha}.$$

By assumption, $A_t \equiv 1$ and $L_t \equiv L$ were treated as constant. The only term that was allowed to grow was K_t. During the transition to the steady-state equilibrium, the capital stock grows according to Eq. (4.19), but at a diminishing rate because of the waning marginal productivity of physical capital. Asymptotically, therefore, the steady state is reached, and the economy stops growing. The clear answer of the simplest formulation of the Solow (1956) model to the question of whether physical capital accumulation alone can explain long-run economic growth is therefore a decided "no."

Solow (1956) shows that the crucial driver of long-run economic growth must be something other than physical capital accumulation and highlights the central role of technological progress; continual improvements in technology (and therefore growth in productivity A) are necessary for sustained growth in per capita GDP. As we will see later, automation changes the described relationship completely because—according to the definition of automation—it indicates that a new type of capital can perfectly substitute for labor. This essentially implies that labor becomes an accumulable production factor through replacement by robots and, thereby, the diminishing returns with respect to physical capital in the production process can be overcome. However, before we enter this discussion, we first illustrate the arguments presented in this section with a graphical illustration of the dynamics of the simple Solow (1956) model, followed by analyses of the Solow (1956) model with population growth and with technological progress.

Figs. 4.1 and 4.2 illustrate the dynamics of the simple Solow model without technological progress and without population growth, plotting the physical capital stock at time $t + 1$ on the vertical axis as a function of the capital stock at time t according to the fundamental Eq. (4.19). Fig. 4.1 displays Eq. (4.19), together with the 45-degree line. Because $K_{t+1} = K_t$ characterizes a steady state, such a steady state must be located on the 45-degree line; every point on this line has exactly this property of constant capital. Because the Cobb—Douglas production function fulfills the conditions for a neoclassical production function, it is strictly concave and has an initial slope that is much steeper than the 45-degree line. The Inada conditions ensure

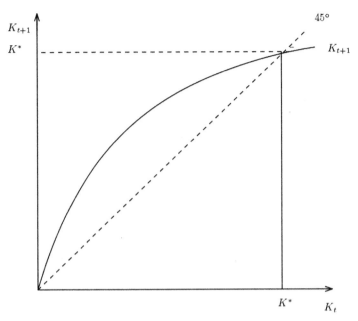

FIGURE 4.1 Steady state of the discrete-time Solow (1956) model, without technological progress and without population growth.

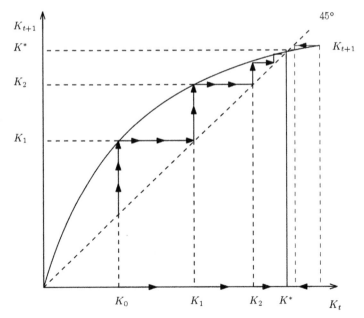

FIGURE 4.2 Dynamics of the discrete-time Solow (1956) model without technological progress and without population growth.

that—after a certain level of the capital stock is surpassed—the slope becomes flatter than the 45-degree line. Altogether, these properties ensure that the K_{t+1} curve intersects the 45-degree line exactly once for a positive capital stock $K_{t+1} > 0$. This intersection is the steady state toward which the economy converges, as the law of motion of the capital stock given by Eq. (4.19) shows.

Now we can analyze the dynamics of the economy outside of the steady state. If the economy starts with a capital stock that is smaller than the steady-state capital stock K^*, then we know from Eq. (4.19) that the capital stock in the next period is larger than the current level (i.e., $K_{t+1} > K_t$) such that physical capital accumulates—grows—over time. Due to the production function (4.9), we know that the economy also expands as long as K grows, and it converges from below to the steady-state level of per capita output associated with K^* via the production function. The further to the left of the steady-state capital stock the economy is, the faster capital accumulates and the faster the economy grows. This dynamic can explain the "growth miracles" of countries after their capital stocks have been destroyed, for example, due to wars. In particular, France, Germany, and Japan from the 1950s to the 1970s are often used as examples for the usefulness of the basic Solow (1956) model in describing such transition phases. In these countries, the capital stock was destroyed in World War II. Nevertheless, subsequent economic growth was very high by historical standards and remained so for several decades, during which their growth rates surpassed those of other industrialized countries with capital stocks that were minimally affected by World War II.

Fig. 4.2 displays the corresponding dynamics of economic development, which are illustrated by the arrows in the graph. If the economy starts with a capital stock K_0, then the capital stock at time $t = 1$ is given by the K_{t+1} curve as K_1 on the vertical axis. One time step corresponds to an inversion of the axes such that the vertical axis becomes the horizontal axis. After the time step, capital at time $t = 1$ is then displayed on the horizontal axis as the value of K_1, projected from the vertical axis to the horizontal axis around the 45-degree line. Then, the capital stock at time $t = 2$ is given by the level on the K_{t+1} curve that corresponds to the value of K_1 on the vertical axis. This amounts to K_2, which is then, again, projected on the horizontal axis, and so on and so forth; the economy clearly converges to the steady state in this situation. Example 4 shows how the steady-state capital stock can be calculated and analyzes its dependence on some crucial underlying parameters.

What happens if, for some reason, the initial capital stock is larger than K^*? In this case, Eq. (4.19) implies that the capital stock in the next period will be smaller than in the current period, that is, $K_{t+1} < K_t$, such that physical capital decumulates (shrinks) over time. Due to the production function (4.9), we know that the economy also shrinks as long as K shrinks, and it converges from above to the steady-state level of per capita output associated with K^*. The central question here is: why would an economy have reached a level of K_t that is above K^* in the first place? One particularly illustrative example is Russia after the collapse of the Soviet Union. During communism, consumption was suppressed, whereas the saving rate and investment were artificially high. After the collapse of the Soviet Union, the saving rate plunged such that capital decumulated, which led to a contracting economy as Russia struggled through its *perestroika*-guided transition from entrenched communism to a mixed market economy and nascent capitalism in the early 1990s.[7]

Example 4
Calculate the steady-state capital stock and analyze its dependence on the saving rate s and on the rate of depreciation δ.

Solution
To calculate the steady-state capital stock, let $K_{t+1} = K_t = K^*$ in the equation that describes the evolution of the capital stock: $K_{t+1} = sK_t^\alpha L^{1-\alpha} + (1 - \delta)K_t$ and then solve for the associated value of K^*. Doing so yields

$$K^* = s(K^*)^\alpha L^{1-\alpha} + (1-\delta)K^* \Leftrightarrow \delta K^* = s(K^*)^\alpha L^{1-\alpha} \Leftrightarrow \delta (K^*)^{1-\alpha} = sL^{1-\alpha} \Leftrightarrow K^* = L\left(\frac{s}{\delta}\right)^{\frac{1}{1-\alpha}}.$$

Obviously, the steady-state capital stock rises with the saving rate (s) and decreases with the rate of depreciation (δ). Mathematically, this can be verified by calculating the partial derivatives $\partial K^*/\partial s$ and $\partial K^*/\partial \delta$. The intuition is straightforward: in case of a higher rate of depreciation, more of the capital stock wears out in each period, such that the steady-state capital stock at which gross investment equals depreciation is diminished. At this lower level, the marginal product of capital is higher, such that the higher depreciation can be sustained. If, by contrast, the saving rate is greater, people save more of their total income, enabling higher gross investment and the given rate of depreciation can be sustained at a higher level of the steady-state capital stock at which the marginal product of capital is lower.

Example 4 shows that different underlying parameter values can lead to different steady states. This implies that countries with different parameter values would also differ in their steady-state capital stocks and in their steady-state per capita GDPs. Thus, the Solow model in its basic form can explain cross-country differences in per capita income levels by cross-country differences in the values of the structural parameters s and δ.

---

7. Another country with a very high saving rate is China. An ongoing debate concerns whether its saving rate might already be inefficiently high such that reducing the saving rate could lead to increases in consumption for current and future generations (this is the topic of dynamic inefficiency that we do not touch upon in this book for lack of space). For a discussion of China and whether its economy might be dynamically inefficient, see Yang, Zhang, and Zhou (2011).

Mankiw, Romer, and Weil (1992) show that, while the Solow model can explain cross-country differences in per capita income to some extent, the empirically observed differences in the parameter values of s and δ cannot generate the vast differences in per capita income levels that we observe. Therefore, Mankiw et al. (1992) augment the Solow model by human capital (i.e., they account for the fact that workforce education levels might also differ among countries) and show that this human capital−augmented version of the Solow model can explain much greater cross-country income differences. More recently, Dalgaard and Strulik (2013) show that considering cross-country differences in the historical timing of the fertility transition also increases the Solow model's power to explain today's cross-country differences in per capita income levels.

The Solow (1956) model in its basic form has very convenient features: it is simple and intuitive, and it delivers reasonable descriptions for economic growth in the medium run. As such, it can explain the economic miracles in France, Germany, and Japan after World War II or the declining Russian economy in the early 1990s. However, and this is quite a serious drawback for a model that aims to explain long-run economic growth, no growth occurs at the long-run steady-state equilibrium at all. So by the standards required of a reasonable economic model, the simplifications are too extreme. By assuming away technological progress, the model economy lacks the property of being able to account for long-run economic growth. In Section 4.3, we allow the stock of technology to grow. This has strong implications for the predicted long-run economic growth rate, such that the assumption $g_A = 0$ is not innocuous. In addition to this generalization, we will allow the population to grow, and we will present a continuous time version of the model.

4.3 The Solow model in continuous time with technological progress and with population growth

Now we introduce population growth at rate n and technological progress at rate g_A into the basic version of the Solow model. Because analyzing the Solow model with population growth and technological progress in discrete time is comparatively difficult, we switch to a continuous time setting. This has the additional advantage of allowing the introduction of differential equations in a simple setting with which the reader is already familiar. In this setting, technological progress and population growth are described by

$$\frac{\dot{A}(t)}{A(t)} = g_A > 0, \qquad \frac{\dot{L}(t)}{L(t)} = n > 0, \qquad (4.20)$$

such that the *particular solutions* of the differential equations for $A(t)$ and $L(t)$ with initial levels $A(0)$ and $L(0)$, respectively, are as follows:

$$A(t) = A(0)e^{g_A \cdot t}, \quad L(t) = L(0)e^{n \cdot t}. \tag{4.21}$$

These particular solutions describe the value of the corresponding variable (in this case technology, A, or labor, L) at each point in time, t, given that the growth process started at the initial values $A(0)$ and $L(0)$ and that the variables have been growing at rates g_A and n, respectively, for exactly t years. If no initial values were given, then we could only get the *general solution* of the differential equations stated in Eq. (4.20), which refers to all possible paths that fulfill the laws of motion implied by Eq. (4.20). However, the differential equations presented in Eq. (4.20) have infinitely many solutions—one for each possible starting value. The imposition of a particular starting value allows the selection of one unique particular solution out of the infinitely many general solutions. For accessible introductions to the analysis of differential equations and difference equations, see, for example, the books by Gandolfo (2010) and Sydsaeter Hammond, Seierstad, & Strom, (2008).

Again, individuals are assumed to save a constant fraction s of their income, such that aggregate capital accumulation is given by

$$\dot{K}(t) = sK(t)^{\alpha}[A(t)L(t)]^{1-\alpha} - \delta K(t). \tag{4.22}$$

Note that, in contrast to the discrete time setting, the right-hand side does not contain the capital stock that is carried over from the previous period. This is because it already shows up on the left-hand side, as $\dot{K}(t)$ is the *change* in the capital stock over time, defined as $\dot{K}(t) = \lim_{\Delta \to 0}(K_t - K_{t-\Delta})$, for which the discrete time formulation is the special case at which Δ attains 1 as the lowest possible value and the change is given by $K_t - K_{t-1}$. In continuous time, Δ can be arbitrarily small and approach zero.

Now we redefine variables in terms of efficiency units of labor (or effective labor) with the available amount of efficiency units of labor in the economy given by $A \cdot L$. Measuring labor in efficiency units takes into account that an increase in labor productivity A allows a given number of workers to produce more output. The transformation into efficiency units is very useful because it enables us to use, again, a graphical illustration of the model around a stationary steady state. If we did not transform variables, we would essentially have to draw a new diagram at each instant to capture a moving steady-state capital stock per worker (which is the untransformed variable).

To this end, we divide all variables by $(A \cdot L)$. We define capital per unit of effective labor as $\hat{k}(t)$, output per unit of effective labor as $\hat{y}(t)$, and consumption per unit of effective labor as $\hat{c}(t)$, such that

$$\hat{k}(t) = \frac{K(t)}{A(t)L(t)}, \quad \hat{y}(t) = \frac{Y(t)}{A(t)L(t)}, \quad \hat{c}(t) = \frac{C(t)}{A(t)L(t)}. \tag{4.23}$$

Assuming again a Cobb−Douglas production function with labor-augmenting technology as before, output per unit of effective labor $\hat{y}(t)$ becomes

$$\hat{y}(t) = \frac{K(t)^{\alpha}[A(t)L(t)]^{1-\alpha}}{A(t)L(t)} = \left[\frac{K(t)}{A(t)L(t)}\right]^{\alpha} = \hat{k}(t)^{\alpha}. \qquad (4.24)$$

We are now looking for a steady state again, but in the transformed variables $\hat{k}$ and $\hat{y}$. Essentially, as we will see later, the nontransformed variables k and y do not exhibit a steady state but grow over time such that, as mentioned earlier, we could not draw similar figures as in Section 4.2 without the transformation.

To explore the evolution of capital per unit of effective labor, we differentiate its expression as defined in Eq. (4.23) with respect to time. Doing so implies that we have to use the quotient rule and the product rule to calculate the derivative because all three variables that define the capital stock per unit of effective labor—$K(t)$, $L(t)$, and $A(t)$—depend on time:

$$\dot{\hat{k}}(t) = \frac{\dot{K}(t)A(t)L(t) - K(t)\left[\dot{A}(t)L(t) + A(t)\dot{L}(t)\right]}{[A(t)L(t)]^2}$$

$$= \frac{\dot{K}(t)}{A(t)L(t)} - \frac{K(t)}{A(t)L(t)}\left[\frac{\dot{A}(t)}{A(t)} + \frac{\dot{L}(t)}{L(t)}\right]$$

$$= \frac{\dot{K}(t)}{A(t)L(t)} - \hat{k}(t)[g_A + n].$$

Next, we substitute for the evolution of aggregate capital from Eq. (4.22) to get

$$\dot{\hat{k}}(t) = \frac{sK(t)^{\alpha}[A(t)L(t)]^{1-\alpha} - \delta K(t)}{A(t)L(t)} - \hat{k}(t)(g_A + n)$$

$$= s\hat{k}(t)^{\alpha} - \hat{k}(t)(n + g_A + \delta). \qquad (4.25)$$

This is the fundamental equation of the Solow (1956) model with technological progress and with population growth. Again, we observe that the first term on the right-hand side is gross investment (now in terms of efficiency units of labor), while the second term on the right-hand side refers to capital depreciation (at rate δ) and effective capital dilution (at rate $g_A + n$). Effective capital dilution is due to the fact that faster technological progress and faster population growth both imply faster growth of the denominator of $\hat{k} = K/(AL)$. As a consequence, equipping every person with the same stock of capital per unit of effective labor requires faster growth of the numerator K.

Now we can solve for the steady state of this economy in terms of capital per unit of effective labor. By definition, $\dot{\hat{k}}(t) = 0$ has to hold at a steady state, such that Eq. (4.25) implies

$$s\left(\hat{k}^*\right)^\alpha = \hat{k}^* (n + g_A + \delta),$$

$$\Leftrightarrow \left(\hat{k}^*\right)^{\alpha-1} = \frac{n + g_A + \delta}{s}$$ (4.26)

$$\Leftrightarrow \hat{k}^* = \left(\frac{s}{n+g_A+\delta}\right)^{\frac{1}{1-\alpha}}.$$

As this expression shows, increasing the saving rate s raises the capital stock per unit of effective labor at the steady state, while increasing n, g_A, and δ reduces the capital stock per unit of effective labor at the steady state. The intuitive arguments to explain this behavior carry over from Section 4.2. What differs from the previous section is that now technological progress and population growth (g_A and n) also dilute the capital stock and thereby function as depreciation by implying a drag on physical capital accumulation measured in efficiency units.

Fig. 4.3 displays the dynamics of the continuous-time Solow (1956) model with technological progress at rate g_A and with population growth at rate n. The crucial difference from the previous case in discrete time is that here the vertical axis displays output per unit of effective labor $\hat{y} = \hat{k}^\alpha$ and gross investment $s \cdot \hat{y} = s \cdot \hat{k}^\alpha$ as a function of the capital stock per unit of effective labor ($\hat{k}$), which is displayed on the horizontal axis. A steady state

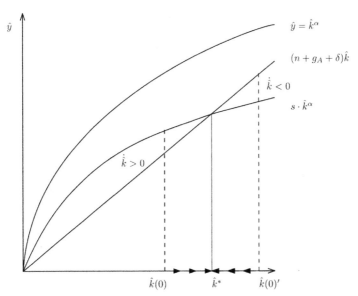

FIGURE 4.3 Dynamics of the continuous-time Solow (1956) model with technological progress at rate g_A and with population growth at rate n.

in the transformed variables is the static point at which $\dot{\hat{k}} = 0$. Eq. (4.25) implies that, at this point, $s \cdot \hat{k}^{\alpha} = (n + g_A + \delta)\hat{k}$, such that gross investment in efficiency units equals effective capital depreciation plus effective capital dilution. Therefore, any steady state of the model will always be located on the line $(n + g_A + \delta)\hat{k}$ starting at the origin. In contrast to the discrete time setting, where the steady state is located on the 45-degree line, we therefore plot the effective capital depreciation and dilution line with slope $(n + g_A + \delta)$ in Fig. 4.3.

Again, arrows indicate the evolution of the economy over time. If the economy starts with a capital stock per unit of effective labor $\hat{k}(0)$ that is lower than the steady-state capital stock per unit of effective labor, then effective capital depreciation and dilution as given by $(n + g_A + \delta)\hat{k}$ is lower than gross investment $s \cdot \hat{k}^{\alpha}$. Thus, capital per efficiency unit of labor accumulates, that is, $\dot{\hat{k}} > 0$. If, by contrast, the economy starts with a capital stock per unit of effective labor $\hat{k}(0)'$ that is higher than the steady-state capital stock per unit of effective labor, then effective capital depreciation and dilution as given by $(n + g_A + \delta)\hat{k}$ is higher than gross investment $s \cdot \hat{k}^{\alpha}$. Thus, capital per efficiency unit of labor decumulates, that is, $\dot{\hat{k}} < 0$. As in discrete time, the economy therefore converges to the steady state, irrespective of whether it starts with a low or a high level of capital per unit of effective labor, with convergence being from below in the former case and from above in the latter.

Next, we derive the growth rates of variables at the steady state and outside the steady state. In doing so, we note that the following relations between variables measured in units of effective labor and variables measured per capita follow from the foregoing definitions of these two types of variables:

$$k(t) = A(t)\hat{k}(t),$$

$$y(t) = A(t)\hat{y}(t) = A(t)\hat{k}(t)^{\alpha},$$

$$c(t) = A(t)(1 - s)\hat{y}(t) = A(t)(1 - s)\hat{k}(t)^{\alpha}.$$

In addition, the following relations hold between variables measured in units of effective labor and aggregate variables:

$$K(t) = A(t)L(t)\hat{k}(t), \tag{4.27}$$

$$Y(t) = A(t)L(t)\hat{y}(t) = A(t)L(t)\hat{k}(t)^{\alpha}, \tag{4.28}$$

$$C(t) = A(t)L(t)(1 - s)\hat{y}(t) = A(t)L(t)(1 - s)\hat{k}(t)^{\alpha}. \tag{4.29}$$

From these equations, it follows that at the steady state at which the variables measured in units of effective labor are constant, per capita variables grow at the rate of technological progress (g_A), while aggregate variables grow at the rate of technological progress plus the rate of population growth $(g_A + n)$. Example 5 shows this result formally.

Example 5
Calculate the growth rates of per capita GDP, $y(t)$, and of aggregate GDP, $Y(t)$. What is the growth rate of per capita GDP and of aggregate GDP if capital per unit of effective labor is at the steady state?

Solution
As demonstrated at the beginning of the chapter, when discussing the computation of a variable's growth rate in continuous time, the growth rate of $y(t)$ can be calculated by first taking the logarithm:

$$\log\left[y(t)\right] = \log[A(t)] + \alpha\log[\hat{k}(t)] \tag{4.30}$$

and then differentiating the result with respect to time, such that

$$g_y = \frac{d\log[y(t)]}{dt} = \frac{\dot{A}(t)}{A(t)} + \alpha\frac{\dot{\hat{k}}(t)}{\hat{k}(t)} = g_A + \alpha\cdot g_{\hat{k}}. \tag{4.31}$$

At the steady state, the growth rate of $\hat{k}(t)$ is, by the definition of a steady state, equal to zero. Consequently, at the steady state of $\hat{k}(t)$, Eq. (4.31) implies that per capita output grows at the rate of technological progress, g_A. Similarly, the growth rates of the capital stock per capita $k(t)$ and of consumption per capita $c(t)$ can be calculated.

To get the growth rate of aggregate output, $Y(t)$, we again take the logarithm:

$$\log[Y(t)] = \log[A(t)] + \log[L(t)] + \alpha\log[\hat{k}(t)] \tag{4.32}$$

and differentiate the result with respect to time, such that

$$g_Y = \frac{d\log[Y(t)]}{dt} = \frac{\dot{A}(t)}{A(t)} + \frac{\dot{L}(t)}{L(t)} + \alpha\frac{\dot{\hat{k}}(t)}{\hat{k}(t)} = g_A + n + \alpha\cdot g_{\hat{k}}. \tag{4.33}$$

At the steady state, the growth rate of $\hat{k}(t)$ is, by the definition of a steady state, equal to zero. Consequently, at the steady state of $\hat{k}(t)$, Eq. (4.33) implies that aggregate output grows at the rate of technological progress plus the rate of population growth $(g_A + n)$. Similarly, the growth rates of aggregate capital $K(t)$ and of aggregate consumption $C(t)$ can be calculated. Doing so would show that they also grow at the rate $(g_A + n)$.

We now integrate the analysis at the steady state with the dynamics outside of the steady state. If an economy starts with a capital stock per unit of effective labor lower than the steady-state capital stock per unit of effective labor (e.g., $\hat{k}(0)$ in Fig. 4.3), growth of $\hat{k}$ occurs during the convergence process toward the steady state but at a declining rate. Consequently, during this transition phase to the steady state, per capita GDP is growing faster than the rate of technological progress, g_A, with the growth rate converging from above to g_A. This is exactly what Germany experienced after World War II until the 1970s.

Thus, in Fig. 4.4, which displays the logarithm of per capita GDP in the United States and in Germany from 1900 to 2010, the model allows us to explain two important stylized facts. Technological progress at the common rate g_A explains the constant long-run trend growth rate in per capita GDP, which is remarkably similar for the United States and Germany. In addition, the model explains the convergence process of Germany after World War II—from 1945 to the end of the 1970s (the "economic miracle")—via the dynamics outside of the steady state when the economy starts with a capital stock per unit of effective labor that is lower than the steady-state level $\hat{k}$. For this case, the model predicts that per capita GDP will grow faster than the rate of technological progress for a prolonged period of time. Eventually, however, the growth rate of per capita GDP slows down and converges to the long-run growth rate g_A from above. This describes well the behavior of the German economy, as displayed in Fig. 4.4.

We can explain Russia's declining economy after the collapse of the Soviet Union with a similar argument. If capital per unit of effective labor is above the steady-state level (e.g., $\hat{k}(0)'$ in Fig. 4.3), $\hat{k}$ declines during the convergence process toward the steady state. Consequently, the economy grows by less than the rate of technological progress g_A and could even decline if $\hat{k}$ falls so strongly that the negative effect of declining capital per

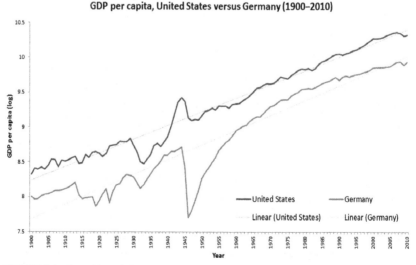

FIGURE 4.4 Logarithm of GDP per capita in the United States (red) and Germany (blue); the dotted lines show a linear trend. *Data from J. Bolt and J. van Zanden, The Maddison Project: collaborative research on historical national accounts, The Economic History Review, 67(3) (2014) 627–651.*

unit of effective labor on the growth rate of per capita GDP outweighs the positive effect of any technological progress that might arise concurrently.

Now we use the Solow (1956) model for a comparative statics analysis that we demonstrate graphically. The first parameter change that we consider is a rise in the saving rate from s to s' (Fig. 4.5). We assume that the economy is initially at the steady state with a capital stock per unit of effective labor of $\hat{k}^*$, indicated by the dashed vertical line, while the original curve related to gross investment is the dashed line $s \cdot \hat{k}^\alpha$. When the saving rate rises to s', the gross investment curve shifts upward to the solid line $s' \cdot \hat{k}^\alpha$, as indicated by the arrows. Correspondingly, the new steady-state capital stock per unit of effective labor is given by the higher value $\hat{k}'^* > \hat{k}^*$. Because output per unit of effective labor is $\hat{y} = \hat{k}^\alpha$, we observe that it also rises with the saving rate. During the transition to the new steady state, the capital stock per unit of effective labor rises and converges to the new steady-state level from below. Note that this behavior is exactly what we can infer analytically from the steady-state expression of the capital stock per unit of effective labor given in Eq. (4.26).

Finally, consider a rise in the population growth rate from n to n' (Fig. 4.6). This change implies that the numerator of all variables that are defined in terms of efficiency units of labor starts to grow faster. Again, we assume that the economy is initially at the steady state with a capital stock per unit of effective labor of $\hat{k}^*$. The original effective capital depreciation

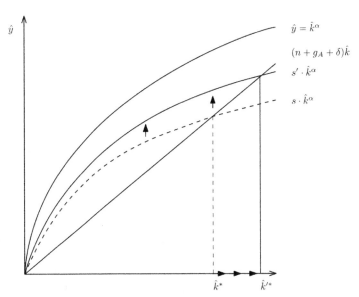

FIGURE 4.5 The effects of a rise in the saving rate from s to s' in the Solow (1956) model with technological progress and population growth.

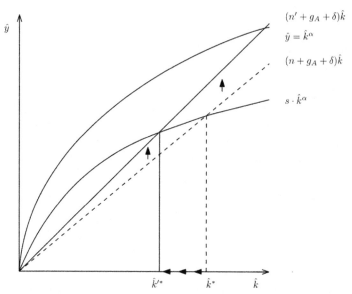

FIGURE 4.6 The effects of a rise in the population growth rate from n to n' in the Solow (1956) model with technological progress and population growth.

and dilution line is the dashed line $(n + g_A + \delta)\hat{k}$. When the population growth rate rises from n to n', the effective capital depreciation and dilution line rotates counterclockwise to the solid line $(n' + g_A + \delta)\hat{k}$, as indicated by the arrows. The new steady-state capital stock per unit of effective labor is given by the lower value $\hat{k}'^{*} < \hat{k}^{*}$. Because output per unit of effective labor is $\hat{y} = \hat{k}^{\alpha}$, we observe that it shrinks if population growth rises. During the transition to the new steady state, the capital stock per unit of effective labor decreases and converges to the new steady-state level from above. Again, this behavior is what we can infer analytically from the steady-state expression of the capital stock per unit of effective labor given in Eq. (4.26).

4.4 The Solow model with automation

Now that we have reviewed the central properties of the Solow (1956) model in discrete and continuous time, we will proceed to consider a basic and straightforward extension of the framework that allows an assessment of the effects of automation. In doing so, we follow the exposition of Prettner (2016, 2019).

Consider an economy with three production factors. Labor L (human workers) and traditional physical capital K (machines, assembly lines, production halls, etc.) are as in the previous sections. In addition, however, we introduce automation capital P (industrial robots, 3D printers, algorithms based on machine learning that perform the tasks of humans, etc.). The notation P derives from the idea that this production factor essentially covers a "programmable" type of labor.[8] In addition, the use of the letter R for "robot" is prohibited by its prominent use throughout the literature to refer to the capital rental rate. Both traditional capital and automation capital can be accumulated and depreciate at rate δ. The central results are robust to a relaxation of this assumption, in the sense that automation capital might depreciate faster than traditional physical capital (for the details, see Prettner, 2019). Labor and traditional physical capital are imperfect substitutes as in the previous section, whereas automation capital is a perfect substitute for labor. The perfect substitutability assumption follows from the strict definition of automation as a full replacement of labor (Merriam-Webster, 2017). Of course, in reality, that replacement often is not full because robots require maintenance, etc. However, the main results are robust to an extension involving a constant elasticity of substitution production function with a high elasticity of substitution between robots and human workers (see, e.g., Lankisch, Prettner, & Prskawetz, 2019; Steigum, 2011).

As in the basic Solow (1956) model, we abstract from modeling the production of traditional physical capital and of automation capital and assume instead that they are directly transformed into the particular production factor out of accumulated savings. For the sake of a simplified exposition, we also abstract from issues such as (1) technological progress in robot production, (2) changes in the relative price of automation capital versus traditional (i.e., nonautomation) capital, (3) a different risk of investment in different forms of capital, (4) irreversible investment decisions, (5) a distinction between capital owners and workers, and (6) that the return on investment in different production factors might be used differently because the owners of the corresponding production factor might have a different propensity to save/invest. For sources that include some of these aspects with and without automation,

---

8. Note that the use of robots in the production process differs from human employment with respect to the time period after which robots become available for production. While robots can be used in the production process rather quickly after they have been produced (and the training of machine learning algorithms often lasts only hours or days), humans do not enter the labor force until decades after their birth, and they require enormous investments in terms of education for years to be able to perform difficult job tasks. This aspect is often neglected when discussing the fact that robots still have difficulties in "learning" certain tasks. In addition, the period of childhood and the later education during young adulthood lead to a strong delay between an increase in population growth and a later rise in workforce growth. This aspect tends to be disregarded when increases in population growth are demanded as a strategy to counter demographic challenges. That this delay is not present for robots leads to interesting implications in relation to automation as a solution to demographic challenges. We will discuss some of these aspects in more detail in Chapter 6 (compare also to Bloom, Canning, & Sevilla, 2003; Bloom & Freeman, 1988; Bloom, Kuhn, & Prettner, 2017).

see, for example, Antony and Klarl (2019), Benzell, Kotlikoff, LaGarda, and Sachs (2015), Foley, Michl, and Tavani (2019), Sachs, Benzell, and LaGarda (2015), and Sachs and Kotlikoff (2012).

Extending the baseline Cobb–Douglas production function by introducing automation capital as a perfect substitute for labor yields

$$Y(t) = K(t)^{\alpha}[L(t)+P(t)]^{1-\alpha}, \tag{4.34}$$

where we again abstract from technological progress by setting $A(t) \equiv 1$, as compared with Eq. (4.9). The reason for this normalization is that one of the central results—the potential for perpetual long-run economic growth that arises because of automation—is best illustrated by abstracting from a second source of long-run growth (compare with the previous section). From the Cobb–Douglas production function with automation, it follows that output per capita is given by

$$y(t) = \frac{Y(t)}{L(t)} = [1+p(t)]^{1-\alpha}k(t)^{\alpha}, \tag{4.35}$$

where lowercase letters again refer to variables measured in per capita terms.

The wage rate and the capital rental rate implied by Eq. (4.34) are given by the marginal value products of labor and traditional physical capital, obtained as the derivative of the production function with respect to the production factor under consideration:

$$w(t) = (1 - \alpha)\left[\frac{K(t)}{L(t)+P(t)}\right]^{\alpha}, \quad r(t) = R(t) - \delta = \alpha\left[\frac{L(t)+P(t)}{K(t)}\right]^{1-\alpha} - \delta. \tag{4.36}$$

Because labor and automation capital are perfect substitutes, automation capital P is compensated by $w(t) - \delta$. As Eq. (4.36) shows, the wage rate decreases with the number of workers *and* with automation, while it increases with the stock of available traditional physical capital. The reverse holds true for the capital rental rate. The reason for the negative effect of automation on the wage rate is the perfect substitutability between automation capital and labor, such that robots and workers are in direct competition.

Again, the assumptions here are that the economy is closed, and there is no government, such that savings at each instant equal gross investment $I(t)$, yielding $I(t) = S(t) = sY(t)$. In contrast to the standard Solow (1956) model, there are two investment vehicles: traditional capital and automation capital. For simplicity, we start by assuming that individuals invest a constant and exogenous share s_K of savings in traditional capital and a share $1 - s_K$ in automation capital. Later, we will show that endogenizing the investment share s_K does not alter any of the main results (compare with Geiger, Prettner, & Schwarzer, 2018; Lankisch et al., 2019).

Altogether, we have the following accumulation equations for the two types of capital:

$$\dot{K}(t) = s_K I(t) - \delta K(t), \qquad \dot{P}(t) = (1 - s_K)I(t) - \delta P(t). \qquad (4.37)$$

Using the production function (4.34), the evolution of traditional physical capital can be written as follows:

$$\dot{K}(t) = s_K s[L(t) + P(t)]^{1-\alpha} K(t)^\alpha - \delta K(t). \qquad (4.38)$$

Using Eq. (4.37), together with the production function (4.34), yields the evolution of automation capital as follows:

$$\dot{P}(t) = (1 - s_K)s[L(t) + P(t)]^{1-\alpha} K(t)^\alpha - \delta P(t). \qquad (4.39)$$

Reformulating the accumulation equations of traditional physical capital and automation capital in per capita terms, we get

$$\frac{\dot{K}(t)}{L(t)} = s_K s[1 + p(t)]^{1-\alpha} k(t)^\alpha - \delta k(t), \qquad (4.40)$$

$$\frac{\dot{P}(t)}{L(t)} = (1 - s_K)s[1 + p(t)]^{1-\alpha} k(t)^\alpha - \delta p(t). \qquad (4.41)$$

Next, we calculate the dynamics of $k(t)$ and $p(t)$ by taking the derivatives of these expressions with respect to time (employing the quotient rule in the derivations):

$$\dot{k}(t) = \frac{d[K(t)/L(t)]}{dt} = \frac{\dot{K}(t)}{L(t)} - \frac{K(t)}{L(t)^2}\dot{L}(t) = \frac{\dot{K}(t)}{L(t)} - k(t)\frac{\dot{L}(t)}{L(t)} = \frac{\dot{K}(t)}{L(t)} - nk(t), \qquad (4.42)$$

$$\dot{p}(t) = \frac{d[P(t)/L(t)]}{dt} = \frac{\dot{P}(t)}{L(t)} - \frac{P(t)}{L(t)^2}\dot{L}(t) = \frac{\dot{P}(t)}{L(t)} - p(t)\frac{\dot{L}(t)}{L(t)} = \frac{\dot{P}(t)}{L(t)} - np(t). \qquad (4.43)$$

Substituting Eqs. (4.40) and (4.41) into Eqs. (4.42) and (4.43) and dividing the results by $k(t)$ and $p(t)$, respectively, yields the growth rates of traditional physical capital per capita and of automation capital per capita as follows:

$$g_k = \frac{\dot{k}(t)}{k(t)} = s_K s\left[\frac{1 + p(t)}{k(t)}\right]^{1-\alpha} - \delta - n, \qquad (4.44)$$

$$g_p = \frac{\dot{p}(t)}{p(t)} = (1 - s_K)s\left[\frac{1 + p(t)}{p(t)}\right]^{1-\alpha}\left[\frac{k(t)}{p(t)}\right]^\alpha - \delta - n. \qquad (4.45)$$

Along a balanced growth path, the growth rates g_k and g_p must be constant by definition. Applying Jones' (1995) method to derive a balanced growth path in the context of research and development based growth models, we calculate the growth rates of the growth rates g_k and g_p and set the result equal to zero (because this implies that the growth rates g_k and g_p are constant).[9] To do so, we reformulate Eqs. (4.44) and (4.45) and take the logarithm such that

$$\log(g_k + \delta + n) = \log(s_K) + \log(s) + (1 - \alpha)\log[1 + p(t)] - (1 - \alpha)\log[k(t)] \tag{4.46}$$

$$\Rightarrow g_{(g_k + \delta + n)} = (1 - \alpha)\frac{\dot{p}(t)}{1 + p(t)} - (1 - \alpha)g_k, \tag{4.47}$$

$$\log(g_p + \delta + n) = \log(1 - s_K) + \log(s) + (1 - \alpha)\log[1 + p(t)]$$
$$- (1 - \alpha)\log[p(t)] + \alpha\log[k(t)] - \alpha\log[p(t)], \tag{4.48}$$

$$\Rightarrow g_{(g_p + \delta + n)} = (1 - \alpha)\frac{\dot{p}(t)}{1 + p(t)} - (1 - \alpha)g_p + \alpha g_k - \alpha g_p. \tag{4.49}$$

At the long-run equilibrium, $p(t)$ is large, so we can use the approximation

$$\frac{\dot{p}(t)}{1 + p(t)} \approx g_p.$$

Equations (4.47) and (4.49) imply that the economy converges to a long-run growth rate with $g_p \approx g_k \equiv g$. Note that, for large $p(t)$ and large $k(t)$, the following relations hold

$$\left[\frac{1 + p(t)}{p(t)}\right]^{1-\alpha} \approx 1, \quad \frac{p(t)}{k(t)} \approx \frac{1 + p(t)}{k(t)} := \xi.$$

By using these approximations, we can rewrite Eqs. (4.44) and (4.45) as follows:

$$g = s_K s \xi^{1-\alpha} - \delta - n, \tag{4.50}$$

$$g = (1 - s_K)s\left(\frac{1}{\xi}\right)^\alpha - \delta - n. \tag{4.51}$$

These are two equations in the two unknown endogenous variables g and ξ that we can solve for. Equalizing the right-hand sides of Eqs. (4.50) and (4.51) yields

$$(1 - s_K)s\left(\frac{1}{\xi}\right)^\alpha = s_K s \xi^{1-\alpha} \Leftrightarrow \frac{1 - s_K}{s_K} = \xi. \tag{4.52}$$

Finally, substituting (4.52) into (4.50) yields the long-run growth rate that holds along the balanced growth path toward which the economy converges.

---

9. Yes, you read correctly, one needs to calculate the growth rate of the growth rate.

On this balanced growth path, GDP per capita and the per capita stocks of traditional capital and automation capital grow at the common constant rate

$$g = s \cdot s_K^{\alpha}(1 - s_K)^{1-\alpha} - \delta - n. \tag{4.53}$$

The solution for which Eq. (4.53) is zero or negative implies a long-run growth rate of zero, as at the steady state in the Solow (1956) model without technological progress. However, if the first term on the right-hand side is large (e.g., because of a sufficiently large saving rate), the growth rate is positive, and we have long-run economic growth that is solely due to the accumulation of different forms of capital. The intuitive explanation for why the long-run growth rate becomes positive in this setting is that labor essentially turns into an accumulable production factor when automation capital is available. Consequently, the diminishing returns with respect to capital accumulation that drive the convergence process, as described previously in relation to the basic Solow (1956) model without automation, do not take hold. Proposition 4.1 summarizes the findings on the long-run growth rate in the Solow (1956) model with automation (see Prettner, 2019).

Proposition 4.1: *If automation is considered a perfect substitute for labor in the Solow (1956) model, then*
●The potential exists for perpetual economic growth driven solely by the accumulation of both types of capital; and
●If long-run growth is perpetual, then the long-run growth rate decreases with the rate of population growth and the rate of capital depreciation and rises with the saving rate.
Proof:
The proof of the proposition follows immediately from inspection of Eq. (4.53).

The first result contrasts not only with the standard Solow (1956) model, but also with the neoclassical growth literature building on Cass (1965), Diamond (1965), Koopmans (1965), and Ramsey (1928), in the sense that perpetual long-run growth fueled solely by the accumulation of capital becomes possible in times of automation. It is important to note that automation makes the production side of the economy similar to the production side of an *AK* type of growth model (Rebelo, 1991; Romer, 1986). This means that output becomes linear in physical capital such that physical capital accumulation alone leads to perpetual economic growth. However, the equilibrium production function turns into an *AK* type of production function not because the declining marginal product of capital is assumed away by introducing a learning-by-doing externality as is usually done in the literature, but because—by the definition of automation—a form of capital can be used instead of labor in the production process. Thus, an economy can produce large amounts of output without the need for labor input (see also Antony & Klarl, 2019; Geiger at al., 2018; Lankisch et al., 2019). This result is also present in the article by Steigum (2011) on robot technology in an optimal growth model, à la Ramsey–Cass–Koopmans, in which households optimally choose the saving rate s. Chapter 5 will discuss this model in more detail.

The second part of Proposition 4.1 is due to the nondiminishing marginal product of overall capital (automation capital and traditional physical capital). As a consequence, variables that reduce the overall accumulation rate of physical capital, such as capital depreciation or capital dilution due to population growth, also reduce the long-run economic growth rate. In contrast to the positive effect of population growth on long-run economic expansion in the semi-endogenous growth literature (see, e.g., Jones, 1995; Kortum, 1997; Segerström, 1998), this result is consistent with the empirical evidence for industrialized countries over the last few decades (Ahituv, 2001; Bloom & Freeman, 1988; Brander & Dowrick, 1994; Kelley & Schmidt, 1995; Li & Zhang, 2007; Herzer, Strulik, & Vollmer, 2012).

Now we turn our attention to the second central result of the model that is a consequence of automation and has implications for the analysis of income distribution. In the standard Solow model, the share of total income that the production factor labor earns is given by $1 - \alpha$ as we have seen previously. Thus, the labor share is always constant, irrespective of the development of all other variables in the model. As mentioned earlier, this has long been considered an advantage of the model because it is consistent with the stylized facts of economic development that Kaldor (1957) observes through the first half of the 20th century. Indeed, until the 1970s, the labor income share remained remarkably constant despite all the technological and structural changes that happened during this period. However, over the last few decades, the labor share in the United States and many other countries has been declining (Elsby, Hobijn, & Sahin, 2013; Karabarbounis & Neiman, 2014; Piketty, 2014), such that more recent developments are no longer consistent with the simple Solow model. We now show that the Solow model with automation is capable of generating a declining long-run labor share of the economy once automation becomes possible. By using the wage rate as given by Eq. (4.36), aggregate labor income can be calculated as follows:

$$w(t)L(t) = (1 - \alpha)\left[\frac{K(t)}{L(t)+P(t)}\right]^{\alpha} L(t). \tag{4.54}$$

Consequently, the labor income share pins down to

$$\frac{w(t)L(t)}{Y(t)} = (1 - \alpha)\frac{L(t)}{L(t) + P(t)}. \tag{4.55}$$

We immediately observe that the accumulation of automation capital reduces the labor income share in such a setting, which we summarize in Proposition 4.2.

Proposition 4.2: *If we consider automation in a standard Solow (1956) model, an increase in the stock of automation capital reduces the labor income share of the economy.*
Proof:
The proof of the proposition follows immediately from inspection of Eq. (4.55).

The intuition for this finding is the following: automation competes with labor, and therefore, its widespread adoption reduces wages. At the same time, the income that automation generates is funneled to capital owners. This leads to a redistribution of overall income away from the production factor labor and toward the production factor capital (including automation capital). Conveniently, the model can also account for the constant labor income share that was seen before the emergence of automation capital. In this case, all the results of the basic Solow model would be valid, which is evident from setting the stock of automation capital to zero ($P = 0$) in Eq. (4.55). Doing so leads to the same version of the Solow model as discussed earlier: without technological progress and without population growth.[10]

At this stage, it is important to note that a crucial difference exists from the case in which the standard Solow model is augmented by immigration instead of automation. In the case of immigration, an additional production factor would also be a perfect substitute for (domestic) workers, namely, foreign workers who choose to migrate and work in the domestic economy. However, immigration increases the number of inhabitants in an economy and, hence, raises the denominator in per capita GDP (y) and in capital per worker (k). Thus, immigration *cannot* overcome the diminishing marginal product of the production factor capital in the Solow model such that perpetual growth would be impossible in a migration-augmented Solow model.[11]

---

10. With an accumulating stock of robots, the long-run labor share would converge to zero. This is a consequence of the simplified model. In more complicated setups with high-skilled labor that is difficult to substitute by robots, the long-run labor share would not be zero (Prettner & Strulik, 2020).
11. Labaj and Dujava (2019) analyze the effects of automation within Mankiw et al.'s (1992) model. With diminishing returns to the aggregate stock of all three types of capital (human capital, traditional physical capital, and automation capital), long-run economic growth cannot emerge. They show, however, that the consideration of automation capital can render convergence nonlinear and even lead to temporary divergence in income per capita.

4.5 Endogenization of the share of investment in traditional physical capital

For the purpose of extending the Solow (1956) model in a straightforward manner, we deliberately kept the analysis simple. Thus, we abstracted from rational investors who decide endogenously how much of their savings they would like to invest in traditional physical capital and how much in automation capital. As long as one of the two investment vehicles delivers a higher rate of return, rational investors would not invest in the other. Thus, investment would only flow into the investment vehicle with the higher rate of return, a process that should ensure long-run equalization of the rates of return between two different assets. In other words, arbitrage opportunities would vanish in any interior equilibrium wherein both types of investments are positive. Hence, for rational investors, only one *optimal* level of the share of investments in physical capital exists: the one for which the no-arbitrage condition between returns of the two types of investments is fulfilled.[12] In this section, we take this no-arbitrage argument into account and thereby endogenize the fraction of investment in traditional physical capital (s_K). The central results of this approach to modeling investment decisions in the automation-augmented Solow (1956) model are that (1) the optimal share of investments diverted to traditional physical capital is equal to $s_K = \alpha$ and (2) the economic implications of the analysis with an exogenous share of investments in automation and in traditional physical capital carry over to the case of an endogenous split of investments.

Recall that the factor rewards in the Solow model with automation are as follows:

$$w(t) = (1 - \alpha)\left[\frac{K(t)}{L(t)+P(t)}\right]^{\alpha}, \quad r(t) = R(t) - \delta = \alpha\left[\frac{L(t)+P(t)}{K(t)}\right]^{1-\alpha} - \delta,$$

$$(4.56)$$

with the remuneration of automation capital being $w(t) - \delta$. Thus, an interior solution in which investment in both types of capital is positive needs to be associated with $w(t) = R(t)$. By using this and the two expressions in Eq. (4.56), we can solve for the stock of automation capital as a function of traditional physical capital, such that

$$P(t) = \left(\frac{1 - \alpha}{\alpha}\right)K(t) - L(t). \quad (4.57)$$

---

12. For articles that are based on the endogenous split between investments in traditional physical capital and in automation capital, see Abeliansky and Prettner (2017), Antony and Klarl (2019), Cords and Prettner (2019), Gasteiger and Prettner (2020), Geiger et al. (2018), Lankisch et al. (2019), and Steigum (2011).

Note that, *ceteris paribus*, automation capital rises with traditional physical capital, which makes sense from an intuitive point of view; if more machines and assembly lines are present in the economy, employing more industrial robots would be associated with a higher rate of return on automation capital, such that a rising $K(t)$ implies a rising $P(t)$. By contrast, if more workers are present in the economy, the stock of automation capital decreases *ceteris paribus*. Again, this is intuitive: in an economy in which labor is abundant, the incentives to automate production are lower.

Substituting Eq. (4.57) into the production function, Eq. (4.34), yields aggregate output as a function solely of the stock of traditional physical capital:

$$Y(t) = \left(\frac{1-\alpha}{\alpha}\right)^{1-\alpha} K(t). \tag{4.58}$$

Obviously, this is the same structure as in an *AK* type of model that implies long-run economic growth solely based on physical capital accumulation (see Rebelo, 1991; Romer, 1986). However, the *AK* structure of the economy with automation does not hinge on learning-by-doing spillover effects. Instead, it follows again in a straightforward manner from the property of automation capital that turns labor into an accumulable production factor and, thereby, overcomes the diminishing marginal productivity of traditional physical capital.

Dividing Eqs. (4.57) and (4.58) by the population size/workforce $L(t)$, we get the corresponding expressions in terms of per capita units:

$$p(t) = \left(\frac{1-\alpha}{\alpha}\right)k(t) - 1, \tag{4.59}$$

$$y(t) = \left(\frac{1-\alpha}{\alpha}\right)^{1-\alpha} k(t). \tag{4.60}$$

Taking the derivative of these expressions with respect to time yields

$$\dot{p}(t) = \left(\frac{1-\alpha}{\alpha}\right)\dot{k}(t), \tag{4.61}$$

$$\dot{y}(t) = \left(\frac{1-\alpha}{\alpha}\right)^{1-\alpha} \dot{k}(t). \tag{4.62}$$

The accumulation of both types of capital at the aggregate level can be described by summing up the individual aggregation equations for both capital types, such that

$$\dot{K}(t) + \dot{P}(t) = sY(t) - \delta[K(t) + P(t)]. \tag{4.63}$$

Dividing this equation by the population size yields

$$\frac{\dot{K}(t)}{L(t)} + \frac{\dot{P}(t)}{L(t)} = sy(t) - \delta[k(t) + p(t)]. \tag{4.64}$$

Note that Eqs. (4.42) and (4.43) do not change in case of an endogenous s_K, such that we can use these expressions to substitute for $\dot{K}(t)/L(t)$ and $\dot{P}(t)/L(t)$ in Eq. (4.64) to arrive at the accumulation equation of both types of capital in per capita terms as follows:

$$\dot{k}(t) + \dot{p}(t) = sy(t) - (n + \delta)[k(t) + p(t)]. \tag{4.65}$$

Finally, we use Eqs. (4.59), (4.60), and (4.61) to substitute for $p(t)$, $y(t)$, and $\dot{p}(t)$ in Eq. (4.65) to get

$$\dot{k}(t) + \left(\frac{1-\alpha}{\alpha}\right)\dot{k}(t) = s\left(\frac{1-\alpha}{\alpha}\right)^{1-\alpha} k(t) - (n + \delta)\left[k(t) + \left(\frac{1-\alpha}{\alpha}\right)k(t) - 1\right]. \tag{4.66}$$

Dividing this expression by the stock of traditional capital per capita and rearranging yields

$$\frac{\dot{k}(t)}{k(t)}\left[1 + \left(\frac{1-\alpha}{\alpha}\right)\right] = s\left(\frac{1-\alpha}{\alpha}\right)^{1-\alpha} - (n + \delta)\left[1 + \left(\frac{1-\alpha}{\alpha}\right) - \frac{1}{k(t)}\right]. \tag{4.67}$$

For a large stock of physical capital per capita, the term $1/k(t)$ vanishes asymptotically. In addition, note that

$$\left[1 + \left(\frac{1-\alpha}{\alpha}\right)\right] = \frac{1}{\alpha}.$$

Dividing the expression in Eq. (4.67) by this term, we arrive at

$$\frac{\dot{k}(t)}{k(t)} = s\left(\frac{1-\alpha}{\alpha}\right)^{1-\alpha}\alpha - (n + \delta). \tag{4.68}$$

From Eqs. (4.59) and (4.60), it eventually follows that per capita traditional capital, per capita automation capital, and per capita output all grow at the common rate

$$g_k = g_p = g_y = s \cdot \alpha^\alpha (1-\alpha)^{1-\alpha} - n - \delta. \tag{4.69}$$

This result shows that the economy's growth rate along the balanced growth path is very similar to the one in Section 4.4, with an exogenous share of investment s_K diverted to the accumulation of traditional physical capital, except that the optimal level of this share, $s_K = \alpha$, appears in Eq. (4.69).

Again, the potential exists that the economy's growth rate is positive in the long run (e.g., when the saving rate s is high), such that perpetual growth without technological progress is feasible. Furthermore, inspection of Eq. (4.69) reveals that the saving rate s, the population growth rate n, and the depreciation rate δ have the same influence on the long-run growth rate as in Section 4.4. Thus, the results of Proposition 4.1 carry over to the case of an endogenous investment share $s_K = \alpha$. Finally, the labor share would again decrease with the accumulation of automation capital, such that the results of Proposition 4.2 also carry over.

4.6 Automation and wage inequality

Up to now, we have shown two of the crucial macroeconomic effects of automation:

1. Automation has the potential to lead to perpetual growth, even in the absence of technological progress.
2. Automation implies a declining labor income share.

However, in the simple framework, we cannot yet analyze the effects of automation on wage inequality, which is a central component of overall income inequality. To address this issue, we need to introduce heterogeneity into the model, which is accomplished by introducing two types of labor: low-skilled and high-skilled workers.

For this purpose, we follow Lankisch et al. (2019)[13] and assume an aggregate production function that allows for the presence of two types of labor, such that

$$Y = \left[(1-\beta)L_s^{\gamma} + \beta(P+L_u)^{\gamma} \right]^{\frac{1-\alpha}{\gamma}} K^{\alpha}, \tag{4.70}$$

where L_s refers to the number of high-skilled workers, L_u refers to the number of low-skilled workers, $\beta \in (0,1)$ is the weight of low-skilled workers in the production process, and $\gamma \in (-\infty, 1]$ determines the elasticity of substitution between both types of workers. For $\gamma = 1$, workers with different skills are perfect substitutes, and for $\gamma \to -\infty$, they are perfect complements. A realistic range for this parameter is $\gamma \in (0,1)$, such that low-skilled and high-skilled workers are gross substitutes (Acemoglu, 2002, 2009; Autor, 2002). In the following analysis, we focus on this realistic parameter range.

In the production process, we assume that automation is a perfect substitute for low-skilled workers L_u, while it is only an imperfect substitute for high-skilled workers L_s. The degree of substitutability between automation and high-skilled labor is the same as the degree of substitutability between low-skilled and high-skilled workers, as determined by γ.[14] This makes sense from an intuitive point of view because automation capital can perform the

---

13. The results that automation leads to faster growth but rising inequality are very robust to different modeling strategies (see, e.g., Berg, Buffie, & Zanna, 2018; Prettner & Strulik, 2020).

14. The central insights from the basic Solow model with automation generalize to the case in which different degrees of substitutability exist betweeen high- and low-skilled workers as long as they remain gross substitutes.

tasks of low-skilled workers in the model. If low-skilled workers, in turn, can perform the tasks of high-skilled workers (albeit imperfectly), then automation capital should be similarly productive in these tasks.[15]

As far as the wages of high-skilled workers (w_s) and the wages of low-skilled workers (w_u) are concerned, we take the derivatives of the production function (4.70) with respect to the two types of workers, such that

$$w_s = \frac{\partial Y}{\partial L_s} = (1 - \alpha)\frac{Y}{L_s^{1-\gamma}}\frac{1 - \beta}{(1 - \beta)L_s^{\gamma} + \beta(P + L_u)^{\gamma}}, \tag{4.71}$$

$$w_u = \frac{\partial Y}{\partial L_u} = (1 - \alpha)\frac{Y}{(P + L_u)^{1-\gamma}}\frac{\beta}{(1 - \beta)L_s^{\gamma} + \beta(P + L_u)^{\gamma}}. \tag{4.72}$$

The skill premium is defined as the ratio between the wages of high-skilled workers and the wages of low-skilled workers, which reduces to

$$\frac{w_s}{w_u} = \frac{1 - \beta}{\beta}\left(\frac{P + L_u}{L_s}\right)^{1-\gamma}. \tag{4.73}$$

As long as $0 < 1$, such that imperfect substitution prevails between the two types of skills, the accumulation of automation capital (an increasing P) raises the skill premium and, thereby, raises wage inequality. This implies the third central macroeconomic result of automation, which we summarize in Proposition 4.3 (see Lankisch et al., 2019).

Proposition 4.3: *If we consider automation in the Solow (1956) model with high-skilled and low-skilled workers and an imperfect substitutability between the two types of workers, an increase in the stock of automation capital raises the skill premium and, thereby, wage inequality.*
Proof:
The proof follows immediately from inspection of Eq. (4.73).

The intuition for this result is that (at least up to now) low-skilled workers are more susceptible to automation than high-skilled workers. Consequently, automation reduces their wages to a larger extent than it does the wages of high-skilled workers. We now show this explicitly by deriving the analytical effect of automation on the wage levels of high-skilled and low-skilled workers.

The effect of an increase in the stock of automation capital on the wages of low-skilled workers is given by

---

15. We focus on the case in which automation capital can replace low-skilled workers more easily than high-skilled workers. For example, an industrial robot can easily be used to replace assembly line workers, whereas replacing doctors, scientists, lawyers, teachers, etc. remains rather difficult. If at some point substituting high-skilled labor with robots becomes easier than substituting low-skilled labor with robots, many of the distributional results of this chapter might reverse (see also Acemoglu & Restrepo, 2018).

$$\frac{\partial w_u}{\partial P} = \frac{(1-\alpha)\beta Y}{(P+L_u)^{2-\gamma}} \frac{\left\{ ((1-\alpha-\gamma)\beta(P+L_u)^\gamma - ((1-\gamma)[(1-\beta)L_s^\gamma + \beta(P+L_u)^\gamma]\right\}}{\left[(1-\beta)L_s^\gamma + \beta(P+L_u)^\gamma\right]^2}.$$

(4.74)

Both the numerator and the denominator of the first term are positive. Because $(1-\alpha-\gamma)\beta(P+L_u)^\gamma < (1-\gamma)\beta(P+L_u)^\gamma$, the numerator of the second term is always negative. Because the denominator of the second term is positive, the whole derivative is therefore negative. This implies that the accumulation of automation capital reduces the wages of low-skilled workers. We summarize this finding in the fourth crucial macroeconomic effect of automation (see Lankisch et al., 2019).

Proposition 4.4: *Consider automation in the Solow (1956) model with high-skilled and low-skilled* workers that are gross substitutes; if automation capital and low-skilled workers are perfect substitutes, an increase in the stock of automation capital reduces the wages of low-skilled workers.
Proof:
The proof follows from Eq. (4.74) and the discussion below this equation.

In principle, this result could help explain why the wages of low-skilled workers in the United States have decreased since the 1970s despite the fact that strong overall productivity growth occurred in all the decades since (see Chapter 2).

We also calculate the effect of an increase in the stock of automation capital on the wages of high-skilled workers as follows:

$$\frac{\partial w_s}{\partial P} = (1-\alpha)Y \frac{(1-\beta)\beta L_s^\gamma}{L_s(P+L_u)^{1-\gamma}} \frac{1-\alpha-\gamma}{\left[(1-\beta)L_s^\gamma + \beta(P+L_u)^\gamma\right]^2} = \left(\begin{array}{l} \geq 0 \text{ for } 1-\alpha \geq \gamma, \\ < 0 \text{ for } 1-\alpha < \gamma. \end{array} \right)$$

(4.75)

The sign of this derivative is ambiguous and depends on the substitutability between both types of workers. If γ is high, such that substitution is easy, increasing the stock of robots would reduce the wages of high-skilled workers. If, by contrast, the substitutability between low-skilled workers and high-skilled workers is low, automation will raise the wages of high-skilled workers.

This result shows that, while automation affects low-skilled workers negatively in this setting, this need not be the case for high-skilled workers. In particular, the effect of automation on high-skilled workers depends on the difficulty of substituting low-skilled workers for high-skilled workers and, thus, the difficulty of employing robots for the tasks that high-skilled workers perform. Altogether, however, the result indicates that high-skilled workers are not immune to the effects of automation's advance, even if—for now—they are not being perfectly replaced by robots.

As far as the long-run evolution of wage inequality in terms of the skill premium is concerned, Lankisch et al. (2019) simulate the model dynamics for the parameter values $s = 0.21$, $n = 0.009$, $\delta = 0.04$, $\alpha = 0.33$, $\beta = 0.5$, and $\gamma = 0.7$, and a share of skilled labor in the total workforce of 23%. These values are either taken as long-run averages for the United States according to World Bank (2019) data or used because they resemble standard values applied in the literature as, for example, in Grossmann, Steger, & Trimborn (2013). Fig. 4.7 depicts the evolution of the skill premium that the model implies in comparison with United States Census Bureau (2017) data. We observe that although the model is rather simple, for example, endogenous skill-upgrading is abstracted from, it approximates the skill premium in the data fairly well.

Finally, it is important to mention that the possibility of long-run economic growth driven by capital accumulation alone carries over to this setting. The easier it is to substitute high-skilled workers by low-skilled workers, the wider is the parameter range for which perpetual growth can emerge.

4.7 The tradeoff between growth and inequality

So far this chapter has shown that basic economic theory suggests two broad effects of automation. On the one hand, we can expect economic growth fueled by automation.[16] This has the potential to raise material well-being and living standards. On the other hand, we expect that automation increases inequality via two channels: (1) a decline in the labor income share and (2) a growing skill premium as long as automation predominantly affects the low-skilled. Thus, automation is unlikely to lead to a Pareto improvement—requiring that nobody is left worse off, while at least someone is better off due to automation—but will create winners and losers (see also Acemoglu & Restrepo, 2018; Berg et al., 2018; Prettner & Strulik, 2020). The extent to which a society stands to gain in aggregate terms thus depends on (1) how averse it is to inequality and (2) how willing and able it is to use the gains of automation to compensate the losers.

The first item is often discussed in the context of a social welfare function. Under certain conditions outlined in detail in Cowell (2011), individual utility levels $u_i(\cdot)$ that might depend on economic characteristics (e.g., on individual consumption or individual income) can be aggregated over all individuals to yield the society's welfare level (see also Adler, 2019). Denoting welfare of the society by W and the contribution of individual i to social welfare by w (u_i), we can then write

---

16. However, at the same time, we could independently witness a decrease in economic growth due to a slowdown in technological progress and other headwinds to economic development such as demographic change. This concern has been voiced, for example, by Gordon (2016). If the described headwinds are strong enough, they can overcompensate for the positive (isolated) effect of automation.

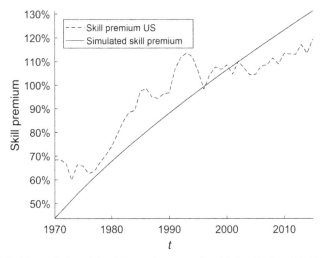

FIGURE 4.7 The evolution of the skill premium as predicted in Lankisch et al.'s (2019) model versus the skill premium in the United States Census Bureau's (2017) data for the United States. This figure is part of Fig. 4.3 in the article by Lankisch et al. (2019) and used here with permission.

$$W = \sum_{i=1}^{N} w(u_i). \tag{4.76}$$

Depending on the shape of the function $w(\cdot)$, which represents society's preferences, inequality in u can have less severe or more severe effects on aggregate welfare. In terms of a specific functional form of $w(\cdot)$, many cases can be described well with the help of so-called isoelastic functions (which Chapter 5 will discuss in more detail). These functions have the following form:

$$w(x_i) = \frac{u_i^{1-\varepsilon} - 1}{1 - \varepsilon}, \tag{4.77}$$

where, in the context given here, the parameter ε measures the degree of society's inequality aversion. If ε equals zero, the function is linear with a slope of one and we are in the utilitarian (Benthamite) case in which inequality in the individual utility level u_i does not matter at all for aggregate social welfare.[17] In this case, aggregate welfare is the sum of individual utility

---

17. We assume here that society is concerned with inequality in utility levels and not with inequality in the variables that determine utility at the individual level. Via the preferences of individuals, further considerations could enter the determination of social welfare (e.g., if individual utility functions are concave, then an equal distribution of the variables/resources that determine utility yields higher aggregate utility levels than an unequal distribution). Furthermore, for the following thought experiments, we assume that utility levels can be

levels with each person receiving the same weight irrespective of her level of utility such that

$$W = \sum_{i=1}^{N} u_i. \tag{4.78}$$

That inequality of utility does not matter for aggregate welfare in this case is evident by considering a transfer of u from an individual with a low level of u to an individual with a high level of u. Such a transfer would not affect aggregate welfare although it would raise inequality.

Consider now an increase in inequality aversion ε in Eq. (4.77). The higher ε is, the more important inequality becomes in the determination of social wefare because the function $w(\cdot)$ becomes increasingly concave. Thus, the effect of an increase in individual utility u_i on aggregate welfare becomes smaller for an individual who already has a high level of u_i than for an individual with a low level of u_i. In this case, the redistribution of utility from a person with a low utility level to a person with a high utility level (as described previously) would lower social welfare.

An important case that is not captured by the aforementioned isoelastic function is the Rawlsian social welfare function, where the utility of the least well-off individual is the sole driver of aggregate welfare. In this case, social welfare is given by

$$W = \min_i u_i \tag{4.79}$$

such that only the lowest level of u_i determines W. In this case, if almost everybody in the society had a high level of u_i, but one person j had a low level of u_j, then aggregate welfare would equal the individual utility of person j. Increases in u_i among those who already have high levels of u_i would not matter at all for aggregate welfare as long as the level of u_j remained unaffected. However, a redistribution of u to person j would raise aggregate welfare. Note that redistributions among all other persons $i \neq j$ who do not have the lowest level of u would not affect welfare even though they could potentially reduce inequality.

This discussion clearly shows that societies in which inequality aversion ε is high or societies with a Rawlsian social welfare function are more likely to be skeptical about automation, whereas societies in which inequality aversion is rather low are more likely to favor automation. Thus, automation would likely be regarded as beneficial if the society adhered to a social welfare function of the utilitarian (Benthamite) type because of higher economic growth and the gains that accrue to high-skilled workers and capital owners.

---

redistributed directly. All of these assumptions help to avoid the need to define nested functions and their properties when discussing the effects of a society's inequality aversion with respect to how favorable it is to the adoption of automation technologies.

However, automation could be regarded as harmful in a society with a higher level of ε or a society that adhered to a Rawlsian social welfare function because low-skilled workers and the asset-poor parts of the population may suffer absolute losses due to automaton. Of course, real-world societies might not be characterized well by these extreme cases.

Because automation will likely produce winners and losers, no Pareto-improvements can be expected. Thus, the discussion so far suggests the application of a different criterion to assess whether automation will be beneficial from an aggregate viewpoint: the criterion of Kaldor—Hicks efficiency (see Hicks, 1939; Kaldor, 1939; Scitovsky, 1941). According to this criterion, a certain change is Kaldor—Hicks efficient if the winners of the change could fully compensate the losers of the change and still be left better off than before the change. Note that this criterion does not require that the compensation of the losers actually happens.[18]

Chapter 7 will discuss policies that could potentially be used to compensate the losers of automation. However, we note here that assessing the preferences of households and the inequality aversion of societies is extremely difficult. Thus, we refrain from making any statements on the optimality of different policies.

4.8 Summary

This chapter introduced key concepts and tools of model building such as the calculation of growth rates, the concept of representative agents, and the aggregate production function. These concepts formed the basis for discussing the standard Solow (1956) model without technological progress and without population growth in discrete time (by means of difference equations). This allowed us to gain first insights into the driving forces of economic growth in the medium run versus the long run. We analyzed the system dynamics by means of diagrams and showed that the model can explain convergence phases such as the "growth miracles" in France, Germany, and Japan after World War II comparatively well, whereas the model fails to explain long-run economic growth dynamics.

This chapter then introduced population growth and technological progress into the basic Solow model and presented the framework in continuous time (by means of differential equations). Introducing technological progress enabled the model to explain long-run growth dynamics in addition to convergence phases: the reason that countries such as Germany and the United States grow in the long run is that technological progress leads to continual

---

18. Please note that throughout the book we assume another distinguishing feature of robots, namely, that they do not experience utility the way that humans do and, more generally, that they do not have free will. Thus, they do not show up as relevant entities in welfare analyses or in decision problems.

increases in productivity. We again analyzed the transitional dynamics implied by the model by means of phase diagrams.

We then introduced automation into the model by assuming the presence of a production factor that is a perfect substitute for labor but is itself physical capital (which can be interpreted as robots). Because this production factor competes directly with workers, it depresses wages. In addition, the income that this production factor earns is funneled to capital owners. Thus, automation decreases the labor income share in the automation-augmented Solow model. Because labor income tends to be more equally distributed than capital income, a declining labor income share leads to a rise in overall income inequality in real-world economies. A second remarkable effect of automation in the Solow model is that it overcomes the declining marginal productivity of labor such that the possibility of sustained long-run economic growth emerges even without the presence of technological progress.

The basic automation-augmented model assumes that the decision of how much to invest in traditional physical capital versus how much to invest in automation capital is exogenous. While consistent with the setting of the Solow (1956) model, rational investors might not choose such an exogenous investment rate. Section 4.5 shows that all important results remain valid in the case of an endogenous split of investment between automation capital and traditional physical capital.

Section 4.6 further generalizes the model by introducing two types of labor: low-skilled workers and high-skilled workers. This allowed us to analyze the effects of automation not only on the labor share but also on wage inequality. We see that automation raises the skill premium (the wedge between the wages of low-skilled workers and the wages of high-skilled workers) and that it typically reduces the wages of low-skilled workers. This model implication is consistent with the evolution of the wages of high-skilled workers and low-skilled workers in the United States since the 1970s. The other implications of the baseline model (the potential for perpetual growth even without technological progress and the declining labor income share) are also present in this extension of the basic model.

Finally, we discussed the issue of changes in social welfare due to automation. This chapter's theoretical discussions suggest that automation will lead to rising growth but at the expense of increasing inequality. The extent to which automation is beneficial to the society thus depends on a society's valuation of inequality. If inequality does not matter at all (the case of a utilitarian or Benthamite social welfare function), automation is likely to be seen as beneficial. In the case of a Rawlsian social welfare function, by contrast, economic well-being of the least well-off person determines the welfare of the society such that automation would likely be seen as harmful. Overall, the actual degree of a society's inequality aversion is very difficult to assess, such that normative judgments cannot be easily made. However, Chapter 7 describes policies that could potentially compensate the losers of automation and discusses the advantages and disadvantages of those policies.

References

Abeliansky, A., & Prettner, K. (2017). Automation and demographic change. Hohenheim Discussion Papers in Business, Economics, and Social Sciences 05-2017.

Acemoglu, D. (2002). Directed technical change. *Review of Economic Studies, 69*(4), 781−809.

Acemoglu, D. (2009). *Introduction to modern economic growth.* Princeton, NJ: Princeton University Press.

Acemoglu, D., & Restrepo, P. (2018). Low-skill and high-skill automation. *Journal of Human Capital, 12*(2), 204−232.

Adler, M. D. (2019). *Measuring social welfare: an introduction.* Oxford, UK: Oxford University Press.

Aghion, P., & Howitt, P. (2008). *The economics of growth.* Cambridge, MA: MIT Press.

Ahituv, A. (2001). Be fruitful or multiply: On the interplay between fertility and economic development. *Journal of Population Economics, 14*(1), 51−71.

Antony, J., & Klarl, T. (2019). The implications of automation for economic growth when investment decisions are irreversible. *Economics Letters* (forthcoming).

Autor, D. (2002). Skill biased technical change and rising inequality: What is the evidence? What are the alternatives? Retrieved from https://economics.mit.edu/files/558. Accessed January 3, 2018.

Barro, R. J., & Sala-i-Martin, X. S. (2003). *Economic growth.* Cambridge, MA: MIT Press.

Benzell, S. G., Kotlikoff, L. J., LaGarda, G., & Sachs, J. D. (2015). *Robots are us: Some economics of human replacement.* Cambridge, MA: National Bureau of Economic Research, NBER Working Paper 20941.

Berg, A., Buffie, E. F., & Zanna, L.-F. (2018). Should we fear the robot revolution? (The correct answer is yes). *Journal of Monetary Economics, 97*, 117−148, August 2018.

Blanchard, O. (2016). *Macroeconomics* (7th ed.). London: Pearson.

Bloom, D. E., Canning, D., & Sevilla, J. (2003). The demographic dividend: A new perspective on the economic consequences of population change. Population Matters. A RAND Program of Policy-Relevant Research Communication, Santa Monica, CA.

Bloom, D. E., & Freeman, R. B. (1988). Economic development and the timing and components of population growth. *Journal of Policy Modelling, 10*(1), 57−81.

Bloom, D. E., Kuhn, M., & Prettner, K. (2017). Africa's prospects for enjoying a demographic dividend. *Journal of Demographic Economics, 83*(1), 63−76.

Bolt, J., & van Zanden, J. (2014). The Maddison Project: Collaborative research on historical national accounts. *The Economic History Review, 67*(3), 627−651.

Brander, J. A., & Dowrick, S. (1994). The role of fertility and population in economic growth. *Journal of Population Economics, 7*(1), 1−25.

Cass, D. (1965). Optimum growth in an aggregative model of capital accumulation. *The Review of Economic Studies, 32*(3), 233−240.

Cords, D., & Prettner, K. (2019). Technological unemployment revisited: Automation in a search and matching framework. GLO Discussion Paper Series 308, Essen.

Cowell, F. (2011). *Measuring inequality* (3rd ed.). Oxford, UK: Oxford University Press.

Dalgaard, C.-J. L., & Strulik, H. (2013). The history augmented Solow model. *European Economic Review, 63*(1), 134−149.

Diamond, P. A. (1965). National debt in a neoclassical growth model. *American Economic Review, 55*(5), 1126−1150.

Elsby, M. W. L., Hobijn, B., & Sahin, A. (2013). The decline of the U.S. labor share. *Brookings Papers on Economic Activity*, 1−63, Fall 2013.

Foley, D., Michl, T. R., & Tavani, D. (2019). *Economic growth and distribution* (2nd ed.). Cambridge, MA: Harvard University Press.

Gandolfo, G. (2010). *Economic dynamics*. Berlin, Heidelberg: Springer.

Gasteiger, E., & Prettner, K. (2020). A note on automation, stagnation, and the implications of a robot tax. Macroeconomic Dynamics (forthcoming).

Geiger, N., Prettner, K., & Schwarzer, J. (2018). Die auswirkungen der Automatisierung, auf Wachstum, Beschäftigung und Ungleichheit. *Perspektiven der Wirtschaftspolitik, 19*(2), 59−77.

Gordon, R. (2016). *The rise and fall of American growth: The U.S. standard of living since the Civil War*. Princeton, NJ: Princeton University Press.

Grossmann, V., Steger, T. M., & Trimborn, T. (2013). Dynamically optimal R&D subsidization. *Journal of Economic Dynamics and Control, 37*(3), 516−534.

Heijdra, B. J. (2017). *Foundations of modern macroeconomics* (3rd ed.). Oxford, UK: Oxford University Press.

Herzer, D., Strulik, H., & Vollmer, S. (2012). The long-run determinants of fertility: One century of demographic change 1900−1999. *Journal of Economic Growth, 17*(4), 357−385.

Hicks, J. (1939). The foundations of welfare economics. *Economic Journal, 49*(196), 696−712.

Jones, C. I. (1995). R&D-based models of economic growth. *Journal of Political Economy, 103* (4), 759−783.

Jones, C. I. (2005). The shape of production functions and the direction of technical change. *Quarterly Journal of Economics, 120*(2), 517−549.

Jones, C. I., & Scrimgeour, D. (2008). A new proof of Uzawa's steady-state growth theorem. *The Review of Economics and Statistics, 90*(1), 180−182.

Jones, C. I., & Vollrath, D. (2009). *Introduction to economic growth* (3rd ed.). New York: W. W. Norton & Company.

Kaldor, N. (1939). Welfare propositions in economics and interpersonal comparisons of utility. *Economic Journal, 49*(195), 549−552.

Kaldor, N. (1957). A model of economic growth. *The Economic Journal, 67*(268), 591−624.

Karabarbounis, L., & Neiman, B. (2014). The global decline of the labor share. *The Quarterly Journal of Economics, 129*(1), 61−103.

Kelley, A. C., & Schmidt, R. M. (1995). Aggregate population and economic growth correlations: The role of the components of demographic change. *Demography, 32*(4), 543−555.

Koopmans, T. C. (1965). On the concept of optimal economic growth. In J. Johansen (Ed.), *The Econometric Approach to Development Planning*. Amsterdam: North Holland.

Kortum, S. (1997). Research, patenting and technological change. *Econometrica, 65*(6), 1389−1419.

Labaj, M., & Dujava, D. (2019). Economic growth and convergence during the transition to production using automation capital. Department of Economic Policy, Faculty of National Economy, University of Economics in Bratislava, Department of Economic Policy Working

Paper Series 017. Retrieved from https://nhf.euba.sk/www_write/files/katedry/khp/working-papers/dep_wp017.pdf. Accessed December 18, 2019.

Lankisch, C., Prettner, K., & Prskawetz, A. (2019). How can robots affect wage inequality? *Economic Modelling*, *81*, 161–169, September 2019.

Li, H., & Zhang, J. (2007). Do high birth rates hamper economic growth? *Review of Economics and Statistics*, *89*(1), 110–117.

Mankiw, N. G. (2015). *Macroeconomics* (9th ed.). New York: Worth Publishers.

Mankiw, N. G., Romer, D., & Weil, D. (1992). A contribution to the empirics of economic growth. *Quarterly Journal of Economics*, *107*(2), 407–437.

Merriam-Webster. (2017). Automation. Retrieved from https://www.merriam-webster.com/dictionary/automation. Accessed March 3, 2017.

Piketty, T. (2014). *Capital in the twenty-first century*. Cambridge, MA: The Belknap Press of Harvard University Press.

Prettner, K. (2016). The implications of automation for economic growth and the labor share of income. Hohenheim Discussion Papers in Business, Economics and Social Sciences. Discussion Paper 18-2016.

Prettner, K. (2019). A note on the implications of automation for economic growth and the labor share. *Macroeconomic Dynamics*, *23*(3), 1294–1301.

Prettner, K., & Strulik, H. (2020). Innovation, automation, and inequality: Policy challenges in the race against the machine. *Journal of Monetary Economics (forthcoming)*.

Ramsey, F. P. (1928). A mathematical theory of saving. *The Economic Journal*, *38*(152), 543–559.

Rebelo, S. (1991). Long-run policy analysis and long-run growth. *Journal of Political Economy*, *99*(3), 500–521.

Romer, D. (2011). *Advanced macroeconomics*. New York: McGraw-Hill.

Romer, P. (1986). Increasing returns and long-run growth. *Journal of Political Economy*, *94*(5), 1002–1037.

Sachs, J. D., Benzell, S. G., & LaGarda, G. (2015). *Robots: Curse or blessing? A basic framework*. Cambridge, MA: National Bureau of Economic Research, NBER Working Paper 21091.

Sachs, J. D., & Kotlikoff, L. J. (2012). *Smart machines and long-term misery*. Cambridge, MA: National Bureau of Economic Research, NBER Working Paper 18629.

Scitovsky, T. (1941). A note on welfare propositions in economics. *Review of Economic Studies*, *9*(1), 77–88.

Segerström, P. S. (1998). Endogenous growth without scale effects. *American Economic Review*, *88*(5), 1290–1310.

Solow, R. M. (1956). A contribution to the theory of economic growth. *The Quarterly Journal of Economics*, *70*(1), 65–94.

Steigum, E. (2011). Robotics and growth. In H. Beladi, & E. K. Choi (Eds.), *Frontiers of economics and globalization: Economic growth and development* (pp. 543–557). Bingley, UK: Emerald Group, Chapter 21.

Sydsaeter, K., Hammond, P., Seierstad, A., & Strom, A. (2008). *Further mathematics for economic analysis* (2nd ed.). Upper Saddle River, NJ: Prentice Hall.

United States Census Bureau. (2017). Historical income tables. Retrieved from https://www.census.gov/data/tables/time-series/demo/income-poverty/historical-income-people.html. Accessed August 14, 2017.

Uzawa, H. (1961). Neutral inventions and the stability of growth equilibrium. *Review of Economic Studies*, 28(2), 117–124.

Weil, D. N. (2012). *Economic growth* (3rd ed.). London: Taylor & Francis.

World Bank. (2019). *World development indicators 1960–2019*. Washington, DC: The World Bank.

Yang, D. T., Zhang, J., & Zhou, S. (2011). *Why are saving rates so high in China?* Cambridge, MA: National Bureau of Economic Research, NBER Working Paper No. 16771.

Chapter 5

Endogenous savings and extensions of the baseline model

5.1 Introduction

This chapter deals with extensions to the basic economic frameworks presented in Chapter 4 and can be covered in more advanced courses on macroeconomics, in general, and on automation, in particular (e.g., at the advanced undergraduate level or at the graduate level). For readers who wish to skip this chapter, doing so is possible without any major consequences for understanding the rest of the book. The following brief description of this chapter's content and the summary at the end of the chapter might nevertheless provide insights for readers who do not wish to delve into the technical details of the model extensions.

First, this chapter provides an overview of important tools for advanced (dynamic) economic analysis, such as solving static optimization problems with equality and inequality constraints and solving dynamic optimization problems in discrete and continuous time. The presentation of these tools is deliberately kept simple and in the form of recipes/cookbook procedures that allow for a straightforward application of the methods to different practical problems at hand. After the basic tools have been introduced, we will present two workhorse models that form the backbone of modern dynamic macroeconomics: (1) the neoclassical growth model of the Ramsey−Cass−Koopmans type (Cass, 1965; Koopmans, 1965; Ramsey, 1928) and (2) the canonical overlapping generations (OLG) model (Diamond, 1965; Samuelson, 1958). These frameworks, and extensions thereof, are widely used in the analysis of

- Business cycle phenomena with real business cycle models and the New Keynesian model containing—at their core—a Ramsey−Cass−Koopmans model (see Galí 2015; Heijdra, 2017; Romer, 2011 for overviews);

Automation and its Macroeconomic Consequences. DOI: https://doi.org/10.1016/B978-0-12-818028-0.00005-3

- Questions related to the causes of long-run economic growth and potential policies to foster economic development (see Acemoglu, 2009; Galor, 2011; Heijdra, 2017 for overviews); and
- The effects of fiscal policies, including those related to social security systems and the sustainability of pension funds (see Auerbach & Kotlikoff, 1987; de la Croix & Michel, 2002; Heijdra, 2017 for overviews).

After presenting the extended baseline frameworks, we will examine the implications of introducing automation into these models. In this context, one new insight will emerge: while the Ramsey−Cass−Koopmans model and the OLG model yield remarkably similar predictions with respect to almost all research questions, the implications of automation are very different from each other. While the Ramsey−Cass−Koopmans model preserves the basic insight that automation can lead to long-run economic growth even in the absence of further technological progress (see Chapter 4), automation-driven long-run growth is impossible in the canonical OLG model. The reason for this diverging implication is that savings/investments are made out of total income (capital income plus labor income) in the former framework, while savings/investments are made exclusively out of labor income in the latter framework. In the canonical OLG model, agents save for retirement when they are young and do not own any capital. Because robots compete with workers on the labor market, the wages of young workers and, hence, their savings decrease in the presence of automation, hampering investment and capital accumulation. Consequently, a vicious cycle emerges: automation puts downward pressure on wages, which are the only source of investment to finance future automation. This happens to the extent that the canonical OLG model with automation predicts long-run economic stagnation.[1]

5.2 Cookbook procedures for static and dynamic optimization

Before analyzing automation in the neoclassical growth model and in the OLG model, we provide the recipes/cookbook procedures (i.e., a presentation of straightforward, step-by-step instructions) for static optimization with equality constraints in Section 5.2.1, static optimization with inequality constraints and nonnegativity constraints on (some of the) choice variables in Section 5.2.2, dynamic optimization in discrete time with two time periods

---

1. Various extensions of the baseline model exist, and some of them weaken this conclusion, for example, the presence of bequests and perfect intergenerational altruism. However, even in the case of these extensions, the qualitative results of the baseline framework are remarkably robust (see Gasteiger & Prettner, 2020).

in Section 5.2.3, and dynamic optimization in continuous time in Section 5.2.4.

5.2.1 The method of Lagrange

Suppose we seek to maximize an objective function $U(\cdot)$, which is typically the utility of an individual or household in economic contexts.[2] This objective function depends on two variables in the simplest case, say x_1 and x_2. In a utility maximization context, these two variables are the consumption levels of good 1 and good 2, respectively. Assuming that utility increases in consumption of the two goods is standard. This is tantamount to the statement that the partial derivatives of the function $U(x_1, x_2)$ with respect to the two input arguments are positive. These partial derivatives are the marginal utilities of x_1 and x_2, i.e., the amount by which utility increases when consumption of one of the input arguments of the function increases to a very small (infinitesimal) extent. In mathematical terms, this can be stated as follows:

$$U_{x_1}(x_1, x_2) \equiv \frac{\partial U(x_1, x_2)}{\partial x_1} > 0, \qquad U_{x_2}(x_1, x_2) \equiv \frac{\partial U(x_1, x_2)}{\partial x_2} > 0,$$

where the short-hand notation for the partial derivatives of a function $U(\cdot)$ with respect to the argument x_i is U_{x_i}.

The additional utility gleaned from additional consumption is usually assumed to decrease. This is equivalent to the statement that the second partial derivatives of the function $U(x_1, x_2)$ with respect to the two input arguments are negative (i.e., marginal utilities decrease). In mathematical terms, this can be stated as follows:

$$U_{x_1 x_1}(x_1, x_2) \equiv \frac{\partial^2 U(x_1, x_2)}{\partial x_1^2} < 0, \qquad U_{x_2 x_2}(x_1, x_2) \equiv \frac{\partial^2 U(x_1, x_2)}{\partial x_2^2} < 0.$$

Intuitively, the assumptions make sense: if a person is hungry, the first slice of pizza delivers relatively high (marginal) utility. However, the 35th slice will likely not provide the same satisfaction, increasing utility by much less than the first few pieces. This comparison holds for many different goods. Again, we need to abstract from reasonable, real-world complications such as (1) additional utility could turn negative for some goods (e.g., the fifth bottle of wine, at least for most of us) and (2) marginal utility could *increase*

---

2. Other common applications are profit maximization and cost minimization, but for the sake of clarity, we focus on utility maximization here. Apart from the different interpretation, the mathematical techniques for profit maximization are the same. Cost minimization also leads to a similar structure when recognizing that the minimization of a function is the same as the maximization of its negative expression.

for certain goods, for example, in cases of addiction (smokers rarely report that their inaugural cigarette tasted good).

In compact terms, the aforementioned assumptions can be summarized by the statement that utility $U(x_1, x_2)$ is *strictly concave* in both input arguments. Graphically, this means that $U(x_1, x_2)$ looks like the curve in Fig. 5.1 for a given level of $x_2 = const.$: if x_1 increases, the value of the function increases strongly for low levels of x_1 (it has a steep slope—or $U_{x_1}(x_1, x_2)$ is high—for small levels of x_1). However, the slope of the function decreases as x_1 increases, such that it becomes flatter for a higher x_1.

To ensure an interior optimum for utility maximization problems, Inada-type conditions (see the discussion of production functions in Chapter 4) are often assumed to also hold for the utility functions:

$$\lim_{x_1 \to 0} U_{x_1}(x_1, x_2) = \infty, \qquad \lim_{x_1 \to \infty} U_{x_1}(x_1, x_2) = 0,$$

$$\lim_{x_2 \to 0} U_{x_2}(x_1, x_2) = \infty, \qquad \lim_{x_2 \to \infty} U_{x_2}(x_1, x_2) = 0.$$

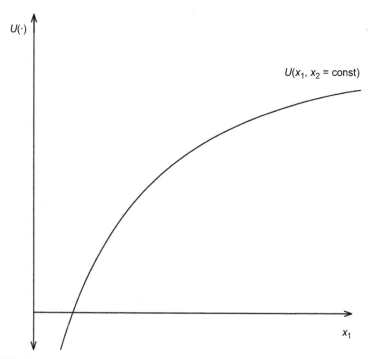

FIGURE 5.1   Illustration of a strictly concave utility function. The slope of the curve is steep for low levels of x_1 and decreases as x_1 increases. Note that the function can be negative for low levels of x_1 (e.g., in case of a logarithmic utility function). If the Inada conditions are fulfilled, utility tends to $-\infty$ as x_1 approaches zero.

These conditions rule out corner solutions—that is, consuming nothing of a certain good is not optimal if income is positive and if the marginal utility of the particular good at a consumption level of zero goes to infinity.

Clearly, if this were the whole story, maximizing utility would call for infinite levels of x_1 and x_2 because the function $U(\cdot)$ is nondecreasing in its arguments. Unfortunately, reality imposes certain constraints, for example, goods are costly to obtain and our budget does not allow us to buy an infinite amount of them. Following the notation of Dixit (1990), the constraints in economic models take the general form $G(x_1, x_2) = I$, where I is the exogenously given budget/income that can be spent on goods 1 and 2. Usually, the prices are also assumed to be exogenously given such that the budget constraint is linear and of the form

$$p_1 x_1 + p_2 x_2 = I.$$

In reality, however, situations could exist in which prices depend negatively on the quantities consumed (quantity discounts) such that the budget constraint becomes concave, or in which prices increase with the quantity consumed (e.g., if the production of the consumption goods requires scarce resources that are progressively more difficult to obtain) such that the budget constraint becomes convex. For simplicity, the following description disregards these cases, and we focus on the standard situation of a linear budget constraint (such that the function $G(\cdot)$ is linear).

Following the descriptions of the utility function and budget constraint, the basic tradeoffs are clear: if a consumer buys more of good 1, then she has less money to spend on good 2. Thus, the consumer will try to allocate her budget to the consumption of both goods in a way that yields the maximum possible utility without violating her budget constraint—inherently, this will be the point at which the additional utility of a slight increase in the consumption of good 1 will exactly balance the utility loss of the concomitant decrease in consumption of good 2 that is necessary because the budget constraint is fulfilled at the initial consumption choice and has to stay fulfilled at the new consumption choice. In other words, at the optimal allocation, each dollar spent must yield the same additional utility, irrespective of whether it is spent on good 1 or good 2—otherwise, a reallocation could raise the overall utility and the given initial allocation would not have been optimal in the first place.

In the following analyses, we look at the method of Lagrange to mathematically derive such optimal choices. We present this (and the other methods) in the form of a recipe/cookbook procedure in which one needs only to follow the successive steps to arrive at the optimal solution. Interestingly, while the contexts of many optimization problems and their interpretations can vary, the mathematical structure is usually quite similar. For most economic problems, following our recipe/cookbook procedure will ensure that the solution can be found easily. For more complex problems, Dixit (1990),

Léonard and van Long (1992), Sundaram (1996), Sydsaeter, Hammond, and Strom (2012), Sydsaeter, Hammond, Seierstad, and Strom (2008) provide further insights into these different methods and the mathematical proofs of why they work (or, in certain situations, might not work).

In the case of the underlying problem of maximizing the function

$$U(x_1, x_2),$$

subject to the constraint

$$G(x_1, x_2) = I,$$

the recipe/cookbook procedure works as follows:

1. Set up the Lagrangian function $\mathcal{L}(x_1, x_2, \lambda)$, which is defined as follows:

$$\mathcal{L}(x_1, x_2, \lambda) = U(x_1, x_2) + \lambda[I - G(x_1, x_2)],$$

where λ is the Lagrange multiplier that, at the optimum, amounts to the additional utility that a marginal relaxation of the budget constraint yields. Consistent with the previous intuitive interpretation, this additional utility of λ has to be the same for both goods x_1 and x_2 at any optimal allocation (see step 2).

Because $U(x_1, x_2)$ is strictly concave and fulfills the Inada conditions, while we assume $G(x_1, x_2)$ to be linear, the Lagrangian $\mathcal{L}(x_1, x_2, \lambda)$ will be strictly concave in x_1 and x_2: subtracting a linear term $[\lambda G(x_1, x_2)]$ from a strictly concave term preserves the strict concavity. The Lagrangian $\mathcal{L}(x_1, x_2, \lambda)$ will therefore increase for low levels of x_1 and x_2 in the corresponding argument, while—for higher levels of x_1 and x_2—it will decrease in x_1 and x_2. The reason is the falling marginal utility of goods 1 and 2 that makes the function $U(x_1, x_2)$ flatter as the arguments increase, whereas the term that is subtracted, $G(x_1, x_2)$, is linear and will dominate from some point onward. Thus, the Lagrangian exhibits a unique interior maximum, as Fig. 5.2 shows, at the point where $\mathcal{L}(x_1, x_2 = \text{const.}, \lambda)$ attains the highest possible value $x_1 = \bar{x}$.

2. Calculate the first-order conditions (FOCs) for an optimum, which are as follows:

$$\frac{\partial \mathcal{L}(x_1, x_2, \lambda)}{\partial x_1} \overset{!}{=} 0, \tag{5.1}$$

$$\frac{\partial \mathcal{L}(x_1, x_2, \lambda)}{\partial x_2} \overset{!}{=} 0, \tag{5.2}$$

$$\frac{\partial \mathcal{L}(x_1, x_2, \lambda)}{\partial \lambda} \overset{!}{=} 0, \tag{5.3}$$

where "$\overset{!}{=} 0$" means that the result should be set equal to zero. The reason these conditions need to be fulfilled at the optimum is that an

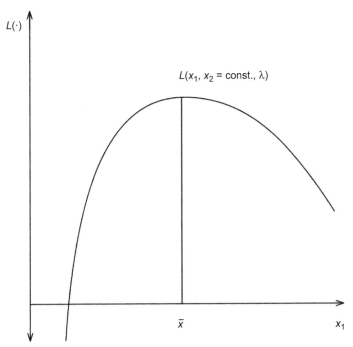

FIGURE 5.2 Illustration of a strictly concave Lagrangian function. The Lagrangian attains its maximum at the point $x_1 = \bar{x}$. In case of a strictly concave Lagrangian, this maximum is unique.

increase in x_1 or in x_2 that still fulfills the budget constraint (i.e., it is paired with a corresponding decrease in the other consumption good) cannot increase overall utility anymore; otherwise the solution would not have been optimal in the first place. Graphically, the optimum is where the function $\mathcal{L}(x_1, x_2, \lambda)$ attains its maximum value in Fig. 5.2. At the maximum, the function $\mathcal{L}(x_1, x_2, \lambda)$ has a slope of zero, which is the point at which the partial derivatives of the Lagrangian with respect to the corresponding input arguments equal zero. In our case, this procedure delivers three equations in the three unknowns x_1, x_2, and λ, such that the system can usually be solved for all the unknowns.

3. Solve the system of equations resulting from the FOCs for the unknowns x_1, x_2, and λ. This yields candidate points for an optimum solution. In our case of a strictly concave Lagrangian, we are done at this point: its strict concavity implies that the Lagrangian can only attain a maximum at one point. Fortunately, many economic applications come with such a strictly concave Lagrangian. If the Lagrangian were not strictly concave, however, we would need to apply the next step.

4. This step is only needed if the Lagrangian is not strictly concave or if the geometric properties of the Lagrangian are unknown. In this step, we need

to analyze the obtained candidate solutions and check whether they are maxima, minima, or neither maxima nor minima of the optimization problem. This process amounts to checking the definiteness of the matrix of the Langrangian's second partial derivatives (the bordered Hessian matrix). If the bordered Hessian at the candidate point is positive definite, the Lagrangian is locally convex at the candidate point, and the corresponding solution is a local minimum. If the bordered Hessian is negative definite at the candidate point, the Lagrangian is locally concave at the candidate point, and the corresponding solution is a local maximum. If the bordered Hessian is indefinite at the candidate point, the corresponding solution is neither a maximum nor a minimum. In our simple case of two choice variables and one constraint, checking the definiteness of the bordered Hessian amounts to calculating its determinant. If the determinant is positive, the bordered Hessian is negative definite and the candidate point is a maximum. If the determinant is negative, the bordered Hessian is positive definite and the candidate point is a minimum. However, checking the definiteness of the bordered Hessian becomes more difficult when we have $n > 2$ choice variables and potentially $m > 1$ constraints, as we will see later. To determine whether a candidate point that has been identified as a *local* maximum/minimum is indeed the *global* maximum/minimum, plug all of the candidate solutions and all solutions at the boundary of the domain into the objective function to check which solution yields the highest and lowest values. These results are then the global maximum and the global minimum, respectively.

Example 1 applies the recipe/cookbook procedure to a basic optimization problem that often confronts economists.

Example 1

Suppose an individual can consume two goods and her utility function has the following form:

$$U(c_1, c_2) = \alpha \ln(c_1) + \beta \ln(c_2),$$

where c_1 and c_2 are the consumption levels of goods 1 and 2, α is the utility weight of good 1, and β is the utility weight of good 2. The budget constraint is linear and reads

$$p_1 c_1 + p_2 c_2 = I.$$

Derive the optimal solutions for c_1, c_2, and λ. Interpret the result, argue why it represents a maximum, and explain why it is unique.

Solution
1. Set up the Lagrangian function:

$$\mathcal{L}(c_1, c_2, \lambda) = \alpha \ln(c_1) + \beta \ln(c_2) + \lambda(I - p_1 c_1 - p_2 c_2).$$

2. Calculate the FOCs:

$$\frac{\partial \mathcal{L}(c_1, c_2, \lambda)}{\partial c_1} = \frac{\alpha}{c_1} - \lambda p_1 \overset{!}{=} 0, \tag{5.4}$$

$$\frac{\partial \mathcal{L}(c_1, c_2, \lambda)}{\partial c_2} = \frac{\beta}{c_2} - \lambda p_2 \overset{!}{=} 0, \tag{5.5}$$

$$\frac{\partial \mathcal{L}(c_1, c_2, \lambda)}{\partial \lambda} = I - p_1 c_1 - p_2 c_2 \overset{!}{=} 0. \tag{5.6}$$

3. Solve the resulting system of three equations for the three unknowns c_1, c_2, and λ. One possible way of doing so is to isolate c_1 and c_2 from Eqs. (5.4) and (5.5) and plugging the results into Eq. (5.6). This yields the value of the Lagrange multiplier at the optimal choice:

$$\lambda = \frac{\alpha + \beta}{I}.$$

Clearly, the Lagrange multiplier decreases with income (I) at the optimal choice because marginal utility of both goods decreases such that a marginal relaxation of the budget constraint yields ever lower additional utility for ever higher income (I). In addition, the Lagrange multiplier increases with the utility weights α and β because, if they are higher, utility increases by more for a marginal increase of consumption.

Next, plugging λ into the expressions derived for c_1 and c_2 yields the (Marshallian) demand functions for the two consumption goods as follows:

$$c_1 = \frac{\alpha I}{(\alpha + \beta)p_1}, c_2 = \frac{\beta I}{(\alpha + \beta)p_2}.$$

The interpretation is straightforward. First, the demand for both goods increases with income (I) because the individual can afford more consumption if she earns more. Second, the demand for both goods decreases with an ascending price of the corresponding good (either p_1 or p_2) because, if the good becomes more expensive, the individual can afford less of it. Third, if the individual likes a specific good more (its utility weight increases), she will *ceteris paribus* purchase more of this good and less of the other good. The latter is required because, at the original point, the budget constraint holds. Increasing consumption of the good for which the utility weight increases can therefore only be afforded by decreasing consumption of the other good. At the new optimum, a marginal dollar spent on either of the two goods must again yield the same additional utility, irrespective of whether it is spent on good 1 or on good 2.

The reason this solution is indeed the global unique maximum is that the Lagrangian is strictly concave. This result can be confirmed graphically by plotting the Lagrangian for a varying consumption of one of the two goods and holding the consumption of the other good fixed. It can also be verified by noting that the utility function is strictly concave in both choice variables, while the budget constraint is linear. As mentioned earlier, subtracting a linear function from a strictly concave function results, again, in a strictly concave function.

The method of Lagrange is easily generalized to a situation with $n > 2$ choice variables and $m > 1$ constraints as long as $n > m$ is fulfilled, which is usually the case in economic problems. The utility function is then $U(x_1, x_2, \ldots, x_n)$ and the system of budget constraints can be written as follows:

$$G^j(x_1, x_2, \ldots, x_n) = I_j \quad \text{for} \quad j = 1, 2, \ldots, m.$$

In this case, the recipe/cookbook procedure looks as follows.

1. Set up the Lagrangian function:

$$\mathcal{L}(x_1, x_2, \ldots, x_n, \lambda_1, \lambda_2, \ldots, \lambda_m) = U(x_1, x_2, \ldots, x_n) + \sum_{j=1}^{m} \lambda_j \left[I_j - G^j(x_1, x_2, \ldots, x_n) \right].$$

2. Calculate the FOCs for an optimum, which are

$$\frac{\partial \mathcal{L}(x_1, x_2, \ldots, x_n, \lambda_1, \lambda_2, \ldots, \lambda_m)}{\partial x_i} \overset{!}{=} 0 \quad \text{for} \quad i = 1, 2, \ldots n, \quad (5.7)$$

$$\frac{\partial \mathcal{L}(x_1, x_2, \ldots, x_n, \lambda_1, \lambda_2, \ldots, \lambda_m)}{\partial \lambda_j} \overset{!}{=} 0 \quad \text{for} \quad j = 1, 2, \ldots m. \quad (5.8)$$

3. Solve the resulting system of $n + m$ equations of FOCs for the $n + m$ unknowns $x_1, x_2, \ldots, x_n$ and $\lambda_1, \lambda_2, \ldots, \lambda_m$.
4. This step is only needed if the Lagrangian is not strictly concave or if the geometric properties of the Lagrangian are unknown. Check whether the candidate solutions are indeed local maxima, minima, or neither maxima nor minima of the optimization problem. Again, we must check the definiteness of the bordered Hessian. In the case of n choice variables and m constraints, this requires checking the sign of the last $n - m$ leading principal minors. We have the following:
   - If the leading principal minors alternate in sign with the last principal minor (the determinant of the bordered Hessian), having the sign $(-1)^n$, then the bordered Hessian is negative definite, the Lagrangian is locally concave, and the candidate point is a local maximum.
   - If the leading principal minors have the same sign $(-1)^m$, then the bordered Hessian is positive definite, the Lagrangian is locally convex, and the candidate point is a local minimum.
   - In all other cases, the bordered Hessian is indefinite, and the candidate point is neither a local maximum nor a local minimum.

To determine whether a candidate point that has been identified as a *local* maximum/minimum is indeed the *global* maximum/minimum, plug all of the candidate solutions and all solutions at the boundary of the domain into the objective function to check which solution yields the highest and the lowest values. These results are then the global maximum and the global minimum, respectively.

5.2.2   The method of Karush−Kuhn−Tucker

The method of Lagrange can also be generalized to deal with (1) nonnegativity constraints on the choice variables and (2) side constraints that need not be fulfilled with strict equality. For example, in the case of consumption goods c_i, requiring that $c_i \geq 0$ for all i might make sense because negative consumption is usually not possible. In addition, a person need not spend her whole budget/income at once. Instead, the budget constraint and other potential constraints could be stated as a set of inequalities

$$G^j(x_1, x_2, \ldots, x_n) \leq I_j \quad \text{for} \quad j = 1, 2, \ldots, m.$$

In the context of a budget constraint, this means that a person cannot spend more than the available budget but can spend less. In this more general case, the recipe/cookbook procedure changes as follows (this is known as the method of Karush−Kuhn−Tucker after Karush, 1939 and Kuhn & Tucker, 1951):

1. Set up the Lagrangian function:

$$\mathcal{L}(x_1, x_2, \ldots, x_n, \lambda_1, \lambda_2, \ldots, \lambda_m) = F(x_1, x_2, \ldots, x_n) + \sum_{j=1}^{m} \lambda_j \left[I_j - G^j(x_1, x_2, \ldots, x_n) \right].$$

2. Calculate the FOCs for an optimum, which are now pairs of inequalities:

$$\frac{\partial \mathcal{L}(x_1, x_2, \ldots, x_n, \lambda_1, \lambda_2, \ldots, \lambda_m)}{\partial x_i} \leq 0, x_i \geq 0 \quad \text{for} \quad i = 1, 2, \ldots n, \quad (5.9)$$

$$\frac{\partial \mathcal{L}(x_1, x_2, \ldots, x_n, \lambda_1, \lambda_2, \ldots, \lambda_m)}{\partial \lambda_j} \geq 0, \lambda_j \geq 0 \quad \text{for} \quad j = 1, 2, \ldots m. \quad (5.10)$$

   These pairs of conditions need to hold with *complementary slackness*, which means that if one of the two conditions for each i and each j holds with a *strict inequality*, the other has to hold with a *strict equality*. Thus, at most one of the two conditions for each i and each j can be slack (fulfilled with strict inequality), while the other then needs to be fulfilled with strict equality.

3. As a consequence of step 2, many possible cases of combinations of equalities and inequalities now exist in the system of FOCs that all need to be solved for and analyzed. Overall, step 2 provides 2^{m+n} cases of different systems of $m + n$ equations in $m + n$ unknowns that all lead to a candidate solution of the optimization problem. Clearly, the task of solving all of them becomes very cumbersome for large n and m. Fortunately, practical applications have shortcuts because many of the cases can be ruled out by a priori economic arguments. For example, if all goods yield a positive marginal utility, leaving money unspent makes no sense such that in this case the budget constraint

will never be slack (i.e., it will always be fulfilled with strict equality).[3] This case rules out all FOCs for which the budget constraint is slack.

4. This step is only needed if the Lagrangian is not strictly concave or if the geometric properties of the Lagrangian are unknown. We need to find out whether the candidate points for a solution are local maxima, minima, or neither maxima nor minima of the optimization problem. The procedure is the same as that described in Section 5.2.1 for the method of Lagrange with n choice variables and m constraints.

5.2.3 Dynamic optimization in discrete time in the case of two time periods

With the standard method of Lagrange, we can also solve simple dynamic optimization problems, which we encounter later in this chapter when we discuss the OLG model. The trick is to assume that the choice variable at different points in time is actually a different variable (e.g., consumption at time t is c_t and consumption at time $t + 1$ is c_{t+1} and so on). Then, one can follow the recipe/cookbook procedure for the method of Lagrange with n choice variables and m constraints. However, for advanced problems with many time periods and in which strategic interactions occur between agents or in which the future is uncertain, more sophisticated methods of *dynamic programming* are required. Dixit (1990), Léonard and van Long (1992), Sorger (2015), Stokey, Lucas, and Prescott (1989), and Sydsaeter et al. (2008), among others, provide good descriptions of these methods. Example 2 applies the method of Lagrange in case of a two-period optimization problem such that $n = 2$ and $m = 1$.

Example 2

Assume that individuals live for two time periods, t and $t + 1$, in which they earn wages w_t and w_{t+1}, respectively. Individuals have an isoelastic utility function over consumption in the two time periods, as given by

$$U(c_t, c_{t+1}) = \frac{c_t^{1-\theta} - 1}{1 - \theta} + \beta \frac{c_{t+1}^{1-\theta} - 1}{1 - \theta}.$$

In this formulation, $\beta \in (0, 1)$ is the discount factor measuring how much weight an individual attaches to future consumption (i.e., it measures impatience). The discount *factor* is determined by the discount *rate*, denoted by $\rho > 0$ via the relationship $\beta = 1/(1 + \rho)$. The parameter θ measures the risk aversion of the

---

3. This, of course, assumes that goods are divisible such that one can buy, say, half a unit of a certain good. In case of indivisibility, money may still be left over because it would be insufficient to buy the full amount of any of the goods left.

individual (i.e., the concavity of the utility function).[4] Its inverse, $1/\theta$, is the elasticity of intertemporal substitution measuring an individual's willingness to depart from consumption smoothing to earn higher interest income.[5] The individual's choice is how much of her income to save in the first period of life to consume more in the second period of life. The savings carried over from the first to the second period earn an asset income at the going interest rate r, and we assume that the individual starts the first period without any assets.

1. Write down the budget constraint that the individual faces.
2. Derive optimal individual consumption in periods t and $t+1$ and use the result to characterize the rule of optimal individual consumption growth.

Solution

Denoting savings by s_t and assuming that individuals start their lives without assets, the choice of individuals has to satisfy

$$c_t + s_t = w_t$$

in the first period such that consumption and savings add up to wage income in the first period. Note that savings can also be negative such that individuals go into debt. In the second period, the choice of consumption has to satisfy

$$c_{t+1} = w_{t+1} + (1 + r)s_t$$

such that consumption in the second period equals wage income in the second period, plus savings from the previous period on which interest is paid. Substituting $s_t = w_t - c_t$ obtained from the first equation and plugging it into the second equation yields

$$c_{t+1} = w_{t+1} + (1 + r)(w_t - c_t).$$

Rearranging all terms involving consumption to appear on the left-hand side leads to the lifetime budget constraint

$$c_t + \frac{c_{t+1}}{1 + r} = w_t + \frac{w_{t+1}}{1 + r}.$$

The left-hand side comprises total discounted lifetime consumption expenditures, while the right-hand side comprises total discounted lifetime income. By using this equation as the constraint, we can solve the given simple dynamic optimization problem by following our recipe/cookbook procedure.

---

4. Note the similarity to the discussion of inequality aversion in Chapter 4. In fact the parameters for inequality aversion and for risk aversion measure the curvature of the utility function. Depending on the context, this curvature can be interpreted as inequality aversion or as risk aversion. According to the latter interpretation, individuals try to avoid situations in which they end up with a low consumption level in one period. This is particularly relevant where uncertainty is present. The more risk-averse individuals are, the more they would be willing to insure themselves against the risk of having low consumption in one of the periods.

5. Using the rule of L'Hospital in the isoelastic utility function in case of $\theta = 1$, one can show that the logarithmic utility function results. Note that the rule of L'Hospital could not be applied to the isoelastic utility function if it were stated without the term " -1 " in the numerator because plugging in $\theta = 1$ would lead to a numerator other than zero. For the utility maximization problem it does not matter whether the term " -1 " shows up in the numerator or not. The reason is that a constant additive term just drops out when taking the derivative to calculate the FOCs.

1. The Lagrangian is

$$\mathcal{L} = \frac{c_t^{1-\theta} - 1}{1 - \theta} + \beta \frac{c_{t+1}^{1-\theta} - 1}{1 - \theta} + \lambda \left(w_t + \frac{w_{t+1}}{1 + r} - c_t - \frac{c_{t+1}}{1 + r} \right).$$

2. The FOCs are

$$L_{c_t} = c_t^{-\theta} - \lambda \overset{!}{=} 0,$$

$$L_{c_{t+1}} = \beta c_{t+1}^{-\theta} - \frac{\lambda}{1 + r} \overset{!}{=} 0,$$

$$L_\lambda = w_t + \frac{w_{t+1}}{1 + r} - c_t - \frac{c_{t+1}}{1 + r} \overset{!}{=} 0.$$

3. Using $c_t^{-\theta} = \lambda$, as implied by the first FOC; plugging it into the second FOC; and reformulating yields the so-called consumption Euler equation:

$$\frac{c_{t+1}}{c_t} = [(1 + r)\beta]^{\frac{1}{\theta}}. \tag{5.11}$$

In this equation, the left-hand side is the growth factor of consumption at the optimum, while the right-hand side is a function of the interest rate, the discount factor, and individuals' risk aversion. Optimal consumption grows over time if the right-hand side is larger than one. This is the case if the interest rate is high in comparison with the discount factor such that the product $(1 + r)\beta$ is larger than one. In this case, the financial market overcompensates for individual impatience by paying a sufficiently high interest rate to induce individuals to save. Saving, in turn, is tantamount to having positive consumption growth, $c_{t+1}/c_t > 1$. Note that consumption growth (saving) is higher if

- The interest rate r is higher.
- Households are more patient (ρ is lower such that β is higher).
- Households are less risk averse (θ is lower). If households are less risk averse, the elasticity of intertemporal substitution is higher, and they are more willing to shift consumption over time to take advantage of the higher interest rate.

5.2.4 Dynamic optimization in continuous time

Finally, we provide the recipe/cookbook procedure for dynamic optimization in continuous time to address the household optimization problem of the standard neoclassical growth model of Ramsey–Cass–Koopmans (Cass, 1965; Koopmans, 1965; Ramsey, 1928). We focus on the simplest structure in which we have one *control variable* (the variable that the individual can choose) and one *state variable* (the variable that past decisions of the individual predetermine and that can change only gradually via the choices of the control variable).[6] In

---

6. This terminology is from the method that we apply to solve dynamic optimization problems, which is called optimal control theory (or Pontryagin's Maximum Principle). It was originally developed to calculate the optimal thrust of rockets to maximize payload. The control variable in this original application is the thrust of the rocket at each moment in time and the state variable is the rocket's velocity (see Pontryagin, Boltyanskii, Gamkrelidze, & Mishchenko, 1962 for more details).

addition, we assume that the objective function only depends on the control variable and that all the functions are well behaved (in terms of concavity/convexity) such that we do not need to check the second-order conditions (SOCs).

Suppose that time t evolves continuously and that individuals aim to maximize their lifetime utility

$$U[c(t)] = \int_0^\infty u[c(t)]e^{-\rho t}dt,$$

where instantaneous utility $u(\cdot)$ depends on the control variable consumption at each moment in time $c(t)$. Instantaneous utility is integrated over the life cycle of the individual (the equivalent of summation over time in the case of a discrete-time variable) to get lifetime utility $U[c(t)]$. In most applications, the boundaries of the integration go from time zero up to infinity, which simplifies matters substantially and is usually justified by the assumption that the utility function belongs to the head of a dynasty with perfect foresight and perfect altruism toward the offspring. The term $e^{-\rho t}$ is the discount factor in continuous time. It ensures that the weight of future instantaneous utility decreases at the rate of impatience (ρ) as the corresponding moment moves away in time.

The constraint of the optimization problem is a dynamic equation (a differential equation) that relates the evolution of the stock of assets to total income and consumption expenditures. It is given by

$$\dot{a}(t) = G[a(t), c(t)],$$

where $a(t)$ denotes the individual's stock of assets, which is the state variable.

Unlike static optimization, where we aim to derive the optimal *consumption level* (a number), here, we aim to derive an optimal *consumption path* (a function depending on time). The recipe/cookbook procedure to solve the optimization problem works as follows:

1. Define the so-called *present-value Hamiltonian*[7] as

$$\mathcal{H}[c(t), a(t), \lambda(t)] = U[c(t)]e^{-\rho t} + \lambda(t)G[a(t), c(t)],$$

where $\lambda(t)$ is the *costate variable*, which essentially has a similar interpretation as the Lagrange multiplier in the method of Lagrange, except that there is a costate variable at each instant. Intuitively, one can think

---

7. The procedure also works with a different formulation, the *current-value Hamiltonian*. In this alternative formulation, the discount factor is assumed to be part of the costate variable. The FOCs of the current-value Hamiltonian change such that the final result is, again, the same as in the case of the present-value formulation. In some cases, however, deriving and solving the FOCs is less cumbersome in the current-value formulation.

of this as having to solve a series of static optimization problems—one at each moment in time—and these problems are linked over time via the state variable $a(t)$ and the costate variable $\lambda(t)$.

2. Derive the FOCs for an interior maximum for which $c(t)$, $a(t)$, and $\lambda(t)$ have to fulfill the following conditions:[8]

$$\frac{\partial \mathcal{H}[c(t), a(t), \lambda(t)]}{\partial c(t)} \overset{!}{=} 0,$$

$$\frac{\partial \mathcal{H}[c(t), a(t), \lambda(t)]}{\partial a(t)} \overset{!}{=} -\dot{\lambda}(t),$$

$$\frac{\partial \mathcal{H}[c(t), a(t), \lambda(t)]}{\partial \lambda(t)} \overset{!}{=} \dot{a}(t).$$

The intuition for the first FOC is that a consumption increase comes with an increase in utility today, but with a decrease in future utility because fewer savings are carried over to afford future consumption. If the first FOC is fulfilled, then the two effects exactly offset each other for a given costate variable $\lambda(t)$. In this case, reallocating consumption over time cannot raise lifetime utility, which is necessary for an optimum. The second FOC is not present in static optimization because it relates to the evolution of the costate variable over time. In case of positive net savings (growing assets) and a strictly concave utility function, the additional utility derived from a marginal relaxation of the budget constraint decreases. For an optimal savings path, this decrease must exactly match the additional utility that the optimizing individual gets out of the additional asset income. Finally, the third FOC replicates the dynamic budget constraint that must hold for a viable solution path.[9]

3. Solve the system of FOCs to get a system of differential equations, either in terms of the state and costate variables [$a(t)$ and $\lambda(t)$] or in terms of the state and control variables [$a(t)$ and $c(t)$]. In economic applications, the solution exhibits a more accessible, intuitive interpretation when the system of equations is in the control-state space of consumption [$c(t)$] and assets [$a(t)$].

Example 3 illustrates a dynamic optimization problem in continuous time that is often encountered in economics and can serve as the building block of a simplified Ramsey−Cass−Koopmans model (as in Section 5.3).

---

8. Formally, the solution must also fulfill an initial condition and a terminal condition (these conditions select the only optimal solution path out of the infinitely many paths that fulfill the FOCs). For expositional reasons, however, we discuss these two additional conditions later.

9. For a more detailed discussion of the intuition behind the FOCs of dynamic optimization in continuous time, see Dorfman (1969).

Example 3

Assume that the head of an infinitely lived dynasty seeks to maximize the utility of the dynasty, whose members have an isoelastic instantaneous utility function over consumption such that

$$U[c(t)] = \int_0^\infty \frac{c(t)^{1-\theta} - 1}{1 - \theta} e^{-\rho t} dt, \tag{5.12}$$

where ρ is the discount rate. The parameter θ again measures risk aversion (i.e., the concavity of the utility function), and its inverse, $1/\theta$, is the elasticity of inter-temporal substitution. Assume that physical capital $k(t)$ is the only savings vehicle such that the dynamic budget constraint is given by

$$\dot{k}(t) = r(t)k(t) + w(t) - c(t),$$

where $\dot{k}(t)$ is the change in the capital stock. The capital stock increases with total income—consisting of capital income $r(t)k(t)$ and wage income $w(t)$—and decreases with total consumption expenditures $c(t)$.[10] If total income is higher than total consumption expenditures, the change in capital ($\dot{k}$) is positive such that capital accumulates and the individual saves. By contrast, if total income is less than total consumption expenditure, the change in capital ($\dot{k}$) is negative such that capital decumulates and the individual dissaves. Derive the optimal individual consumption path over time and interpret the result.

Solution

1. First, we set up the present-value Hamiltonian:

$$\mathcal{H}[c(t), k(t), \lambda(t)] = \frac{c(t)^{1-\theta} - 1}{1 - \theta} e^{-\rho t} + \lambda(t)[r(t)k(t) + w(t) - c(t)].$$

2. Second, we derive the necessary FOCs:

$$\frac{\partial \mathcal{H}[c(t), k(t), \lambda(t)]}{\partial c(t)} \overset{!}{=} 0 \Leftrightarrow c(t)^{-\theta} e^{-\rho t} = \lambda(t),$$

$$\frac{\partial \mathcal{H}[c(t), k(t), \lambda(t)]}{\partial k(t)} \overset{!}{=} -\dot{\lambda}(t) \Leftrightarrow \dot{\lambda}(t) = -\lambda(t)r(t),$$

$$\frac{\partial \mathcal{H}[c(t), k(t), \lambda(t)]}{\partial \lambda(t)} \overset{!}{=} \dot{k}(t) \Leftrightarrow \dot{k}(t) = r(t)k(t) + w(t) - c(t).$$

3. The second and third FOCs already represent a system of two differential equations in the two unknowns $k(t)$ and $\lambda(t)$, that is, in the state-costate space. However, the economic meaning of the solution in the state-costate space is difficult to grasp. Therefore, we use the first FOC to derive the solution in the control-state space. To do so, we take the logarithm of the first FOC

$$\log[\lambda(t)] = -\theta \cdot \log[c(t)] - \rho t$$

---

10. The usual assumption is that the interest rate trajectory $[r(t)]$ and the wage rate trajectory $[w(t)]$ cannot be influenced by the optimizing individual, that is, the individual is *atomistic* or price-taking.

and differentiate it with respect to time to obtain

$$\frac{\dot{\lambda}(t)}{\lambda(t)} = -\theta \frac{\dot{c}(t)}{c(t)} - \rho. \tag{5.13}$$

In this derivation, we used the fact that the time derivative of the logarithm of a variable is the growth rate of the variable under consideration (see Chapter 4). From the second FOC, we get

$$\frac{\dot{\lambda}(t)}{\lambda(t)} = -r(t). \tag{5.14}$$

Plugging Eq. (5.14) into Eq. (5.13) eliminates the costate variable and yields

$$\frac{\dot{c}(t)}{c(t)} = \frac{r(t) - \rho}{\theta}. \tag{5.15}$$

This is the consumption Euler equation in continuous time. The interpretation is similar to the interpretation of Eq. (5.11): The left-hand side is now the growth *rate* of consumption at the optimum, while the right-hand side is again a function of the interest rate, the discount rate (impatience), and the risk aversion of individuals. Optimal consumption now grows over time if the right-hand side of the consumption Euler equation is greater than zero. This is the case if the interest rate is high in comparison with the discount rate such that $r(t) > \rho$. In this case, the financial market overcompensates for individual impatience by paying a sufficiently high interest rate to induce individuals to save. Saving is, in turn, tantamount to having positive consumption growth $\dot{c}(t)/c(t) > 0$. Consumption growth (saving) is higher if

- The interest rate $r(t)$ is higher.
- Households are more patient (ρ is lower).
- Households are less risk averse (θ is lower). If households are less risk averse, they are more willing to shift consumption over time to take advantage of the higher interest rate.

Interestingly, while the mathematical techniques to handle dynamics in discrete and continuous time differ substantially, the meaning and implications of the consumption Euler equation are similar—irrespective of which time formulation the problem is expressed in. Together with the capital accumulation equation, the consumption Euler equation forms a system of two differential equations in the two variables $c(t)$ and $k(t)$ that can be solved for the general solution (infinitely many paths that fulfill the laws of motion given by the system) and the particular solution (one particular path that is pinned down out of the general solutions by two additional conditions). For details on this, see, for example, Gandolfo (2010) or Sydsaeter et al. (2008). However, deriving explicit solutions is very cumbersome, and often impossible, due to the nonlinearity of the system of differential equations. Thus, such systems of differential equations are often analyzed numerically; we do not go into the details here, but refer readers to the excellent treatment of numerical solutions of these types of models by Trimborn, Koch, and Steger (2008) and Trimborn (2013).[11] An alternative method to characterize the solution paths of two-dimensional systems of differential equations is to draw a *phase diagram*. We will employ this approach when discussing the Ramsey–Cass–Koopmans model in the following section.

Now we have all the necessary tools to begin analyzing neoclassical economic growth models and OLG models in the following sections.

5.3   Endogenous savings in the Ramsey–Cass–Koopmans model

The frameworks analyzed in Chapter 4, which are based on the Solow (1956) model, have one crucial disadvantage: they assume that individuals save a constant fraction s of their income. Because s is a parameter in these models, households cannot choose it. In reality, however, the household consumption-savings choice is one of the most important economic decisions. As such, it is one of the crucial behavioral aspects of households at the microeconomic level that determines the dynamics of aggregate economies at the macroeconomic level. The reason is that savings determine the capital stock of a society and, in more elaborated models of long-run economic growth driven by endogenous research and development (R&D) investments, the very incentives to invest in new technologies. Accordingly, individual consumption-savings behavior is more accurately explained endogenously within a general equilibrium growth model.

Two attempts have been made to endogenize the saving rate in the macroeconomic literature, and both attempts have led to very successful frameworks that constitute the backbone of modern dynamic macroeconomics. The first is the Ramsey–Cass–Koopmans model (the neoclassical growth model), in which a single, infinitely lived representative agent (or the head of a dynasty) decides—at each moment in time—how much income to consume and how much to save (Cass, 1965; Koopmans, 1965; Ramsey, 1928). The second is the OLG framework, in the canonical formulation of which individuals live for two time periods, earning a wage income in the first period while saving for their retirement in the second period (Diamond, 1965; Samuelson, 1958). This section covers the Ramsey–Cass–Koopmans model, and the following section extends it to include automation. Subsequent sections will address the OLG model and the OLG model with automation.

---

11. The authors also provide Matlab and Mathematica codes for solving many common (systems of) dynamic equations numerically. For the sources, see https://sites.google.com/site/timotrimborn/software and https://www.wiwi.uni-siegen.de/vwli/forschung/relaxation/the_relaxation_method.html.

For brevity, we suppress time arguments in analyzing the Ramsey–Cass–Koopmans model whenever this does not impair the clarity of the exposition. Example 3 fully describes the consumption side of the model. From there, we know that in the case of a representative agent with an isoelastic utility function, the consumption Euler equation reads

$$\frac{\dot{c}}{c} = \frac{r - \rho}{\theta}. \tag{5.16}$$

Together with the capital accumulation equation,

$$\dot{k} = rk + w - c, \tag{5.17}$$

which is the second central equation of the Ramsey–Cass–Koopmans model, and the consumption Euler equation forms a system of two differential equations in the two unknowns c and k. This system describes the behavior of the household side of the economy; its intuitive interpretation is known from Example 3. To analyze the behavior of the whole economy at the general equilibrium, however, we still need to determine the equilibrium interest rate r and the equilibrium wage rate w, which are endogenous variables that are determined by the interactions between households and firms. To derive the general equilibrium, we need to specify the firm side of the economy, which we do next.

Recall that the Cobb–Douglas production function with technology normalized to unity is given by

$$Y = K^{\alpha} L^{1-\alpha},$$

where, as in Chapter 4, Y is aggregate output, K is the aggregate capital stock, L is labor input, and α is the elasticity of output with respect to capital input. Under perfect competition and assuming that capital depreciates at the rate δ, we get the following factor rewards that equal the marginal (value) products of each production factor:

$$w = \frac{\partial Y}{\partial L} = (1 - \alpha)L^{-\alpha}K^{\alpha} = (1 - \alpha)k^{\alpha},$$

$$r = \frac{\partial Y}{\partial K} - \delta = \alpha K^{\alpha-1}L^{1-\alpha} - \delta = \alpha k^{\alpha-1} - \delta.$$

Plugging these expressions for r and w into the system of differential equations formed by Eqs. (5.16) and (5.17) yields

$$\dot{c} = \left(\frac{\alpha k^{\alpha-1} - \delta - \rho}{\theta}\right)c, \tag{5.18}$$

$$\dot{k} = \left(\alpha k^{\alpha-1} - \delta\right)k + \left(1 - \alpha\right)k^{\alpha} - c = k^{\alpha} - \delta k - c. \tag{5.19}$$

This two-dimensional system of differential equations in the two variables, consumption (c) and capital (k), fully describes the evolution of the model economy because interactions between the household and the firm side are considered and because the representative household can be treated as equivalent to the aggregate economy. Thus, consumption per worker and aggregate consumption and capital per worker and aggregate capital coincide ($c \equiv C$ and $k \equiv K$).

We can analyze the dynamics implied by the system of the two differential Eqs. (5.18) and (5.19) by means of a phase diagram in the c-k space (the control-state space). Fig. 5.3 shows the first step in constructing the phase diagram, where we plot the capital stock on the horizontal axis and consumption on the vertical axis. To derive the steady-state equilibrium of the economy—in which consumption and capital no longer change—we set the left-hand sides of the differential Eqs. (5.18) and (5.19) equal to zero to yield

$$0 \overset{!}{=} \left(\frac{\alpha k^{\alpha-1} - \delta - \rho}{\theta} \right) c \Leftrightarrow \alpha k^{\alpha-1} = \delta + \rho, \tag{5.20}$$

$$0 \overset{!}{=} k^\alpha - \delta k - c \Leftrightarrow c = k^\alpha - \delta k. \tag{5.21}$$

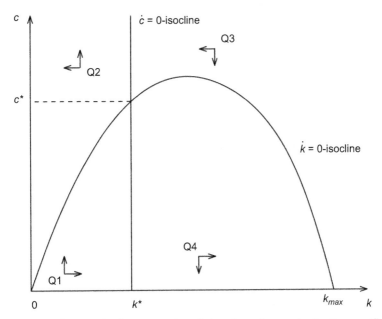

FIGURE 5.3 First step in the construction of the phase diagram in the Ramsey–Cass–Koopmans model. The $\dot{c} = 0$ isocline depicts the capital stock k for which Eq. (5.18) equals zero, and the $\dot{k} = 0$ isocline depicts the combinations of c and k for which Eq. (5.19) equals zero. At the intersection of the two isoclines, both equations equal zero and the economy is at its steady state, associated with $c = c^*$ and $k = k^*$. The isoclines divide the c-k space into four quadrants, Q1–Q4, in which the corresponding arrows illustrate the evolution of c and k, as described in the text.

These equations represent *isoclines* or *level curves* of combinations between c and k for which the corresponding variable does not change over time. In Fig. 5.3, the $\dot{c} = 0$ isocline depicts the combinations of c and k for which Eq. (5.18) equals zero such that consumption does not change, and the $\dot{k} = 0$ isocline depicts the combinations of c and k for which Eq. (5.19) equals zero and capital does not change. At the intersection of the two isoclines, both differential equations equal zero, consumption and capital do not change, and the economy is at its steady state. We denote the steady-state values of consumption and capital by $c = c^*$ and $k = k^*$, respectively.

The steady state of the economy will not be reached immediately if we start off with a capital stock $k(0) \neq k^*$. Therefore, we have to characterize how the economy behaves outside of the steady state. For this purpose, we recognize that the two isoclines in Fig. 5.3 divide the c-k space into four quadrants, Q1−Q4, in which c and k exhibit the following dynamics:

- Quadrant Q1: Consumption lies below the level of the $\dot{k} = 0$ isocline such that Eq. (5.19) is positive because income is higher than consumption expenditures and the representative individual therefore saves. Thus, capital increases in this quadrant, as indicated by the arrow pointing to the right. At the same time, capital lies below the level of the $\dot{c} = 0$ isocline such that Eq. (5.18) is positive [note that the exponent of k in Eq. (5.18) is negative]. Thus, consumption increases in this quadrant, as indicated by the arrow pointing upward. The economic intuition for increasing consumption is that the high interest rate induces the representative individual to sacrifice some consumption today for the ability to consume more in the future (implying a rising consumption path).

- Quadrant Q2: Consumption lies above the level of the $\dot{k} = 0$ isocline such that Eq. (5.19) is negative because income is lower than consumption expenditures, and the representative individual therefore dissaves. Thus, capital decreases in this quadrant, as indicated by the arrow pointing to the left. At the same time, capital lies below the level of the $\dot{c} = 0$ isocline such that Eq. (5.18) is positive. Thus, consumption increases further in this quadrant, as indicated by the arrow pointing upward. Again, the high and increasing interest rate induces the representative individual to sacrifice some consumption today for the ability to consume more in the future (implying a rising consumption path). However, in this case, the level of consumption is already so high that capital decumulates and becomes zero at some point. The chosen consumption path would therefore not be feasible in the long run. It could be sustained only by borrowing ever more and paying back the borrowed money with even higher debt. As we discuss subsequently, financial markets would not enable such a solution.

- Quadrant Q3: Consumption lies above the level of the $\dot{k} = 0$ isocline such that Eq. (5.19) is negative because income is lower than consumption expenditures, and the representative individual therefore dissaves. Thus, capital decreases in this quadrant, as indicated by the arrow pointing to the left. At the same time, capital lies above the level of the $\dot{c} = 0$ isocline such that Eq. (5.18) is negative. Thus, consumption also decreases in this quadrant, as indicated by the arrow pointing downward. The economic intuition here is that the interest rate is so low that individuals prefer to consume more today and—in conjunction with the associated dissaving—less in the future (implying a falling consumption path).

- Quadrant Q4: Consumption lies below the level of the $\dot{k} = 0$ isocline such that Eq. (5.19) is positive because income is higher than consumption expenditures, and the representative individual therefore saves. Thus, capital increases in this quadrant, as indicated by the arrow pointing to the right. At the same time, capital lies above the level of the $\dot{c} = 0$ isocline such that Eq. (5.18) is negative. Thus, consumption decreases in this quadrant, as indicated by the arrow pointing downward. Again, the reason for decreasing consumption is that the interest rate is so low that individuals prefer to consume more today and less in the future (implying a falling consumption path). However, in contrast to quadrant Q3, the level of consumption is so low that the capital stock still rises, which reduces the interest rate further. In this quadrant, the representative individual converges to a situation in which she would save all income and consume nothing. Clearly, such a path cannot be optimal from an individual perspective, as we also discuss later.

As mentioned and as discussed in more detail later, optimal behavior of the representative individual will rule out ever choosing a path in quadrants Q2 and Q4 or a path leading into these quadrants when the path starts in quadrants Q1 or Q3.

For each combination of values c and k at the initial point, the economy will follow one solution path of the system of differential Eqs. (5.18)–(5.19). Because one could start with infinitely many combinations of c and k, there are also infinitely many *general solution* paths. However, the system of differential Eqs. (5.18)–(5.19) must fulfill two conditions in the case of an economy populated by rational agents, and these two conditions select one unique initial combination of c and k that leads to the one and only *particular solution*; this is the only viable solution path.

The first of the two conditions is an initial condition on the capital stock at which the economy starts. We denote this initial capital stock by $k(0)$, and Fig. 5.4 shows the possible dynamics emerging from $k(0)$ for different initial levels of consumption $c(0)$. All remaining viable solution paths for this initial condition have to start at the vertical dashed line at the level $k(0)$ of the capital stock. If the representative agent chooses an initial consumption level of $c(0)_1$, consumption is so high that the capital stock in the economy declines. As time goes by, the economy converges to the vertical axis at which the

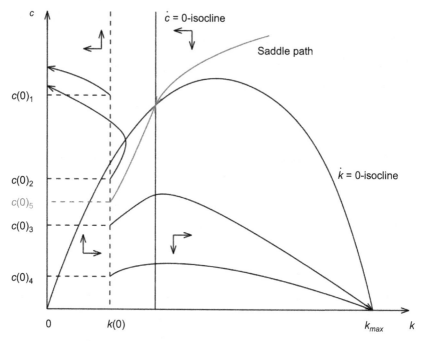

FIGURE 5.4 Second step in the construction of the phase diagram in the Ramsey–Cass–Koopmans model. Potential solution paths of the economy in the c-k space are depicted for a given initial capital stock $k(0)$ and different initial consumption levels $c(0)$. Only the solution with the initial condition $k = k(0)$ and $c = c(0)_5$ fulfills the transversality condition and lies on the saddle path such that the economy converges to the long-run steady-state equilibrium at which $k = k^*$ and $c = c^*$.

capital stock becomes zero and the economy ceases to exist. Similar dynamics hold for a slightly lower initial consumption level of $c(0)_2$ for which, however, the capital stock grows initially until the solution path crosses the $\dot{k} = 0$ isocline. After this point, consumption is again unsustainably high such that the capital stock decreases and the economy converges toward the vertical axis with a zero capital stock. Clearly, these solution paths cannot be optimal as individuals would strive for ever higher consumption without any resources left for its production. Suppose now that the representative agent chooses a lower initial consumption level $c(0)_3$ or $c(0)_4$. In both cases, the agent saves a large amount and the capital stock increases quickly. However, oversaving would occur to the extent that—in the long run—all income would be used to sustain the high level of the capital stock and no income would remain for consumption. Clearly, these paths cannot be optimal either.

Exactly one initial consumption level, $c(0)_5$, puts the economy onto the red solution path that goes exactly toward the long-run steady state. This particular solution path is called the *saddle path*, and it is the only solution path that is consistent with the optimal behavior of rational agents. All solution paths with higher initial consumption violate the "no-Ponzi game condition": agents would want to increase consumption by assuming ever higher debt. However, financial markets would not allow a solution in which debtors continually escalate their debt, refinancing their obligations by taking out ever higher loans. By contrast, all solution paths with lower initial consumption levels than $c(0)_5$ would lead to oversaving—also not optimal from the agent's perspective. The condition that simultaneously rules out Ponzi games and oversaving is called the *transversality condition*. It is given by

$$\lim_{t \to \infty} k(t) e^{-\int_0^t [\alpha k(\tau)^{\alpha-1} - \delta] d\tau} = 0$$

in our setting. This equation states that the present value of assets must converge to zero asymptotically, and it is the second condition on the system of differential equations that pins down the only viable combination of initial values $c(0)_5$ and $k(0)$ such that the economy moves along the saddle path toward its long-run steady state.[12]

In a mathematically sloppy, but intuitively accessible interpretation, the time point $t = \infty$ could be thought of as the point when the economy "dies." Clearly, having a positive capital stock $k(t)$ left at that point would not be optimal, because in this case, one could have increased lifetime utility by saving less and consuming more. However, and this is also clear, financial markets would not allow people to plan to die indebted. Otherwise, the financial sector would end up in bankruptcy. Therefore, the only solution that is consistent with optimizing agents is the one at which the transversality condition holds with equality and the economy is on the saddle path.

Although the solution of this model is much more difficult to obtain compared with the solution of the standard Solow (1956) model, the central results are remarkably similar. The economy that a Ramsey–Cass–Koopmans model describes similarly converges to a steady-state solution in which the capital stock and gross domestic product (GDP) per worker and per capita do not grow in the absence of technological progress. This is the steady-state solution, c^* and k^*, at which the two isoclines intersect and to which the saddle path leads. As in the Solow model, there is convergence to the steady state (along the saddle path), and this convergence is associated with a high economic growth rate if it starts with a capital stock that is far below its steady-state level. During the convergence process, the capital

---

12. The transversality condition is a terminal condition in the sense that it specifies where the system needs to end up. In the example of maximizing the payload of a rocket that should end up in the earth's orbit, the transversality condition ensures that the final speed of the payload is exactly the one at which the centrifugal forces and gravity offset each other. Only in this case will the payload circle the earth.

stock per worker increases, and the interest rate decreases, until the following equation,

$$r - \rho = \alpha k^{\alpha-1} - \delta - \rho = 0,$$

holds at the steady state. At this point, consumption ceases to grow according to the consumption Euler Eq. (5.16). This feature is important because the discussion of automation within this model will show that the forces that lead the interest rate to converge to the steady state solution in the standard model might be switched off in the presence of automation.

Altogether, the closer the economy moves toward its steady-state solution, the more the growth rate of capital (and hence the growth rate of GDP) slows down. The aspects that we have discussed in the context of the Solow model, such as the economic miracle in Germany after World War II and the economic decline after the collapse of the Soviet Union, can therefore also be explained by the more sophisticated Ramsey–Cass–Koopmans model with endogenous savings choices.

5.4 Automation in the Ramsey–Cass–Koopmans model

Steigum (2011) introduces automation capital into the setting of a neoclassical Ramsey–Cass–Koopmans model by assuming a production function of the form

$$Y = AK^{\alpha}[\nu(\varepsilon P)^{\mu} + (1-\nu)L^{\mu}]^{\frac{1-\alpha}{\mu}},$$

where Y is aggregate output, K is traditional physical capital, P is automation capital, L is labor, A and ε are efficiency parameters with the latter referring to the productivity of automation capital, ν and $1-\nu$ are the production weights, μ determines the elasticity of substitution between workers and robots, and α is the elasticity of output with respect to traditional capital as in the previous models. Normalizing the production weight ν to $\nu \equiv \beta/(1-\alpha)$ with $0 < \beta < 1-\alpha$ and assuming perfect substitutability between robots and workers, the production function becomes

$$Y = AK^{\alpha}\left[\frac{\beta \varepsilon P}{1-\alpha} + \left(1 - \frac{\beta}{1-\alpha}\right)L\right]^{1-\alpha}.$$

Taking the derivatives of this expression with respect to K and P yields the rates of return on investment in traditional physical capital and in automation capital as, respectively,

$$r_K = A\alpha K^{\alpha-1}\left[\frac{\beta \varepsilon P}{1-\alpha} + \left(1 - \frac{\beta}{1-\alpha}\right)L\right]^{1-\alpha},$$

$$r_P = \beta \varepsilon A K^\alpha \left[\frac{\beta \varepsilon P}{1 - \alpha} + \left(1 - \frac{\beta}{1 - \alpha} \right) L \right]^{-\alpha}.$$

Because the model features rational investors and the two types of capitals are perfect substitutes, their return on investment has to be equal (as in the extension of the automation-augmented Solow model of Chapter 4). Setting $r_K = r_P$ and solving the resulting expression for the stock of robots P yields

$$P = K \left(\frac{1 - \alpha}{\alpha} \right) - \frac{L(1 - \alpha - \beta)}{\beta \varepsilon}.$$

Plugging this into the expressions for r_P or r_K and assuming that both assets depreciate at the rate δ, Steigum (2011) derives the common interest rate for both saving vehicles (traditional physical capital and automation capital) as

$$r = A \alpha^\alpha (\varepsilon \beta)^{1-\alpha} - \delta.$$

Because all right-hand side variables are constant parameters in this expression, the interest rate no longer converges toward the steady-state level as the economy grows. The reason is that the automation capital stock grows along the solution path of the economy together with the traditional physical capital stock. This prevents the diminishing returns of physical capital from taking hold—similar to the models considered in Chapter 4. As a consequence of the constant interest rate, three outcomes are now possible:

- In the case of $r < \rho$, consumption shrinks over time. In this case, the households do not save/invest enough to ensure long-run economic growth.
- If $r = \rho$, the growth rate is zero. In contrast to the standard neoclassical Ramsey−Cass−Koopmans model described previously, the case $r = \rho$ can only happen by sheer coincidence because no convergence forces lead to the steady state.
- Finally, if $r > \rho$, growth of the economy is perpetual. This is evident in the consumption Euler Eq. (5.16), which is always positive in this case.

Altogether, Steigum (2011) shows that, similar to the models described in Chapter 4, long-run economic growth becomes possible in the neoclassical growth model even without the presence of technological progress. Furthermore, the labor income share decreases as automation progresses because the production function has a similar structure as in the Solow model with automation as long as the substitutability between automation capital and labor is high/perfect. Therefore, two central implications of automation in the Solow model carry over to a setting in which the saving rate is determined endogenously according to the neoclassical growth model of Ramsey– Cass–Koopmans. However, Steigum (2011) does not introduce different skill levels into the model such that wage-related inequality cannot be analyzed in his setting.

5.5 Endogenous savings in the OLG model

Another workhorse model of modern dynamic macroeconomics is the OLG framework, which originates with the works of Diamond (1965) and Samuelson (1958). Here, we describe the canonical model of Diamond (1965), simplified to lead to analytically tractable solutions that allow easily extending the model to analyze the implications of automation in Section 5.6.

In contrast to the Ramsey–Cass–Koopmans type of neoclassical growth model, time is assumed to evolve discretely such that $t = 1, 2, \ldots, \infty$ and individuals are assumed to live for two time periods with certainty. One time period does not refer to a year but to a generation, corresponding to 20–30 years depending on the application of the model and potential calibrations to the real-world data. In the first period of life, individuals work and earn a wage income, while in the second period of life, they are retired, do not earn a wage income, and have to live off of the savings that they carried over from the previous period. These generations differ with respect to their asset holdings (wealth) such that the OLG model features crucial age-specific heterogeneities: young individuals do not own any assets and have to save for retirement out of their labor income. Old individuals, by contrast, hold assets because they saved when they were young. However, they do not work anymore and, thus, receive no labor income.

Fig. 5.5 summarizes the model's basic demographic structure. Time periods (generations) are depicted on the horizontal axis, where an individual who is born at time t is young until time $t + 1$. At the beginning of period $t + 1$, this individual becomes old and retires. Finally, at the end of period $t + 1$, the individual dies with certainty. In each period, a new young generation is born that replaces the cohort that was young in the previous period. The vertical axis refers to the structure of the population within an economy at any particular point in time. At each of these time points, two generations are alive: the young and the old. Any aggregation to derive aggregate consumption, aggregate assets, etc., must account for this structure and sum up the generation-specific variables over all generations that are currently alive. Note that this implies a crucial difference from the representative agent setting in the previous sections, in which one agent can be treated as representing the aggregate economy.

The canonical OLG model can be easily generalized to account for more than two generations. However, models with more than three generations can usually not be solved analytically. These large-scale models—which can

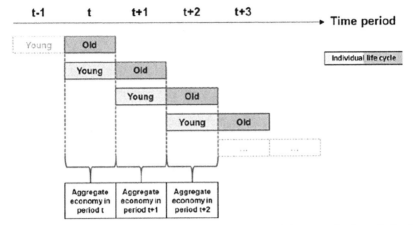

FIGURE 5.5 Structure of the canonical OLG model. Time periods (generations) are depicted on the horizontal axis, and the aggregate economy at time t can be characterized by summing over the two generations that are alive at that point in time.

consist of up to 100 generations such that one time period refers to 1 year—are called computable OLG models. They are frequently used to analyze questions related to the sustainability of social security systems and pension funds and the extent to which different cohorts benefit or suffer from different policy measures (see, for example, Auerbach & Kotlikoff, 1987; Krueger & Ludwig, 2007).

In the canonical OLG model, the utility function of individuals who are born at time t is given by

$$U_t(c_{1,t}, c_{2,t+1}) = u(c_{1,t}) + \beta u(c_{2,t+1}).$$

The utility function has the same structure as the utility function in Example 2, except that we use two subscripts for the choice variables: the first subscript indicates the phase of an individual's life cycle (1 referring to the working phase and 2 referring to the retired phase) and the second subscript indicates time periods. The first index has to be introduced to distinguish consumption of those who are young in period t ($c_{1,t}$) from consumption of those who are old in period t ($c_{2,t}$).

The aforementioned utility function is stated in general terms, that is, no specific structure is assumed on $u(\cdot)$. If we assume an isoelastic utility function, as in Example 2, solving the model analytically would become difficult. A useful simplification often made is to assume a logarithmic utility function of the following form instead:

$$U(c_{1,t}, c_{2,t+1}) = \log(c_{1,t}) + \beta \log(c_{2,t+1}). \tag{5.22}$$

The logarithmic utility function is the special case of an isoelastic utility function in which $\theta = 1$. Applying L'Hospital's rule to the isoelastic utility function from Example 2 for the case $\theta = 1$ shows this mathematically (see also Footnote 5). The crucial advantage of the logarithmic utility function is that income and substitution effects exactly offset each other. The income effect refers to the fact that a higher interest rate implies higher capital income, which would allow individuals to shift consumption from the second period to the first, that is, to save *less*. The substitution effect, by contrast, refers to the fact that a higher interest rate implies a higher return on saving, inducing individuals to save *more*. If both of these effects are of the same magnitude, they cancel each other out. The resulting demand functions are then much simpler than in a situation in which the corresponding terms need to be considered (for the mathematical details, see the later solution to the utility maximization problem).

The budget constraint is modified from Example 2 to take into account that (1) the individual is retired in the second period of life and, thus, earns no labor income in period $t + 1$ and (2) the interest rate in the OLG model is endogenously determined (because the model is a general equilibrium framework), so it is a variable that depends on time. The budget constraint then reads

$$c_{1,t} + \frac{c_{2,t+1}}{1 + r_{t+1}} = w_t. \tag{5.23}$$

Again, the left-hand side comprises total discounted lifetime consumption expenditures, while the right-hand side comprises lifetime income (consisting only of wage income in the first period of the individual's life).

We solve the individual's choice problem of maximizing (5.22) subject to (5.23) by means of the previously described method of Lagrange:

1. We set up the Lagrangian function of the optimization problem:

$$\mathcal{L} = \log(c_{1,t}) + \beta\log(c_{2,t+1}) + \lambda\left(w_t - c_{1,t} - \frac{c_{2,t+1}}{1 + r_{t+1}}\right). \tag{5.24}$$

2. We calculate the FOCs:

$$\mathcal{L}_{c_{1,t}} = \frac{1}{c_{1,t}} - \lambda \overset{!}{=} 0 \Leftrightarrow \frac{1}{c_{1,t}} = \lambda,$$

$$\mathcal{L}_{c_{2,t+1}} = \frac{\beta}{c_{2,t+1}} - \frac{\lambda}{1 + r_{t+1}} \overset{!}{=} 0 \Leftrightarrow \frac{\beta(1 + r_{t+1})}{c_{2,t+1}} = \lambda,$$

$$\mathcal{L}_\lambda = w_t - c_{1,t} - \frac{c_{2,t+1}}{1 + r_{t+1}} \overset{!}{=} 0 \Leftrightarrow c_{1,t} + \frac{c_{2,t+1}}{1 + r_{t+1}} = w_t.$$

Note that the third FOC again restates the budget constraint. We have a system of three equations for the three unknowns $c_{1,t}$, $c_{2,t+1}$, and λ that we can solve by applying straightforward algebra.

3. We combine the first two of the FOCs, which yields again the consumption Euler equation:

$$\frac{c_{2,t+1}}{c_{1,t}} = \beta(1 + r_{t+1}).$$

This equation has the standard interpretation that we know both from Example 2 and the Ramsey–Cass–Koopmans framework (although it is stated in continuous time there): consumption growth (saving) rises with the patience of individuals (β) and with the interest rate (r_{t+1}). The elasticity of intertemporal substitution does not show up here, however, because we simplified by assuming a logarithmic utility function, that is, by setting θ to unity.[13] Using the budget constraint (5.23), we can calculate consumption and savings in period t explicitly by noting that the budget constraint implies

$$c_{2,t+1} = (w_t - c_{1,t})(1 + r_{t+1}).$$

Substituting this into the consumption Euler equation, we get

$$\frac{(w_t - c_{1,t})(1 + r_{t+1})}{c_{1,t}} = \beta(1 + r_{t+1}) \Leftrightarrow c_{1,t} = \frac{w_t}{1 + \beta}.$$

Thus, consumption in the first period of the life cycle is a fraction of labor income, which decreases with β. This is intuitively clear: if individuals are more patient (β is higher), they consume less in the first period of their lives, that is, they save more to be able to consume more in the second period of their lives. Note that the interest rate dropped out in the derivation, which is very convenient. That the interest rate dropped out is a consequence of the logarithmic utility function ensuring that income and substitution effects exactly offset each other.

Next, we apply the definition of savings $s_t = w_t - c_{1,t}$ to arrive at

$$s_t = w_t - \frac{w_t}{1 + \beta} = \frac{\beta}{1 + \beta} w_t.$$

Taking the derivative of s_t with respect to β yields $[1/(1+\beta)^2]w_t > 0$, such that savings increase with the discount factor. Again, this is intuitively clear because individuals with greater patience will shift more consumption from the first period to the second period of their lives, that is, they would save more.

4. Because the utility function is strictly concave and the budget constraint is linear, the Lagrangian is strictly concave in the choice variables such

---

13. Note that the interpretation of the Euler equation differs a bit in case of a logarithmic utility function than in case of a more general isoelastic utility function because the effect that the interest rate exerts originates solely in the income that savings generate. If the interest rate is higher, second-period consumption will be higher because, for given savings, the individual will have more income to spend on second-period consumption. The savings behavior itself is, however, unaffected by changes in the interest rate.

that the candidate solution found by solving the FOCs indeed represents the unique maximum; we do not need to check the SOCs.

In the canonical OLG model, population growth at rate n is allowed. The cohort size, which equals the size of the workforce, therefore evolves according to the following difference equation:

$$L_t = (1 + n)L_{t-1} \Rightarrow L_t = (1 + n)^t L_0. \qquad (5.25)$$

Thus, the cohort size and the population size at any time t can always be calculated if we know the initial cohort size L_0 (note the analogy to the general solution and the specific solution in case of differential equations).

Until now, we have analyzed the household side of the model. To close the model and solve for its general equilibrium, we need to specify the firm side, derive the wage rate, and plug it into the savings expression to get to the equilibrium capital accumulation equation.[14] For this purpose, we again use a Cobb–Douglas specification of the production function in which we normalize technology to unity such that

$$Y_t = K_t^\alpha L_t^{1-\alpha},$$

where Y_t is aggregate output at time t, K_t is the aggregate capital stock at time t, L_t is labor input at time t, and α is the elasticity of output with respect to capital input. Using this production function, the wage rate is given as the marginal (value) product of labor:

$$w_t = \frac{\partial Y_t}{\partial L_t} = (1 - \alpha)K_t^\alpha L_t^{-\alpha} = (1 - \alpha)k_t^\alpha, \qquad (5.26)$$

where k_t is capital per worker at time t.

Now we derive the capital accumulation equation and, as is standard in the OLG literature, assume that physical capital fully depreciates over the course of one generation such that $\delta = 1$. In this case, aggregate capital at time $t + 1$ is given by $K_{t+1} = s_t L_t$.[15] Dividing K_{t+1} by the size of the workforce at time $t + 1$, L_{t+1}, we get the evolution of capital per worker as follows:

$$k_{t+1} = \frac{s_t}{1 + n} = \frac{\beta}{(1 + \beta)(1 + n)} w_t.$$

---

14. Note that we do not need to derive the interest rate in this case (and in contrast to the Ramsey–Cass–Koopmans model) because we assumed a logarithmic utility function such that the interest rate dropped out in the savings expression.
15. The capital stock of the previous period does not feature in this expression because the capital stock is assumed to depreciate fully over the course of one generation. Note that the capital accumulation equation essentially implies that the savings of the old generation determine the wages of the young generation.

In the next step, we substitute wages from Eq. (5.26) into this expression such that

$$k_{t+1} = \frac{\beta(1 - \alpha)}{(1 + \beta)(1 + n)} k_t^{\alpha}. \tag{5.27}$$

This difference equation is the fundamental equation of the canonical OLG model and allows for the analysis of the economy's dynamics in terms of capital per worker (k_t). We depict this function, which is concave as in the Solow model, in a diagram in which we have capital per worker at time t on the horizontal axis and capital per worker at time $t + 1$ on the vertical axis (Fig. 5.6). The dynamics are very similar to the Solow model without technological progress and without population growth in discrete time (see Chapter 4). The main difference is that we now allow for population growth such that we must plot the dynamics of the transformed variable "capital per worker" (k_t) instead of "aggregate capital" (K_t) in Fig. 5.6. While individuals optimally choose the saving rate in the canonical OLG model but not in the Solow model, this does not affect the qualitative graphical analysis.

The arrows in the graph again illustrate the development of the economy. If the economy starts with a capital stock per worker k_0, then the capital stock at time $t = 1$ is given by the k_{t+1} curve as k_1 on the vertical axis. As in

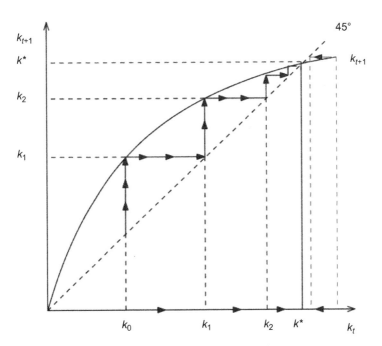

FIGURE 5.6 Dynamics of the canonical OLG model without technological progress.

Chapter 4, one time step corresponds to a projection of the vertical axis around the 45-degree line such that the vertical axis becomes the horizontal axis in the next time period. After the first time step, capital at time $t = 1$ is displayed on the horizontal axis as the value of k_1 projected from the vertical axis to the horizontal axis around the 45-degree line. The capital stock per worker at time $t = 2$ is then again given by the level on the k_{t+1} curve that corresponds to the value of k_1 on the vertical axis. This amounts to k_2, which is again projected onto the horizontal axis and so on and so forth. As in Chapter 4, the economy converges from below to the steady-state solution k^*. If the economy starts out with a very high capital stock, by contrast, then convergence to the steady state comes from above and the economy contracts. Overall, these dynamics can again explain the economic miracle in Germany after World War II and the declining economy of Russia after the collapse of the Soviet Union.

Next, we derive the model's steady-state solution, which means that we focus on the solution in which capital per worker no longer changes. To get this solution, we set $k_{t+1} = k_t = k^*$ in Eq. (5.27) and isolate k^* on the left-hand side such that

$$k^* = \left[\frac{\beta(1-\alpha)}{(1+\beta)(1+n)} \right]^{\frac{1}{1-\alpha}}. \tag{5.28}$$

Because per worker GDP (y_t) is given by

$$y_t = k_t^\alpha$$

as in the Solow model with a Cobb–Douglas production function and without technological progress, we again see that changes in k_t affect per-worker GDP directly. Thus, if k_t increases, per-worker GDP also increases, and vice versa.

With the help of Eq. (5.28), we can derive the following results that hold at the steady state:

- If the population growth rate n increases, capital per worker, GDP per worker, consumption per worker, and wages per worker decrease.
- If individuals become more patient (β decreases), capital per worker, GDP per worker, consumption per worker, and wages per worker increase.
- Note that $\delta = 1$ and $\theta = 1$ such that neither depreciation nor the coefficient of relative risk aversion show up explicitly in k^*.

Altogether, the transitional dynamics and the steady-state implications of the OLG model are remarkably similar to both the Solow and the Ramsey–Cass–Koopmans models. Thus, these frameworks usually lead to similar insights when it comes to analyzing the effects of different policy measures or attempts to uncover the driving forces behind long-run economic growth. However, when we discuss the OLG model with automation, the implications of automation differ quite significantly between the Solow model and the Ramsey–Cass–Koopmans model on the one hand and between the canonical OLG model on the other hand. This is the task to which we turn next.

5.6 Automation in the OLG model

To discuss the implications of automation in the OLG model, we follow Gasteiger and Prettner (2020) and consider an economy similar to the one in Section 5.5, except that this production function includes automation capital (P_t) and reads

$$Y_t = K_t^\alpha (L_t + P_t)^{1-\alpha}. \tag{5.29}$$

Individuals face the logarithmic utility function (5.22) and the standard budget constraint (5.23). We also allow for population growth at rate n as in Eq. (5.25). Thus, the individual optimization problem does not change such that we can characterize the consumption-saving behavior by the standard consumption Euler equation:

$$\frac{c_{2,t+1}}{c_{1,t}} = \beta(1 + r_{t+1}). \tag{5.30}$$

In addition, we get the expressions for consumption and savings as before:

$$c_{1,t} = \frac{1}{1+\beta} w_t, \quad s_t = \frac{\beta}{1+\beta} w_t. \tag{5.31}$$

When investing their savings, households can choose to buy traditional physical capital or automation capital as in the articles by Geiger, Prettner, and Schwarzer (2018), Lankisch, Prettner, and Prskawetz (2019), and Steigum (2011).

While the consumption side is similar to the canonical OLG model, we allow for automation capital on the economy's production side. Under perfect competition in goods and factor markets, all three production factors earn their marginal value products such that

$$w_t \equiv R_t^p = (1-\alpha)\left(\frac{K_t}{L_t + P_t}\right)^\alpha, \tag{5.32}$$

$$R_t^k = \alpha\left(\frac{L_t + P_t}{K_t}\right)^{1-\alpha}, \tag{5.33}$$

where we distinguish between the rate of return on automation capital R_t^p and the rate of return on traditional physical capital R_t^k. Again, we observe that increasing automation capital raises the rate of return on traditional physical capital but puts downward pressure on worker's wages because of the direct competition from robots and three-dimensional (3D) printers.

Checking Eqs. (5.32) and (5.33), we observe that

$$\lim_{P_t \to 0} R_t^p = (1 - \alpha) \left(\frac{K_t}{L_t} \right)^{\alpha} \quad \text{and} \quad \lim_{K_t \to 0} R_t^k = \infty, \qquad (5.34)$$

such that the Inada conditions are *violated* in the case of automation capital. This allows for a corner solution in which automation capital is zero: if both stocks of capital are low, rational investors would prefer to invest in traditional capital because its return will definitely be higher than the return on automation capital. If the traditional physical capital stock is sufficiently large, an interior equilibrium emerges in the capital market in which rational investors will want to invest in both types of capital. This interior equilibrium of the capital market again has to be associated with a no-arbitrage relationship stating that $R_t^k = R_t^p$; otherwise, rational investors would only want to invest in one type of capital—the one that delivers a higher return on investment. From the no-arbitrage condition, the familiar relationship between P_t and K_t from Chapter 4 emerges again

$$P_t = \left(\frac{1 - \alpha}{\alpha} \right) K_t - L_t. \qquad (5.35)$$

Considering the possibility of corner solutions in which individuals do not invest in automation capital, the stock of automation capital can be written as follows:

$$P_t = \max \left\{ 0, \left(\frac{1 - \alpha}{\alpha} \right) K_t - L_t \right\}. \qquad (5.36)$$

If $P_t = 0$, the production function is simply the one from the previously described standard canonical OLG model, in which both the steady-state capital stock per worker and the steady-state income per worker are constant.

To solve the model for the steady state with an interior capital market equilibrium, we substitute the no-arbitrage relationship (5.35) into the production function (5.29) to get

$$Y_t = \left(\frac{1 - \alpha}{\alpha} \right)^{1 - \alpha} K_t. \qquad (5.37)$$

This is again similar to an *AK*-type production technology, where $A \equiv [(1 - \alpha)/\alpha]^{1 - \alpha}$ as in Chapter 4 (compare with Rebelo, 1991; Romer, 1986). Thus, we would expect the possibility for long-run economic growth in the automation-augmented OLG model without technological progress because the diminishing marginal product of capital, which is responsible for the convergence to a no-growth steady-state equilibrium, does not take hold.

Thus far, both representative-agent neoclassical growth models with automation and the Solow model with automation imply the possibility of automation-driven long-run growth precisely because automation turns their aggregate production functions into those of an *AK* model (Lankisch et al., 2019; Prettner, 2019; Steigum, 2011).

However, in case of the OLG model, the fact that the aggregate production function exhibits the structure of an *AK* model is *not* sufficient to sustain long-run growth. Assuming that both types of capital fully depreciate over the course of one generation such that the aggregate stock of both types of capital at time $t + 1$ is determined by aggregate investment in period t yields

$$K_{t+1} + P_{t+1} = s_t L_t = \frac{\beta(1-\alpha)}{1+\beta}\left(\frac{K_t}{L_t + P_t}\right)^\alpha L_t. \tag{5.38}$$

Dividing Eq. (5.38) by the size of the cohort L_{t+1} and substituting in the no-arbitrage condition (5.35), we get the following result for capital per worker:

$$k_t = \alpha + \alpha\left(\frac{\beta}{1+\beta}\right)\left(\frac{1-\alpha}{1+n}\right)\left(\frac{\alpha}{1-\alpha}\right)^\alpha. \tag{5.39}$$

Clearly no transitional dynamics are present because the right-hand side does not depend on time t. Thus, the capital-to-labor ratio of the economy is given by $k_{t+1} = k_t = k^*$, as in Eq. (5.39). Because the right-hand side of this equation only depends on constant parameters, the capital-to-labor ratio cannot grow. It follows that GDP per worker stagnates and no potential exists for long-run economic growth. Proposition 5.1 summarizes these results (see Gasteiger & Prettner, 2020).

Proposition 5.1:
In the canonical OLG model with automation,

- *The production side of the economy has the structure of an AK type of growth model; and*
- *Irrespective of the previous point, the economy stagnates and no potential exists for long-run economic growth.*

Proof:
The proof of the proposition follows immediately from inspection of Eqs. (5.37) and (5.39).

The results summarized in Proposition 5.1 sharply contrast the neoclassical growth model of automation with a representative agent and Solow-type growth models with automation (Lankisch et al., 2019; Prettner, 2019; Steigum, 2011). The intuition behind this result is the following: in both the Solow and the Ramsey−Cass−Koopmans frameworks, individuals save/invest out of their total income (capital income plus wage income), whereas in the

OLG framework, they save/invest exclusively out of their labor income. The reason for the latter is that individuals enter the economy without assets in the canonical OLG model. However, automation capital puts downward pressure on labor incomes and thereby reduces the only source of investment in the model. This vicious cycle among investment, automation, and declining wages prevents the economy from taking off and featuring positive long-run growth, even though the production side of the economy has an *AK* structure. This result for the canonical OLG model explains why automation models that rely on an OLG structure of the economy (such as Benzell, Kotlikoff, LaGarda, & Sachs, 2015; Sachs & Kotlikoff, 2012; Sachs, Benzell, & LaGarda, 2015) tend to yield much more pessimistic results with respect to the effects of automation on economic development compared with the Solow model and the neoclassical growth model with a representative agent.

5.7 Discussion of extensions

5.7.1 Endogenous technological progress and automation

All the frameworks described so far have assumed away the role of R&D-driven technological progress in long-run economic growth. However, we have known since at least the seminal contribution of Romer (1990), and many works that followed afterward in endogenous, semi-endogenous, Schumpeterian, and unified growth theory, that technological progress is the most important driver of long-run economic development.[16] Focusing on the models of Solow (1956), Ramsey−Cass−Koopmans (Cass, 1965; Koopmans, 1965; Ramsey, 1928), and Diamond (1965) is justified by our aim to provide an accessible introduction to the potential effects of automation. In this section, we want to provide a glimpse into the likely effects of automation in more sophisticated frameworks with endogenous technological progress. To this end, we briefly discuss the results of the recent works of Acemoglu and Restrepo (2018), Hémous and Olsen (2018), and Prettner and Strulik (2020), who analyze the interrelations between R&D-based innovations and automation, as well as the effects of innovation and automation on economic growth and inequality. The three studies differ in their theoretical setup, but most of the crucial results are remarkably similar from a

---

16. For a nonexhaustive list of contributions in these areas, see Aghion and Howitt (1992, 1999, 2009), Bucci (2008), Cervellati and Sunde (2005), Connolly and Peretto (2003), Dalgaard and Kreiner (2001), Dinopoulos and Thompson (1998), Funke and Strulik (2000), Galor (2005, 2011), Galor and Weil (2000), Grossman and Helpman (1991), Grossmann, Steger, and Trimborn (2013), Howitt (1999), Jones (1995), Jones and Williams (1998, 2000), Kortum (1997), Peretto (1998), Peretto and Saeter (2013), Prettner (2013), Segerström (1998), Strulik (2005), Strulik, Prettner, and Prskawetz (2013), Prettner and Trimborn (2017), and Young (1998).

qualitative perspective and show that many of the insights of the simpler models with automation carry over to the more elaborate ones.

Acemoglu and Restrepo (2018) and Hémous and Olsen (2018) base their analyses on a representative agent framework without endogenous education, while Prettner and Strulik (2020) consider an OLG structure of the economy in which young workers can invest to upgrade their skills (endogenous higher education). This reflects the race between education and technology (Acemoglu & Autor, 2012; Goldin & Katz, 2009). On the firm side, Acemoglu and Restrepo (2018) focus on settings with various work tasks and Hémous and Olsen (2018) focus on various differentiated intermediate goods, which are then used to produce final goods. Irrespective of the particular setting, the different tasks/varieties can be performed/produced by labor or by robots that fully replace low-skilled workers. In the first step, the R&D sector creates new varieties or tasks that are initially unautomated. In the second step, firms can choose to invest in automating the production of the tasks/varieties. Within this setting, low-skilled workers benefit from new innovations because they increase the range of unautomated tasks/varieties. Automation itself could even be beneficial for low-skilled workers because an increasing share of automated tasks/varieties could lead to higher incentives to innovate and thereby to introduce new tasks/varieties that are initially unautomated. By contrast, Prettner and Strulik (2020) assume that automation technologies (the patents for labor-saving machines) are generated directly by new innovations, which is consistent with Mann and Püttmann's (2017) data, who show that the share of automation-related patents increased from 25% in 1976 to 67% in 2014.

While the frameworks of Acemoglu and Restrepo (2018) and Hémous and Olsen (2018) are a bit more optimistic regarding the effects of automation on low-skilled workers, the general results of the three papers are strikingly similar. Briefly, automation tends to lead to faster economic growth, higher wage inequality, and a decrease in the labor income share (see also Berg, Buffie, & Zanna, 2018). Thus, these frameworks also support the main predictions made in Chapter 4 and in the first part of this chapter, based on the simpler frameworks without endogenous innovation.

Somewhat less-related in terms of focus is the contribution by Chu, Cozzi, Furukawa, and Liao (2018). They augment a Schumpeterian R&D-based growth model with automation and quantify the extent to which R&D subsidies and automation subsidies affect economic growth and welfare. As is intuitive, R&D subsidies raise innovation and decrease automation, whereas the reverse holds true for automation subsidies. Overall, the growth effects of both types of subsidies are of an inverted-U shape. Calibrating the model to the United States, Chu et al. (2018) show that R&D subsidies are too high, whereas automation subsidies are too low from the perspective of maximizing economic growth. They also show that changing both subsidies to their socially optimal levels would be associated with welfare gains equivalent to an increase of 3.8% in terms of consumption.

An interesting aspect that all these contributions do not cover is the extent to which new intelligent technologies will speed up R&D itself. Venturini (2019) shows that new technologies such as *deep learning*—which leads to highly accurate prediction methods—could greatly enhance the efficiency of the production of R&D itself in the long run (see also Pratt, 2015). Incorporating these findings into R&D-based growth models is surely a promising avenue for further research and might allow analysis of the extent to which predictions such as the Singularity that we discussed in Chapter 1 (see Kurzweil, 2005) are theoretically plausible.

5.7.2 Technological unemployment

One of the fears that surrounds the emergence of new technologies, in general, and the rapid progress of automation, in particular, is that mass unemployment might follow as fewer workers are needed to produce the goods (and to some extent also the services) that the individuals in an economy consume (see, e.g., Arntz, Gregory, & Zierahn, 2017; Bloom, McKenna, & Prettner, 2018, 2019; Ford, 2015; Frey & Osborne, 2017; *The Economist*, 2014; and many others). We have already discussed many of the channels and general equilibrium adjustment mechanisms by which technological progress and automation have, thus far, not led to visible signs of increasing technological unemployment (Hansen, 1931) or substantial reductions in working hours toward the 15-hour working week predicted by Keynes (1930a, 1930b) for the year 2030. This section discusses additional channels by which increasing technology-driven unemployment might either emerge or be choked off based on labor market models with automation.

In general, surprisingly little analysis has emerged on the possibilities of technological unemployment in growth models that account for automation. The main reason is that in the simpler frameworks of Solow, Ramsey—Cass—Koopmans, and Diamond, labor supply is inelastic such that workers are willing to supply all of their available working time to the labor market at any given wage rate. Of course, in reality this is not true, and elastic labor supply might lead to voluntary unemployment because decreasing wages (predominantly of low-skilled workers) might induce those with the highest disutility of work to quit their jobs. Thus, a substantial part of the impact of automation might materialize in terms of adjustments in employment instead of adjustments in wages.

Prettner and Strulik (2017) model this in a very simple way: social security benefits are primarily paid to workers with lower wages because they are disproportionately in need of them and, relatedly, disproportionally affected by unemployment. If social security is financed out of taxes on overall labor income—including the high-skilled workers whose wages rise with automation—then we have the following situation: the resources available for social security do not fall to the same extent as the wages of low-skilled workers. Thus, the outside option for low-skilled workers becomes relatively more attractive over time such that more and more low-skilled workers would find that they cannot earn their reservation wage anymore. In this case, a growing proportion of low-skilled workers are incentivized to quit their jobs and live off social security benefits rather than wage income. While this mechanism could raise voluntary unemployment, this might be less of a concern than involuntary unemployment.

To analyze the extent to which involuntary unemployment could increase in the wake of automation, a model needs to exhibit an equilibrium wage rate that is above the marginal value product of labor such that labor markets do not clear. Many possible ways to model such a wage premium in conjunction with involuntary unemployment exist, for example, search frictions on labor markets that make advertising and filling a vacancy expensive for firms (Mortensen & Pissarides, 1994; Pissarides, 2000) or efficiency wages that are higher than the reservation wage to induce full effort of workers (Akerlof & Yellen, 1990; Shapiro & Stiglitz, 1984). In an extension of their model, Prettner and Strulik (2020) introduce equilibrium unemployment according to the fair wage theory of Akerlof and Yellen (1990): because the wages of high-skilled workers increase with innovation-driven growth in their framework, whereas the wages of low-skilled workers stagnate, low-skilled workers would perceive their wages as increasingly unfair compared with those of high-skilled workers. Thus, low-skilled workers would demand wages that are higher than their market-clearing wages, which leads to equilibrium unemployment. As automation progresses, the wedge between the market-clearing wage rate and the equilibrium wage rate would increase, leading, *ceteris paribus*, to higher technological unemployment.

However, Prettner and Strulik's (2020) model has a counteracting force: low-skilled individuals have a second strategy to escape stagnating wages, namely to upgrade their skills (Acemoglu & Autor, 2012; Goldin & Katz, 2009). If more individuals upgrade their skills, the pool of low-skilled workers decreases such that the downward pressure on their wages, and the upward pressure on low-skilled unemployment, could ease. In a calibration of their model, Prettner and Strulik (2020) show that low-skilled unemployment could even decrease for a prolonged period in such a setting because skill upgrading can overcompensate for automation effects under reasonable parameter settings (if the pool of initially low-skilled workers was large). This mechanism of skill upgrading is consistent with the stylized fact of an increasing share of college-educated workers over the past few decades and could partly explain why we do not yet observe increasing technological unemployment due to automation.

Cords and Prettner (2019) and Guimarães and Mazeda Gil (2019) base their analyses of automation-driven unemployment on the search-and-matching model of Mortensen and Pissarides (1994). In the study by Cords and Prettner (2019), there are low-skilled workers and high-skilled workers, and, consistent with the evidence to date, low-skilled workers are easier than high-skilled workers to replace by robots. Cords and Prettner (2019) derive the equilibrium unemployment rates on both labor markets (low-skilled and high-skilled) and show that automation decreases the labor market tightness in the low-skilled labor market and increases it in the high-skilled labor market. As a consequence, automation tends to not only raise unemployment of low-skilled workers but also decrease unemployment of high-skilled workers. Interestingly, for a calibration of the model to German data, the authors find that the effect on high-skilled workers is stronger, such that overall unemployment decreases due to automation. The reason is that, in this setting, firm creation reacts endogenously to labor market tightness. The increase in firm creation due to the availability of robots compensates for part of the increase in low-skilled unemployment. In addition, the decrease in high-skilled unemployment due to firm creation in the high-skilled sector then overcompensates for the remaining increase in low-skilled unemployment. The overall result of rising employment and decreasing unemployment due to automation is consistent with the empirical findings of Autor and Salomons (2017, 2018) and Gregory, Salomons, and Zierahn (2016) that more jobs have emerged due to automation in major Organisation for Economic Co-operation and Development countries than have vanished.

While Guimarães and Mazeda Gil (2019) abstract from skill differences between different workers, their results for a calibration of the labor market to that of the United States lead to similar conclusions. In addition, Guimarães and Mazeda Gil (2019) focus on the implications of automation on the labor income share and show that, similar to the results derived in Chapter 4, the labor income share decreases due to automation.

Altogether, the results of Cords and Prettner (2019) and Guimarães and Mazeda Gil (2019) could add another piece to the puzzle to explain why we do not yet see increasing technological unemployment.

5.7.3 International trade, foreign direct investment, and automation

As a final extension, we discuss the possible effects of automation on international trade and foreign direct investment (FDI). In this context, globalization has led to a trend of offshoring production to low-wage countries in recent decades.[17] Decreasing transport costs made shifting production (or some parts thereof) to poorer countries and exporting goods back to

---

17. See, for example, Baldwin (2017), Feenstra and Jensen (2012), Grossman and Rossi-Hansberg (2008), Naghavi and Ottaviano (2009), Ottaviano, Peri, and Wright (2013, 2014), and Rodriguez-Clare (2010).

consumers in richer countries more profitable for firms. This has allowed firms to benefit from lower wages and, thus, lower production costs in poor countries.

Most recently, however, a trend toward reshoring emerged, where some firms started to shift production back to rich countries (see, e.g., Carbonero, Ernst, & Weber, 2018; Chu, Cozzi, & Furukawa, 2013; Krenz, Prettner, & Strulik, 2018; Tate, 2014; *The Economist*, 2013). One reason for this shift might be rising wages in low-income and middle-income countries, particularly in China, to the extent that the cost advantage of offshoring started to disappear. However, automation also seems to have made it possible to produce a range of goods—which previously required many workers—with a much lower need for labor input at home (Krenz et al., 2018).

To capture this effect, Abeliansky, Martinez-Zarzoso, and Prettner (2020) introduce 3D printing technology into the trade and FDI model proposed by Helpman, Melitz, and Yeaple (2004)—which is itself an extension of Melitz (2003)—to take FDI into account. The blueprints for the production by means of a 3D printer can be sent across the world instantaneously. Physical capital in the form of the 3D printer could then print the corresponding object wherever it is desired (of course, also in the home country). This form of production is particularly useful for infrequently needed customized products that have required a substantial amount of specialized labor input in the past. The 3D printing technology implies that firms using it are less and less reliant on labor supply in the locations where they produce, potentially threatening the strategy of export-led growth in poorer countries that relied on FDI from richer countries. While Abeliansky et al. (2020) concede that it is still too early and the technology is not yet sophisticated enough to envision these implications on a large scale, they provide the first tentative evidence in favor of this view for industries in which many 3D printers are employed.

More generally, the emergence of automation technologies could have exerted downward pressure on wages in rich countries that reduced the incentives for offshoring in the first place. Krenz et al. (2018) propose a model of production with low-skilled and high-skilled labor in which robots are not very productive initially when the technology is still young. Thus, some firms that face low trade costs benefit from offshoring production to low-wage countries at that stage. With an increasing productivity of robots, however, the incentives to offshore decrease and reshoring becomes more attractive. As firms start to return to high-wage countries, it is, however, predominantly the production factor of skilled labor that benefits, whereas robots replace low-skilled workers. Increasing tariffs can speed up the process of reshoring in this model, but it cannot help the low-skilled workers who are only replaced faster by robots in the case of increasing tariffs.

Krenz et al. (2018) provide evidence that, indeed, in the sectors that are using robots more intensively, reshoring is more pronounced. In addition, they provide evidence for a positive effect of reshoring on the wages of high-skilled workers but not on the wages of low-skilled workers. Altogether, the findings in this paper also suggest that the export-led growth strategy could become less and less viable for low-wage countries.

Although the wage rates for low-skilled workers decline in the face of automation in both high-income and low-income economies, reshoring would have more severe effects on the wages of low-skilled workers in low-income countries. The reason is that the firms that relocate production back to high-income countries tend to have a large workforce employed in low-income countries. Setting off such large numbers of workers in low-wage countries when the firms are reshoring production to high-income countries would put a downward pressure on wages in low-income countries. This, in turn, could lead to a situation in which the incentives to migrate from low-income countries to rich countries rises as Zhou, Bloom, and Tyers (2019) show.

5.8 Summary

This chapter first provides an easy-to-apply guide to static optimization by means of the methods of Lagrange (for optimization problems with equality constraints) and Karush–Kuhn–Tucker (for optimization problems with inequality constraints and potential nonnegativity constraints on various choice variables). In addition, it provides the recipes/cookbook procedures for dynamic optimization in discrete time by means of the method of Lagrange (in the case of two time periods) and in continuous time by means of optimal control theory. These methods were then used to set up the two workhorse models of modern dynamic macroeconomics: the neoclassical Ramsey–Cass–Koopmans model and the OLG framework. These models form the core of almost all dynamic macroeconomic models currently used to analyze questions related to long-run economic growth and business cycle fluctuations.

We extend these models' basic frameworks by including automation capital to analyze the implications of automation for economic growth and the labor income share. We observe that some of the central implications of the simpler frameworks presented in Chapter 4 carry over to the more sophisticated frameworks, for example, that automation implies an *AK* structure of the production side of the automation-augmented neoclassical growth model and the automation-augmented OLG model. However, we also observe one crucial difference between the implications of the Ramsey–Cass–Koopmans model with automation and the OLG model with automation. Strikingly, even though most of the predictions of the two model classes without automation are qualitatively very similar, their predictions with respect to the growth effects of automation are different. While the Ramsey–Cass–Koopmans model with automation implies that long-run economic growth without technological progress becomes feasible (similar to the automation-augmented Solow model), the canonical OLG model rules out this possibility. The reason is that individuals save/invest out of their total incomes in the Ramsey–Cass–Koopmans model, while they save only out of their wage income in the first period of life in the OLG model. While total income can grow in the case of progressing automation due to growing capital income, wage income tends to decrease. This means that, in the OLG model, automation reduces the only source of saving/investment and, thereby, prevents automation-driven growth from taking place.

Finally, this chapter discusses three additional topics: (1) the implications of automation within a setting of endogenous innovation-driven technological progress, (2) technological unemployment, and (3) the implications of automation for international trade and FDI. Regarding models of automation with endogenous technological progress, we observe that most of the basic model results carry over to these frameworks (that automation enhances economic growth, that it reduces the labor income share, and that it has the potential to increase wage inequality and, with it, income inequality). However, the models of automation with endogenous technological progress allow for a richer analysis that considers endogenous R&D investments and different innovation sectors. The downside is that they are more complicated and, thus, not easily accessible for less-technically-inclined readers.

There are various ways to introduce technological unemployment into the basic models. For example, voluntary unemployment could be a consequence of stagnating or declining wages in connection with constant, or even increasing, social security benefits. Involuntary unemployment could result from search frictions or from efficiency wage considerations. Interestingly, in both cases of involuntary unemployment—search-and-matching frictions and efficiency wage considerations—model calibrations show that automation can go hand in hand with *decreasing* unemployment for reasonable parameter settings and long time periods. This outcome can help to explain why we do not yet see declining employment and rising unemployment as the density of automation increases.

Finally, we examined the implications of automation and 3D printing for international trade and FDI. Emergence of the 3D printer increasingly enables the production of customized products and parts without the need for specialized labor input. Thus, more products could be produced locally as low wages become less relevant for firms' location decisions. This shift could imply that local production will substitute for some trade in the future. In addition, signs indicate that the trend toward offshoring has slowed and a trend toward reshoring has emerged; automation has made producing in rich countries cheaper, while at the same time, wages in many poorer countries have recently begun to increase strongly. Altogether, the forces described in this context could weaken the strategy of export-led growth that many low-income countries have followed over the past decades.

References

Abeliansky, A. L., Martinez-Zarzoso, I., & Prettner, K. (2020). 3D printing, international trade, and FDI. *Economic Modelling, 85*, 288–306.

Acemoglu, D. (2009). *Introduction to modern economic growth*. Princeton, NJ: Princeton University Press.

Acemoglu, D., & Autor, D. (2012). What does human capital do? A review of Goldin and Katz's the race between education and technology. *Journal of Economic Literature, 50*(2), 426–463.

Acemoglu, D., & Restrepo, P. (2018). The race between man and machine: Implications of technology for growth, factor shares and employment. *American Economic Review, 108*(6), 1488–1542.

Aghion, P., & Howitt, P. (1992). A model of growth through creative destruction. *Econometrica: Journal of the Econometric Society, 60*(2), 323–351.

Aghion, P., & Howitt, P. (1999). *Endogenous economic growth*. Cambridge, MA: MIT Press.

Aghion, P., & Howitt, P. (2009). *The economics of growth*. Cambridge, MA: MIT Press.

Akerlof, G., & Yellen, J. (1990). The fair wage-effort hypothesis and unemployment. *Quarterly Journal of Economics, 105*(2), 255–283.

Arntz, M., Gregory, T., & Zierahn, U. (2017). Revisiting the risk of automation. *Economics Letters, 159*(C), 157–160.

Auerbach, A. J., & Kotlikoff, L. J. (1987). *Dynamic fiscal policy*. Cambridge, UK: Cambridge University Press.

Autor, D., & Salomons, A. (2017). Robocalypse now—Does productivity growth threaten employment? In European Central Bank Conference Proceedings. Retrieved from http://conference.nber.org/confer/2017/AIf17/Autor.pdf. Accessed on 30.12.19.

Autor, D., & Salomons, A. (2018). Is automation labor-displacing? Productivity growth, employment, and the labor share. In BPEA Conference Drafts. Retrieved from https://www.brookings.edu/wp-content/uploads/2018/03/1_autorsalomons.pdf. Accessed 30.12.19.

Baldwin, R. (2017). *The great convergence. Information technology and the new globalisation*. Cambridge, MA: Harvard University Press.

Benzell, S. G., Kotlikoff, L. J., LaGarda, G., & Sachs, J. D. (2015). Robots are us: Some economics of human replacement. NBER Working Paper 20941, National Bureau of Economic Research, Cambridge, MA.

Berg, A., Buffie, E. F., & Zanna, L.-F. (2018). Should we fear the robot revolution? (The correct answer is yes). *Journal of Monetary Economics, 97*, 117–148.

Bloom, D., McKenna, M., & Prettner, K. (2018). Demography, unemployment, automation, and digitalization: implications for the creation of (decent) jobs, 2010–2030. NBER Working Paper 24835, National Bureau of Economic Research, Cambridge, MA.

Bloom, D., McKenna, M., & Prettner, K. (2019). Global employment and decent jobs, 2010–2030: The forces of demography and automatio. n. *International Social Security Review, 72*(3), 43–78.

Bucci, A. (2008). Population growth in a model of economic growth with human capital accumulation and horizontal R&D. *Journal of Macroeconomics, 30*(3), 1124–1147.

Carbonero, F., Ernst, E., & Weber, E. (2018). Robots worldwide: The impact of automation on employment and trade. ILO Research Department Working Paper No. 36, International Labour Organisation, Geneva.

Cass, D. (1965). Optimum growth in an aggregative model of capital accumulation. *The Review of Economic Studies, 32*(3), 233–240.

Cervellati, M., & Sunde, U. (2005). Human capital formation, life expectancy, and the process of development. *American Economic Review, 95*(5), 1653−1672.

Chu, A. C., Cozzi, G., & Furukawa, Y. (2013). A simple theory of offshoring and reshoring. University of St. Gallen, School of Economics and Political Science, Department of Economics, Working Paper 2013-09. St. Gallen, Switzerland.

Chu, A. C., Cozzi, G., Furukawa, Y., & Liao, C.-H. (2018). Should the government subsidize innovation or automation? University Library of Munich, MPRA Paper 88276, Munich, Germany.

Connolly, M., & Peretto, P. (2003). Industry and the family: Two engines of growth. *Journal of Economic Growth, 8*(1), 115−148.

Cords, D., & Prettner, K. (2019). Technological unemployment revisited: Automation in a search and matching framework. GLO Discussion Paper Series 308, Global Labor Orgnaozation, Essen, Germany.

Dalgaard, C., & Kreiner, C. (2001). Is declining productivity inevitable? *Journal of Economic Growth, 6*(3), 187−203.

de la Croix, D., & Michel, P. (2002). *A theory of economic growth: Dynamics and policy in overlapping generations*. Cambridge, UK: Cambridge University Press.

Diamond, P. A. (1965). National debt in a neoclassical growth model. *American Economic Review, 55*(5), 1126−1150.

Dinopoulos, E., & Thompson, P. (1998). Schumptarian growth without scale effects. *Journal of Economic Growth, 3*(4), 313−335.

Dixit, A. (1990). *Optimization in economic theory* (2nd ed.). Oxford, UK: Oxford University Press.

Dorfman, R. (1969). An economic interpretation of optimal control theory. *American Economic Review, 59*(5), 817−831.

Feenstra, R., & Jensen, J. (2012). Evaluating estimates of materials offshoring from US manufacturing. *Economics Letters, 117*(1), 170−173.

Ford, M. (2015). *Rise of the robots: Technology and the threat of a jobless future*. New York: Basic Books.

Frey, C. B., & Osborne, M. A. (2017). The future of employment: How susceptible are jobs to computerisation? *Technological Forecasting and Social Change, 114*(C), 254−280.

Funke, M., & Strulik, H. (2000). On endogenous growth with physical capital, human capital and product variety. *European Economic Review, 44*(3), 491−515.

Galí, J. (2015). *Monetary policy, inflation, and the business cycle: An introduction to the new Keynesian framework and its applications* (2nd ed.). Princeton, NJ: Princeton University Press.

Galor, O. (2005). From stagnation to growth: Unified growth theory. In P. Aghion, & P. Durlauf (Eds.), *Handbook of economic growth* (Volume 1, pp. 171−293). Amsterdam: Elsevier, Chapter 4.

Galor, O. (2011). *Unified growth theory*. Princeton, NJ: Princeton University Press.

Galor, O., & Weil, D. (2000). Population, technology, and growth: From Malthusian stagnation to the demographic transition and beyond. *The American Economic Review, 90*(4), 806−828.

Gandolfo, G. (2010). *Economic dynamics*. Berlin Heidelberg: Springer.

Gasteiger, E., & Prettner, K. (2020). A note on automation, stagnation, and the implications of a robot tax. Macroeconomic Dynamics (forthcoming).

Geiger, N., Prettner, K., & Schwarzer, J. (2018). Die auswirkungen der Automatisierung, auf Wachstum, Beschäftigung und Ungleichheit. *Perspektiven der Wirtschaftspolitik, 19*(2), 59−77.

Goldin, C., & Katz, L. (2009). *The race between education and technology.* Boston: Harvard University Press.

Gregory, G., Salomons, A., & Zierahn, U. (2016). Racing with or against the machine? Evidence from Europe. ZEW Discussion Paper No. 16−053, Zentrum für Europäische Wirtschaftsforschung, Mannheim.

Grossman, G., & Rossi-Hansberg, E. (2008). Trading tasks: A simple theory of offshoring. *American Economic Review, 98*(5), 1978−1997.

Grossman, G. M., & Helpman, E. (1991). Quality ladders in the theory of economic growth. *Review of Economic Studies, 58*(1), 43−61.

Grossmann, V., Steger, T. M., & Trimborn, T. (2013). Dynamically optimal R&D subsidization. *Journal of Economic Dynamics and Control, 37*(3), 516−534.

Guimarães, L., & Mazeda Gil, P. (2019). Explaining the labor share: automation vs labor market institutions. Queen's University, Economics Working Papers 19-01, Queen's Management School, Belfast, UK.

Hansen, A. (1931). Institutional frictions and technological unemployment. *Quarterly Journal of Economics, 45*(4), 684−698.

Heijdra, B. J. (2017). *Foundations of modern macroeconomics* (3rd ed.). Oxford, UK: Oxford University Press.

Helpman, E., Melitz, M. J., & Yeaple, S. R. (2004). Exports vs. FDI with heterogeneous firms. *American Economic Review, 94*(1), 300−316.

Hémous, D., & Olsen, M. (2018). The rise of the machines: Automation, horizontal innovation and income inequality. Retrieved from https://papers.ssrn.com/sol3/papers.cfm?abstract_id = 2328774. Accessed 30.12.19.

Howitt, P. (1999). Steady endogenous growth with population and R&D inputs growing. *Journal of Political Economy, 107*(4), 715−730.

Jones, C. I. (1995). R&D-based models of economic growth. *Journal of Political Economy, 103* (4), 759−784.

Jones, C. I., & Williams, J. C. (1998). Measuring the social return to R&D. *The Quarterly Journal of Economics, 113*(4), 1119−1135.

Jones, C. I., & Williams, J. C. (2000). Too much of a good thing? The economics of investment in R&D. *Journal of Economic Growth, 5*(1), 65−85.

Karush, W. (1939). Minima of functions of several variables with inequalities as side constraints. Unpublished master thesis, University of Chicago.

Keynes, J. (1930a). Economic possibilities for our grandchildren. *The Nation and Athenaeum, 48* (2), 36−37.

Keynes, J. (1930b). Economic possibilities for our grandchildren. *The Nation and Athenaeum, 48* (3), 96−98.

Koopmans, T. C. (1965). On the concept of optimal economic growth. In J. Johansen (Ed.), *The Econometric Approach to Development Planning.* North Holland: Amsterdam.

Kortum, S. (1997). Research, patenting and technological change. *Econometrica: Journal of the Econometric Society, 65*(6), 1389−1419.

Krenz, A., Prettner, K., & Strulik, H. (2018). Robots, reshoring, and the lot of low-skilled workers. CEGE Discussion Paper 351, Center for European, Governance and Economic Development Research, University of Göttingen, Germany.

Krueger, D., & Ludwig, A. (2007). On the consequences of demographic change for rates of returns on capital, and the distribution of wealth and welfare. *Journal of Monetary Economics, 54*(1), 49−87.

Kuhn, H., & Tucker, A. (1951). *Nonlinear programming. Proceedings of the Second Berkeley Symposium on Mathematical Statistics and Probability* (pp. 481−492). Berkeley, CA: University of California Press.

Kurzweil, R. (2005). *The singularity is near: When humans transcend biology.* London: Penguin Books.

Lankisch, C., Prettner, K., & Prskawetz, A. (2019). How can robots affect wage inequality? *Economic Modelling, 81*(September 2019), 161−169.

Léonard, D., & van Long, N. (1992). *Optimal control theory and static optimization in economics.* Cambridge, UK: Cambridge University Press.

Mann, K., & Püttmann, L. (2017). Benign effects of automation: New evidence from patent texts. Discussion Paper, Bonn University, Germany.

Melitz, M. (2003). The impact of trade on intra-industry reallocations and aggregate industry productivity. *Econometrica: Journal of the Econometric Society, 71*(6), 1695−1725.

Mortensen, D., & Pissarides, C. (1994). Job creation and job destruction in the theory of unemployment. *Review of Economic Studies, 61*(3), 397−415.

Naghavi, A., & Ottaviano, G. (2009). Offshoring and product innovation. *Economic Theory, 38* (3), 517−532.

Ottaviano, G., Peri, G., & Wright, G. (2013). Immigration, offshoring, and American jobs. *American Economic Review, 103*(5), 1925−1959.

Peretto, P. F. (1998). Technological change and population growth. *Journal of Economic Growth, 3*(4), 283−311.

Peretto, P. F., & Saeter, J. J. (2013). Factor-eliminating technical change. *Journal of Monetary Economics, 60*(4), 459−473.

Pissarides, C. A. (2000). *Equilibrium unemployment theory* (2nd ed.). Cambridge, MA: MIT Press.

Pontryagin, L., Boltyanskii, V., Gamkrelidze, R., & Mishchenko, E. (1962). *The mathematical theory of optimal processes.* Hoboken, NJ: John Wiley.

Pratt, G. A. (2015). Is a Cambrian explosion coming for robotics? *Journal of Economic Perspectives, 29*(3), 51−60.

Prettner, K. (2013). Population aging and endogenous economic growth. *Journal of Population Economics, 26*(2), 811−834.

Prettner, K. (2019). A note on the implications of automation for economic growth and the labor share. *Macroeconomic Dynamics, 23*(3), 1294−1301.

Prettner, K., & Strulik, H. (2017). The lost race against the machine: Automation, education, and inequality in an R&D-based growth model. Hohenheim Discussion Papers in Business, Economics, and Social Sciences 08−2017.

Prettner, K., & Strulik, H. (2020). Innovation, automation, and inequality: Policy challenges in the race against the machine. *Journal of Monetary Economics.* (forthcoming).

Prettner, K., & Trimborn, T. (2017). Demographic change and R&D-based economic growth. *Economica, 84*(336), 667−681.

Ramsey, F. P. (1928). A mathematical theory of saving. *The Economic Journal, 38*(152), 543−559.

Rebelo, S. (1991). Long-run policy analysis and long-run growth. *Journal of Political Economy, 99*(3), 500−521.

Rodriguez-Clare, A. (2010). Offshoring in a Ricardian world. *American Economic Journal: Macroeconomics, 2*(2), 227−258.

Romer, D. (2011). *Advanced macroeconomics.* New York: McGraw-Hill.

Romer, P. (1986). Increasing returns and long-run growth. *Journal of Political Economy, 94*(5), 1002−1037.

Romer, P. (1990). Endogenous technological change. *Journal of Political Economy, 98*(5), 71−102.

Sachs, J. D., Benzell, S. G., & LaGarda, G. (2015). Robots: Curse or blessing? A basic framework. NBER Working Paper 21091, National Bureau of Economic Research, Cambridge, MA.

Sachs, J. D., & Kotlikoff, L. J. (2012). Smart machines and long-term misery. NBER Working Paper 18629, National Bureau of Economic Research, Cambridge, MA.

Samuelson, P. A. (1958). An exact consumption-loan model of interest with or without the social contrivance of money. *Journal of Political Economy, 66*(6), 467−482.

Segerström, P. S. (1998). Endogenous growth without scale effects. *American Economic Review, 88*(5), 1290−1310.

Shapiro, C., & Stiglitz, J. (1984). Equilibrium unemployment as a worker discipline device. *American Economic Review, 74*(3), 433−444.

Solow, R. M. (1956). A contribution to the theory of economic growth. *The Quarterly Journal of Economics, 70*(1), 65−94.

Sorger, G. (2015). *Dynamic economic analysis.* Deterministic models in discrete time.. Cambridge, UK: Cambridge University Press.

Steigum, E. (2011). Robotics and growth. In H. Beladi, & E. K. Choi (Eds.), *Frontiers of economics and globalization: Economic growth and development* (pp. 543−557). Bingley, UK: Emerald Group, Chapter 21.

Stokey, N., Lucas, R., & Prescott, E. (1989). *Recursive methods in economic dynamics.* Cambridge, MA: Harvard University Press.

Strulik, H. (2005). The role of human capital and population growth in R&D-based models of economic growth. *Review of International Economics, 13*(1), 129−145.

Strulik, H., Prettner, K., & Prskawetz, A. (2013). The past and future of knowledge-based growth. *Journal of Economic Growth, 18*(4), 411−437.

Sundaram, R. (1996). *A first course in optimization theory.* Cambridge, UK: Cambridge University Press.

Sydsaeter, K., Hammond, P., Seierstad, A., & Strom, A. (2008). *Further mathematics for economic analysis* (2nd ed.). Upper Saddle River, NJ: Prentice Hall.

Sydsaeter, K., Hammond, P., & Strom, A. (2012). *Essential mathematics for economic analysis* (4th ed.). Upper Saddle River, NJ: Prentice Hall.

Tate, W. (2014). Offshoring and reshoring: U.S. insights and research challenges. *Journal of Purchasing & Supply Management, 20*(1), 66−68.

The Economist, (2013). Reshoring manufacturing: Coming home. January 19, 2013.

The Economist, (2014). Immigrants from the future. A special report on robots. March 27, 2014.

Trimborn, T. (2013). Solution of continuous-time dynamic models with inequality constraints. *Economics Letters, 119*(3), 299−301.

Trimborn, T., Koch, K.-J., & Steger, T. M. (2008). Multidimensional transitional dynamics: A simple numerical procedure. *Macroeconomic Dynamics, 12*(3), 301−319.

Venturini, F. (2019). Intelligent technologies and productivity spillovers: Evidence from the Fourth Industrial Revolution. Retrieved from https://www.researchgate.net/publication/324819823_Intelligent_technologies_and_productivity_spillovers_Evidence_from_the_Fourth_Industrial_Revolution. Accessed 18.12.19.

Wright, G. (2014). Revisiting the employment impact of offshoring. *European Economic Review, 66*(February 2014), 63−83.

Young, A. (1998). Growth without scale effects. *Journal of Political Economy, 106*(5), 41−63.

Zhou, Y., Bloom, D. E., & Tyers, R. (2019). Implications of automation for global migration. In Paper presented at the 11th International Symposium on Human Capital and Labor Markets in Beijing, December 13−14, 2019.

Chapter 6

Automation as a potential response to the challenges of demographic change

6.1 Introduction and stylized facts

Over the past several decades, fertility rates have been falling, both in high-income countries and globally (Bloom, 2011, 2020). Fig. 6.1 plots World Bank (2019) data on the total fertility rate (TFR) from 1960 to 2015. The TFR is defined as the number of children a representative woman would expect to have if the age-specific fertility rates prevailing in a given year were to hold steady throughout her childbearing years. The solid line refers to the world as a whole, while the dashed line refers to the Organisation for Economic Co-operation and Development (OECD) and represents the case of high-income countries. The figure indicates that the TFR decreased from five children per woman worldwide in 1960 to 2.45 in 2015, a decline of more than half. Among OECD countries, the rate fell from 3.23 children per

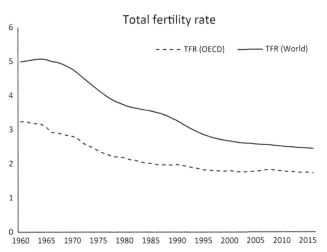

FIGURE 6.1   TFR per woman, in the OECD (*dashed line*) and worldwide (*solid line*).

Automation and its Macroeconomic Consequences. DOI: https://doi.org/10.1016/B978-0-12-818028-0.00006-5
163

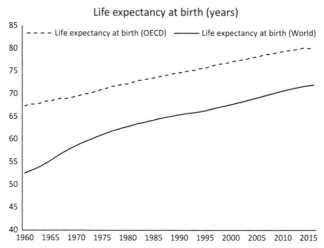

FIGURE 6.2   Life expectancy at birth, in the OECD (*dashed line*) and worldwide (*solid line*).

woman to 1.74 children per woman over the same time period. Thus, in the OECD, the TFR today is already well below the long-run replacement rate of approximately 2.1, which implies a stationary population in the long run and in the absence of net migration (Preston, Heuveline, & Guillot, 2001). The replacement rate does not equal 2.0 for two reasons: (1) mortality before completing the childbearing years and (2) the boy-to-girl sex ratio at birth is above 1.[1] Regarding the effect of mortality, which is higher in low-income countries, it is interesting that the replacement rate is close to 2.0 in high-income countries with a low mortality rate, but it can be substantially above 2.0 in countries with a higher mortality rate, for example, in India.

It is important to understand that even in a no-migration setting, the population growth rate can be positive for some time when the TFR is below the replacement rate. The explanation is rooted in the age structure of the population: if many women are in the prime childbearing years, births can exceed deaths even if age-specific birth rates translate into a TFR that is less than 2.1. Eventually, the age structure of the population converges and does not change anymore. Along the route to that age distribution, population growth stabilizes at zero or some negative number, depending on whether the TFR is 2.1 or less.

While fertility rates have declined substantially, life expectancy at birth has increased. Fig. 6.2 displays this trend, plotting life expectancy at birth from 1960 to 2015 according to World Bank (2019) data. Global average life expectancy at birth rose from 53 years in 1960 to 72 years in 2015. The

---

1. For example, for 2015–2020, the United Nations (2019a) estimates a global sex ratio at birth of 1.07:1 in favor of boys.

OECD increase started from a higher base of 67 years and rose to 80 years over the same time frame. While the increase in life expectancy in low-income countries was mainly due to falling child mortality, in high-income countries it was mainly due to falling mortality at older ages (see, e.g., Deaton, 2013).

Table 6.1 summarizes the change in the demographic indicators "TFR" and "life expectancy at birth" for the Group of Seven (G7) countries plus China and Russia from 1960 to 2015. Without exception, the TFR was well above the long-run replacement rate in these countries in the year 1960 but dropped below the long-run replacement rate by 2015. The only country in which the TFR is close to the replacement rate in 2015 is France; in all other countries, the TFR is far below the replacement rate. As far as life expectancy at birth is concerned, the smallest increase—five years—over the time period observed occurred in Russia. Most countries enjoyed an increase in life expectancy of about 10 years, while Japan and China stand out with gains of 16 and 32 years, respectively.

How increasing life expectancy affects the population's age structure depends strongly upon which age group is affected by declining mortality. If child mortality declines, more children survive to older ages, which has the somewhat paradoxical effect of *increasing* life expectancy and *reducing* the mean age of the population at the same time. Declining child mortality strongly affects life expectancy because a child whose death is averted has a long remaining life expectancy, in contrast to the relatively smaller effect on

TABLE 6.1 TFR and life expectancy at birth (rounded) in the G7 countries plus China and Russia in 1960 and 2015, according to World Bank (2019).

Country	TFR		Life expectancy at birth	
	1960	2015	1960	2015
Canada	3.81	1.60	71	82
China	5.75	1.62	44	76
France	2.85	1.96	70	82
Germany	2.37	1.50	69	81
Italy	2.37	1.35	69	83
Japan	2.00	1.45	68	84
Russia	2.52	1.75	66	71
United Kingdom	2.69	1.80	71	81
United States	3.65	1.84	70	79

life expectancy of a mortality reduction at older ages. Thus, declining child mortality raises overall life expectancy disproportionally. If mortality at the working age decreases, say due to improved treatment of cardiovascular diseases, this change tends to have a smaller effect on the population's age structure because it mainly benefits people closer to the mean age of the population. Finally, if mortality at old age decreases, say due to improved cancer treatment, this tends to lead to a (slightly) higher mean age of the population because it raises the number of people who are older than the existing mean age. For a discussion of the many different, and sometimes subtle, ways in which changing mortality can affect the demographic structure of a society, see Preston et al. (2001).[2]

The described changes in fertility and mortality rates are the main drivers of the population's age structure, jointly determining the relative size of the working-age population (conventionally defined as the population aged 15−64 years) versus the non-working-age population (children under age 15 plus older adults from age 65 upward). Another important factor that influences the relative size of the working-age population is the past age structure, which establishes how many fecund women are represented in the population, which in turn determines the number of births in each year and, thus, changes in the proportion of the population under age 15. Worker migration also contributes to this fluctuating age structure. For a decomposition of population aging into portions attributable to declining fertility, increasing longevity, and changes in the relative size of cohorts reaching the older ages see, for example, Sudharsanan and Bloom (2018).

Fig. 6.3 depicts the combined effect of demographic changes on the relative size of the working-age population, for the world as a whole and for the OECD, from 1960 to 2015. A slight decrease in the fraction of the working-age population in the world appears in the 1960s due to the beginning demographic shift in poorer countries, which started with, a decline in infant and child mortality that triggered a subsequent lagged decline in fertility. This slight decrease was followed by a consistent increase, starting in the 1970s,

---

2. One particularly interesting effect is that a population's overall death rate, measured as the number of deaths per 1,000 persons, could even *increase* if the age-specific mortality rates *decrease* for every age group in this population. The reason for this paradox is that a decrease in mortality at each age group implies that more people survive to an older age. An older age, however, tends to be associated with a higher mortality rate such that the shift in the population's age structure that is induced by lower age-specific mortality, leads—*ceteris paribus*—to a higher overall mortality rate. If this effect is strong enough, it overcompensates for the fall in age-specific mortality to the extent that the total effect is a rise in mortality. To put it differently, the population's death rate can be expressed as a population-weighted average of age-specific death rates. As such, changes in the age structure and changes in age-specific death rates will both affect the population's death rate. If the former effect is strong enough, one could observe an increase in the population's death rate together with a decrease in the age-specific death rates of all age groups.

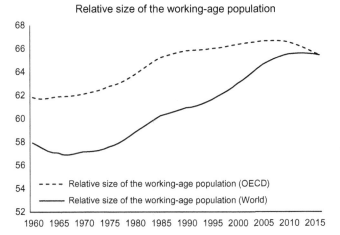

FIGURE 6.3 Relative size of the workforce (percent of the population aged 15−64 years), in the OECD (*dashed line*) and worldwide (*solid line*).
Notes: The shifts are even sharper if we plot the ratio of the working-age population to the non-working-age populations. In this case, however, the interpretation in percentage terms would be lost. Please note that not everyone below the age of 15 or above the age of 65 is nonworking and that not everyone between ages 15 and 65 is working. Finally, please keep in mind that the patterns vary by country and time period.

due to falling fertility and to the falling mortality of the working-age population. The increase started to ebb in the 1990s, when the smaller cohorts gradually entered the working age, and actually reversed in 2011.

The OECD began with a higher fraction of its population in the working ages in the 1960s, mainly due to the lower fertility rate and lower child mortality in the past, such that the relative size of the workforce was larger than in low-income countries. The fraction of the working-age population in the OECD increased further until the beginning of the twenty-first century due to falling fertility and to falling mortality in the working ages, but the increase slowed down markedly in the mid-1980s. At that time, the working-age population gap between the world and the OECD began to shrink. Finally, in 2008, the relative size of the working-age population started to fall in the OECD. This decline happened at a faster pace than the fall in the world's working-age population that started in 2011. As a consequence, the gap between the world and the OECD vanished.

Because migration between Earth and other planets is not yet an issue for demographers, migration cannot influence the world's age structure. However, inward and outward migration could affect the age structure of individual countries and groups of countries like the OECD. Overall, the number of migrants worldwide is relatively small (the United Nations, 2019b, classifies 3.4% of the total world population as international migrants not currently living in their country of birth), such that the impact of migration on the age structure of large countries or country groups tends to be dwarfed by fertility and mortality dynamics. Exceptions to this general picture are small countries that rely strongly on foreign workers, such as the United Arab Emirates, where migrants constitute 88% of the total population (United Nations, 2019b).

6.2 Demographic change and its economic consequences

What are the economic consequences of these demographic developments? Falling fertility implies a reduction in population growth and, practically, fewer children to care for (for families and societies alike). At the family level, this means that more resources are available for each family member, and typically, a substantial part of these resources is invested in the education and health of each child (Bloom, Kuhn, & Prettner, 2020; Li & Zhang, 2007). This shift from having many children with a low education level, and often poor health status, toward having fewer but better-educated and healthier children is related to the quantity–quality tradeoff (Becker & Lewis, 1973; Becker & Tomes, 1976; Becker, 1993; Galor, 2005, 2011; Galor & Weil, 2000). Typically, replacing child quantity with child quality induces positive effects on long-run economic growth at the macroeconomic level via faster human capital accumulation and, thus, faster individual productivity growth (Baldanzi, Bucci, & Prettner, 2019; Galor & Weil, 2000; Lee & Mason, 2010; Prettner, Bloom, & Strulik, 2013; Strulik, Prettner, & Prskawetz, 2013; Prettner, & Strulik, 2016, 2017a, 2017b, 2018).[3]

At the economy-wide level, the reduction in fertility decreases the dependency ratio (the ratio between those who are not in the labor force, technically outside the "working ages," to those who are in the labor force, technically those who fall within the "working ages"). Given this decrease in the dependency ratio, per-capita gross domestic product (GDP) has the potential to rise even for a constant per-worker GDP. To see this, take the definition of the per-capita GDP as Y_t/N_t, where N_t is the population size, and recognize that it can be rewritten as

$$\frac{Y_t}{N_t} = \frac{Y_t}{L_t} \cdot \frac{L_t}{N_t},$$

---

3. In earlier models of research and development (R&D) based growth, a decline in population growth, or a decreasing population size, has a negative effect on economic growth (see, e.g., the frameworks of Aghion & Howitt, 1992; Grossman & Helpman, 1991; Jones, 1995; Kortum, 1997; Romer, 1990; Segerström, 1998). However, this implication is hard to reconcile with the available empirical evidence that supports a negative relation between fertility and economic growth (Ahituv, 2001; Bloom & Freeman, 1988; Brander & Dowrick, 1994; Kelley & Schmidt, 1995; Li & Zhang, 2007). In addition, a positive effect of population growth, or a larger population, runs against the findings in the models of Solow (1956) and Diamond (1965) that are discussed in previous chapters and to their extensions that account for automation.

where L_t is employment (under the assumption that the labor force is fully employed). In this expression, Y_t/L_t is GDP per worker, while L_t/N_t is the ratio of workers to the total population (and, thus, an inverse measure of the dependency ratio). If GDP per worker stays constant but L_t/N_t increases such that the dependency ratio shrinks, per capita GDP rises.

In addition to the previously outlined effect, a decrease in the dependency ratio implies that more governmental resources become available as the fraction of those who pay taxes rises. These additional resources can be spent in many domains, among them education, health, infrastructure, or R&D (Bloom, Khoury, Kufenko, & Prettner, 2019; Prettner & Werner, 2016; Prettner, 2014). If such investments are made wisely, a demographic dividend in terms of faster economic growth may emerge, as has been observed in East Asian "tiger economies," including China, and in Ireland (Bloom & Canning, 2003; Bloom & Finlay, 2009; Bloom & Williamson, 1998; Bloom, Canning, & Sevilla, 2003; Bloom, Kuhn, & Prettner, 2017). Behavioral changes of households—such as increases in female labor force participation when fertility falls, or increases in savings when life expectancy increases—reinforce the demographic dividend (Bloom, Canning, Fink, & Finlay, 2009; Bloom, Canning, Mansfield, & Moore, 2007). If it emerges, the demographic dividend implies fast economic growth. However, no guarantee exists that the demographic dividend will, in fact, emerge: if corruption is high, institutions are extractive or badly developed, macroeconomic management in general is inferior, or labor and capital markets work poorly or are interfered with through counterproductive policies, then the demographic dividend might just go unrealized (Acemoglu & Robinson, 2012; Acemoglu, Johnson, & Robinson, 2001, 2002, 2005a,b; Bloom & Canning, 2000, 2001; Bloom et al., 2017).

Having discussed the economic consequences of declining fertility, we now focus on the corresponding impact of declining mortality and rising life expectancy. Here, the effects depend strongly on the age group in which mortality is decreasing: (1) If child mortality decreases, for example, at the onset of the demographic transition (Cervellati & Sunde, 2005, 2011; Reher, 2004), the TFR tends to decrease as well, and more than proportionally, because of a reduction in precautionary fertility (Doepke, 2005; Kalemli-Ozcan, 2003). If the reduction in the TFR is strong enough, then the initial reduction in child mortality comes with a reduction of the net reproduction rate (the number of surviving daughters per woman). This, in turn, implies a slowdown of population growth and the corresponding positive economic effects described previously kick in. (2) If working-age adult mortality decreases, for example, because of reductions in cardiovascular diseases, the dependency ratio decreases and worker productivity increases via the reduction in disease-related morbidity. Both of these changes have positive effects on economic growth (Bloom et al., 2003; Bloom, Chen et al., 2018; Suhrcke & Urban, 2010). (3) If old-age mortality decreases, predominantly retirees are affected such that the positive effects of declining mortality on economic growth are dampened, whereas the number of retirees increases and so, too, does the dependency ratio. In isolation, the latter tends to generate a negative impulse with respect to its effect on economic growth (Bloom, Khoury, Algur, & Sevilla, 2020; Bloom, Kuhn, & Prettner, 2019). For an overview of the economic effects of health in terms of mortality and morbidity, and for the many mechanisms that matter in this context, see Bloom and Canning (2000), Shastry and Weil (2003), Weil (2007, 2014), Kuhn and Prettner (2016), and Bloom, Canning, Kotschy, Prettner, and Schünemann (2018), Bloom, Kuhn et al. (2019).

Apart from the direct effects of decreasing mortality on the size of the labor force and on labor productivity, an important indirect effect emerges due to the Ben-Porath mechanism (Ben-Porath, 1967). If individuals enjoy a longer life, incentives to invest in education rise because this investment is more likely to pay off the longer an individual works. Because education investments early in life translate into higher labor productivity later on, this tends to raise economic growth.[4] Intuitively, this effect would be strongest when the life expectancy of working-age individuals increases. In this context, life expectancy *per se* is not what matters, but rather healthy life expectancy, which determines how long an individual will stay active in the labor market (see Cervellati & Sunde, 2013; Hazan, 2009; Strulik & Werner, 2016 for discussions).

However, even if lower fertility and mortality result in an initial boost to economic growth, the long-run consequence is an increase in the fraction of older workers and retirees as compared with the total population—i.e., an increase in the dependency ratio. Economists and policymakers are concerned about the following effects that are beginning to surface in many high-income countries: (1) fewer and fewer workers will have to produce the goods consumed by a larger dependent population (see, for example, Gertler, 1999; Gruescu, 2007; *The Economist*, 2009); (2) retirement funds and social security systems might be underfunded and ill-prepared for the demographic challenges ahead (see, e.g., Bloom et al., 2007; Bloom, Canning, & Fink, 2010; Bloom, Canning, & Moore, 2014; Gruber & Wise, 1998; Heijdra & Romp, 2009; Prettner & Canning, 2014); (3) output per worker could decline because older workers might not be as productive as younger workers (see Bloom & Sousa-Poza, 2013; Börsch-Supan & Weiss, 2016; Green & Riddell, 2013; Mahlberg, Freund, Crespo-Cuaresma, & Prskawetz, 2013; Skirbekk, 2008 for discussions on whether this is the case); (4) investment could decline when the members of older cohorts retire and spend down their assets (Mankiw & Weil, 1989; Schich, 2008); and (5) older societies might

---

4. See, for example, the studies by Becker and Woessmann (2009), Cohen and Soto (2007), Hanushek and Woessmann (2012, 2015), de la Fuente and Doménech (2006), Krueger and Lindahl (2001), and Lutz, Cuaresma, and Sanderson (2008) for empirical evidence.

not be as inventive and risk-taking as younger ones, which could reduce technological progress and firm creation (see Baldanzi, Prettner, & Tscheuschner, 2019; Borghans & ter Weel, 2002; Canton, de Groot, & Hahuis, 2002; Gehringer & Prettner, 2019; Irmen & Litina, 2016; McConnell & Sunde, 2019 for different views).

In response to these concerns, many economists claim that behavioral reactions to declining fertility and rising life expectancy and thoughtful economic policies could mitigate some of the negative economic effects of these looming demographic changes (Bloom, 2019). We have already discussed that families with fewer children will invest more in education and health such that average human capital increases (Prettner et al., 2013; Strulik et al., 2013). This effect is reinforced by increasing life expectancy in conjunction with the Ben-Porath mechanism, which means that educational investments become more worthwhile (Ben-Porath, 1967; Cervellati & Sunde, 2005, 2013; Strulik & Werner, 2016). These effects are further magnified by governmental investments in health and education due to the demographic dividend (Bloom, Khoury, Kufenko, et al., 2019; Prettner, 2014). Apart from these aspects, people tend to retire later—and governments tend to raise the retirement age—when (healthy) life expectancy rises, such that the negative effect of aging via the dependency ratio is compensated to some (nontrivial) extent (Bloom et al., 2007; Prettner & Canning, 2014).[5] In addition, the labor supply of parents rises with falling fertility because less time is required for child care (Ashraf, Weil, & Wilde, 2013; Bloom et al., 2009; Bloom, Kuhn et al., 2020; Bloom, McKenna, & Prettner, 2018, 2019). Finally, individuals might save and invest more if they live longer, raising the physical capital stock of an economy and perhaps also boosting incentives to invest in R&D (Baldanzi, Prettner, et al., 2019; Gehringer & Prettner, 2019; Heijdra & Mierau, 2011; Heijdra & Romp, 2008, 2009; Prettner & Trimborn, 2017; Prettner, 2013).

This general summary of the potential economic effects of demographic change and survey of the literature that analyzes these effects sets the stage for us to now address the question of whether automation could also alleviate some of the concerns raised by demographic change (Abeliansky & Prettner, 2017; Abeliansky, Algur, Bloom, & Prettner, 2020; Acemoglu & Restrepo, 2017b, 2018; Leitner & Stehrer, 2019; *The Economist*, 2019).

---

5. This is not inconsistent with the observation that actual retirement ages have decreased in many countries over the past decades. The reason is that increasing incomes might have induced individuals to increase their demand for leisure and therefore for earlier retirement. If the effect is strong enough, it will overcompensate for the contemporaneous effect of an increase in healthy life expectancy. In addition, the design of pension systems also matters because it often includes incentives for early retirement (Bloom et al., 2007; Gruber & Wise, 1998; Prettner & Canning, 2014).

6.3 How robots can help

Clearly, one of the concerns of the current demographic challenges in OECD countries is that fewer "workers" will be available to produce the goods consumed in an economy, i.e., the dependency ratio will rise.[6] At the same time, and as we have seen in previous chapters, many people are concerned that automation could lead to a rise in technological unemployment. Reconciling these antithetical concerns—not enough workers on the one hand, workers are rendered unemployed by technology on the other—is difficult. In the following section, we sketch a pathway by which demographic change might spur automation and discuss the empirical evidence to date on whether automation actually follows trends in demography and is thus, to a considerable extent, a phenomenon driven by economic/demographic conditions rather than a sweeping, independent, and predestined technological development.[7]

Consider again (as in Chapter 4 and Chapter 5) the Cobb–Douglas production function given by

$$Y_t = K_t^{\alpha}(L_t + P_t)^{1-\alpha},$$

where Y_t denotes aggregate output, K_t the stock of traditional physical capital, L_t is the labor force (we abstract from unemployment), P_t is the stock of automation capital, and $\alpha \in (0, 1)$ refers to the elasticity of output with respect to traditional physical capital. Assuming perfect competition, the production factors are remunerated according to their marginal value products such that the wage rate and the rates of return on automation capital and on traditional physical capital are given by, respectively,

$$w_t = (1 - \alpha)\left(\frac{K_t}{L_t + P_t}\right)^{\alpha}, \tag{6.1}$$

$$R_{t+1}^{autom} = (1 - \alpha)\left(\frac{K_t}{L_t + P_t}\right)^{\alpha}, \tag{6.2}$$

$$R_{t+1}^{trad} = \alpha\left(\frac{L_t + P_t}{K_t}\right)^{1-\alpha}. \tag{6.3}$$

---

6. In this context, two aspects need to be remembered. First, "workers" are not synonymous with "working-age people" because the labor force participation rate is generally lower than one and because of unemployment. Second, not working for pay is not synonymous with being a non-worker in the sense of not producing things of value (see, e.g., Bloom, Khoury et al., 2020).

7. Please note that different parts of the human capital distribution might be affected differently by automation and by demographic change. For example, life expectancy gains are largest among the more educated and skilled, whereas technological unemployment will disproportionately affect the less skilled as long as automation is a better substitute for low-skilled workers than for high-skilled workers.

We observe that, *ceteris paribus*, faster labor force growth leads to a decrease in the wage rate and in the return on automation capital, whereas it leads to an increase in the return on traditional physical capital (Abeliansky & Prettner, 2017). Thus, we would expect to see higher incentives to invest in automation in countries in which the labor force increases more slowly or even decreases. Because one of the main drivers of an expansion of the labor force is population growth (which, in turn, depends on fertility), this observation implies that countries in which fertility is low and the population is older should experience a faster increase in robot density (robots per 1,000 workers). This is, indeed, what a first glimpse of the data suggests, and it is also what empirical studies on the relationship between automation and demographic change—either measured in terms of population growth or by means of an increase in the old-age dependency ratio—find (Abeliansky & Prettner, 2017; Acemoglu & Restrepo, 2017b, 2018).[8]

Fig. 6.4 follows Abeliansky and Prettner (2017) and shows a world map of robot density. The countries with a dark green color exhibit a higher robot density, while the robot density is lower in countries with a light green color. Some countries are also in white, indicating no data are available in the database of the International Federation of Robotics (2018). However, limited data availability suggests a low stock of robots in those countries that appear in white. We observe that, consistent with the previously outlined theoretical considerations, robot density is highest in countries that are aging fast, such as Germany, Italy, Japan, and South Korea. By contrast, robot density is lower in countries that are not aging as quickly, such as France (mainly because of its comparatively high fertility rate), the North American Free Trade Agreement (NAFTA) countries (which tend to have inward migration and higher fertility than Germany, Italy, Japan, and South Korea), and the United Kingdom (mainly because of high inward migration from Eastern Europe). Please note that the International Federation of Robotics collects the data for NAFTA countries jointly such that we cannot provide disaggregated data for Canada, Mexico, and the United States.

Acemoglu and Restrepo (2018) define aging as an increase in the share of the population above the age of 56 (compared with those aged 21−55 years) and show that a 10-percentage point increase in this aging variable leads to 0.9 additional industrial robots per 1,000 workers. This compares with an increase in the stock of robots per 1,000 workers between 1993 and 2014 of three units. Given the observed aging in terms of their indicator, Acemoglu and Restrepo (2018) calculate that population aging explains 40−65% of the observed adoption of industrial robots. These results are qualitatively in line with the results of Abeliansky and Prettner (2017), who

---

8. In addition to the higher demand for robots from firms in aging societies, households might also demand more service robots that reduce the need for household labor and could allow them to raise the labor force participation rate.

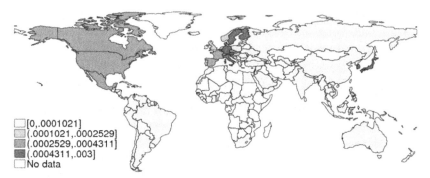

FIGURE 6.4 Map of robot density (average in the years 2011–13). The darker a country's color is, the higher is its robot density. For countries represented in white, no data are available in the International Federation of Robotics (2018) database.

show that a decrease in population growth by 1% leads to an increase in the robot density growth rate by 2%. Both studies control for several other important drivers of the adoption of automation, in particular, for income (in terms of per capita GDP) and investment.

Altogether, these results indicate that population aging creates the incentives for automation and, thereby, the conditions for counteracting one of its negative effects, a shortage of labor. Acknowledging that automation is (at least partly) an endogenous response to demography-driven labor shortages could help to explain why, up to now, we observe neither decreasing employment in the face of automation nor a labor shortage in the face of population aging.

Apart from these considerations, robots could also be helpful in addressing other aging-related concerns and alleviating some of the burdens of an aging population. For example, robotic exoskeletons might help an aging workforce to cope with the decline of physical strength that comes with age. Exoskeletons might also help care assistants and nurses to lift patients and, thereby, contribute to better working conditions for different occupations in the health sector—occupations that are expected to be in high demand in the future of aging societies. "Medical robots," which are already very proficient in diagnosing diseases and screening X-rays, could bring considerable relief to the medical profession in dealing with the expected increase in age-related noncommunicable diseases such as cancer (Bloom et al., 2011; Bloom Cafiero-Fonseca, et al., 2014, 2018b; Chen, Kuhn, Prettner, & Bloom, 2018). The three-dimensional (3D) printing of medical implants, prostheses, hearing aids, replacement teeth, and other medical products demanded predominantly by older adults could bring the prices of these products down and, contemporaneously, improve their quality. Autonomous cars could be a boon to seniors, who may not feel confident driving a car on their own anymore but who still demand mobility. Even loneliness at old age could be countered to some extent by robots, as the therapeutic furry seal "Paro" and the humanoid robot "Pepper" have demonstrated. Finally, wearable sensors are already used to help with adherence to medication plans, to monitor changes in gait, and to summon help when an individual falls (for these and many more examples, see Abeliansky, Martinez-Zarzoso, & Prettner, 2020; *Financial Times*, 2019; Ford, 2015; *The Economist*, 2016, 2019).

6.4 Future employment projections based on automation

But how large is the potential of automation to replace workers? As discussed in previous chapters, the potential effects of automation on employment are often estimated in terms of the technological feasibility of the substitution of workers/tasks by robots. While the corresponding estimates vary widely, the number of jobs that are deemed susceptible to automation is generally rather high (Arntz, Gregory, & Zierahn, 2017; Frey & Osborne, 2017; McKinsey Global Institute, 2017; Nedelkoska & Quintini, 2018). However, the decision to replace workers with robots relies on case-specific economic considerations because replacing an inexpensive long-lived worker with an expensive (and relatively short-lived) robot may not be economical. Furthermore, producing robots requires time and resources, and producing all the robots necessary to replace the 47% of the labor force that Frey and Osborne (2017) estimate to be technically substitutable by robots will likely not be feasible in the near future. In addition, producing and employing such a large "army" of robots comes with considerable material resource and electricity input requirements.[9]

Considering the economic argument, Abeliansky, Algur, et al. (2020) base their projections of the number of jobs that robots could substitute on the potential supply of robots, given current trends in robot production as indicated by International Federation of Robotics (2018) data. Abeliansky, Algur, et al. (2020) calculate a baseline scenario, extrapolating the current trend in the growth rate of robots (observed from 2010 to 2017) to 2030. In addition, they allow for a low robot adoption scenario, in which the growth rate of the stock of robots decreases by 50%, and a high robot adoption scenario, in which the growth rate of the stock of robots increases by 50%, and compare both with the baseline scenario. By contrast, Bloom, McKenna et al. (2018, 2019) extrapolate the somewhat bolder projections of the International Federation of Robotics (2018) of a 14% growth rate of the stock of industrial robots until 2030. In the next step, Bloom, McKenna et al. (2018, 2019) and Abeliansky, Algur, et al. (2020) apply the replacement of manufacturing workers by industrial robots that Acemoglu and Restrepo (2017a) estimate for the United States and Dauth, Findeisen, Suedekum, and

---

9. All this could lead to an additional challenge of automation in terms of its contribution to environmental degradation and climate change (Kuhn & Prettner, 2020).

Woessner (2017) estimate for Germany to calculate how many workers the projected stock of robots will replace in 2030. Because Acemoglu and Restrepo (2017a) find a rather high number of 6.2 manufacturing workers being displaced by one industrial robot in the United States, while Dauth et al. (2017) find that only two manufacturing workers are displaced by one industrial robot in Germany, this procedure delivers a range of plausible estimates between a high-replacement and a low-replacement scenario.

Using this methodology, Bloom, McKenna et al. (2018, 2019) and Abeliansky, Algur, et al. (2020) find that in the high-displacement scenario of Acemoglu and Restrepo (2017a), 38−64 million jobs worldwide could be substituted by robots in the year 2030. Using the low-displacement scenario based on the estimates of Dauth et al. (2017), Abeliansky, Algur, et al. (2020) estimate that only 12 million workers could be replaced by robots in 2030, whereas the results of Bloom, McKenna et al. (2018, 2019) suggest a number close to 20 million. Irrespective of the underlying methodology to project the stock of robots or the choice of displacement scenario, these results are substantially lower than those derived relying on the technological feasibility of substitution (Arntz et al., 2017; Frey & Osborne, 2017; McKinsey Global Institute, 2017; Nedelkoska & Quintini, 2018). Even at the lower end of the estimates based on technological feasibility, robots could replace about 300 million workers worldwide in the next 10 to 20 years. To get some feeling for these numbers, the 38 million people of the baseline estimates of Abeliansky, Algur, et al. (2020) correspond to the population size of countries such as Canada and Poland, whereas the 300 million people of the estimates based on technological feasibility would approximately equal 90% of the population of the United States or the populations of Australia, France, Germany, and Japan combined (2018 population numbers according to World Bank, 2019).

6.5 The reverse channel: could robots affect demography?

Demographic changes affect the incentives to invest in automation predominantly because a smaller workforce relative to dependent segments of the population drives up wages, which induces firms to look for ways to substitute workers with robots, 3D printers, etc. This section briefly discusses some potential reverse causal channels by which automation technologies can affect fertility decisions. This might happen in some obvious ways, and some less direct mechanisms also exist.

As far as the rather obvious effects are concerned, if sex robots were to become widespread and their availability were to affect marriage and partnership formation negatively, this would be a plausible channel by which automation might exert a direct negative impact on fertility. In addition, as we have seen, automation will likely exert downward pressure on the wages of (predominantly low-skilled) workers and thereby affect their fertility decisions via the standard channels known from the family economics literature. A frequently-made argument put forward, for example, by Becker (1965) is that parents' time input is one of the crucial costs of fertility. If wages decrease, the opportunity costs of children should decrease, which could lead to an increase in the fertility rate. However, if wages are already comparatively low, households might just not be able to afford children such that automation could decrease fertility in such a situation (Galor, 2005, 2011). Moreover, new technologies imply that parents would want to invest more in their children's education to help them escape technological unemployment or sluggish wage growth. This increase in education investments implies a switch toward child quality instead of child quantity in standard models in which education and fertility choices are both endogenous (Becker, 1960; Galor & Weil, 2000; Prettner & Strulik, 2016, 2018). This mechanism could also drive fertility rates down.

Apart from these rather direct effects or effects that are well known from the family economics literature, other less direct effects may also exist. For example, robots could reduce the demand for children that emerges in countries in which social security systems are not well developed and where children often care for their parents (cf., Willis, 1980). In addition, children often contribute to household income by means of child labor in poorer countries (Edmonds, 2016). These aspects become less important for households if automation is widespread such that child labor would become less likely to pay off and therefore less valuable. In addition, robot caregivers could reduce the need to have children to take care of people at old age. Altogether, these arguments suggest that fertility might decrease with automation.

In sum, a range of plausible arguments indicate that fertility would decrease in the face of automation, but one argument also indicates that fertility might actually rise.[10]

6.6 Summary

This chapter provides an overview of the demographic changes of the last several decades, identifying declining fertility, increasing life expectancy, and the progression of large-sized cohorts to the older ages as the main drivers of demographic change globally and across individual countries.

---

10. As far as the gender-specific effects of automation are concerned, we know of the following two studies that come to very different conclusions. Acemoglu and Restrepo (2017a, 2020) use data on the United States and find that the adverse effects of automation on employment are greater for men than for women. By contrast, Brussevich et al. (2018) use different data and a different definition of automation and conclude that automation harms women more. This is based on their observation that women participate less in sectors that are intensive in science, technology, engineering, and mathematics (which are deemed to be automation-proof in the near future) and that they perform more routine tasks.

The economic consequences of these developments are wide-ranging and diverse. In the short to medium run, a decline in fertility can generate a demographic dividend that—if reaped and invested wisely—has the potential to lift an economy out of poverty and onto a path of sustained long-run income growth. Increasing life expectancy can, at the same time, foster educational investments and improve labor productivity.

In the very long run, however, declining fertility and rising life expectancy lead to population aging with various potential consequences that concern many economists and the wider public, including (1) fewer workers to produce goods for a larger dependent population; (2) underfunding of retirement funds and social security systems; (3) declines in productivity growth due to older workers not being as productive as younger workers; (4) reduction in investment when wealthier, older cohorts retire and spend down their assets; and (5) older societies that are not as inventive and risk-taking as younger ones. All of this could have negative effects on economic growth.

However, also discussed were behavioral changes by the individuals in aging societies that (partly) mitigate the negative economic effects of population aging, including (1) families with fewer children investing more in the education and health of each child such that average human capital and worker productivity increase; (2) rising life expectancy inducing more investments in education via the Ben-Porath mechanism; (3) the labor supply of parents rising with falling fertility because of the reduced time requirement for child care; and (4) individuals saving and investing more if they live longer, which raises the physical capital stock and might also boost incentives to invest in R&D. Until now, these mechanisms seem to have counterbalanced the potentially negative effects on economic growth of demographic change (Acemoglu and Restrepo, 2017b).

Finally, we discussed the possibility that automation can help to reduce the negative economic effects of population aging. Simple theoretical considerations imply that a lower (or negative) growth rate of the labor force leads to more automation; empirical evidence suggesting that a higher fraction of the population above the age of 55 and lower population growth both boost the adoption of industrial robots supports this implication (Abeliansky & Prettner, 2017; Acemoglu & Restrepo, 2018). Altogether, calculations based on the extrapolation of past trends in robot production suggest that by 2030, robots could substitute for 12−64 million workers (Abeliansky, Algur, et al., 2020; Bloom, McKenna et al., 2018, 2019). In addition, automation-related technologies might help to cope with loneliness, depression, and dementia; they might help healthcare workers with the more physically demanding parts of their jobs; they might help to drive older people with a demand for mobility; they might help to produce high-quality medical implants, prostheses, hearing aids, and teeth that are even cheaper than today; and they might help to relieve the health sector of an expected rise in workload due to higher demand driven by the aging-related illnesses of an aging society.

References

Abeliansky, A., Algur, E., Bloom, D., & Prettner, K. (2020). The Future of Work: Meeting the Global Challenge of Demographic Change and Automation. International Labour Review (forthcoming).

Abeliansky A. L., Martinez-Zarzoso, I., & Prettner K. (2020). 3D printing, international trade, and FDI. *Economic Modelling 85(C)*, 288−306.

Abeliansky, A. & Prettner, K. (2017). Automation and demographic change. Hohenheim Discussion Papers in Business, Economics, and Social Sciences 05-2017, University of Hohenheim, Germany.

Acemoglu, D., Johnson, S., & Robinson, J. A. (2001). The colonial origins of comparative development: An empirical investigation. *American Economic Review, 91*(5), 1369−1401.

Acemoglu, D., Johnson, S., & Robinson, J. (2002). Reversal of fortune: Geography and institutions in the making of the modern world income distribution. *The Quarterly Journal of Economics, 117*(4), 1231−1294.

Acemoglu, D., Johnson, S., & Robinson, J. A. (2005a). Institutions as a fundamental cause of long-run growth. In P. Aghion, & S. Durlauf (Eds.), *Handbook of economic growth* (pp. 386−472). Amsterdam: Elsevier, chapter 6.

Acemoglu, D., Johnson, S., & Robinson, J. (2005b). The rise of Europe: Atlantic trade, institutional change, and economic growth. *American Economic Review, 95*(3), 546−579.

Acemoglu, D., & Restrepo, P. (2017a). Robots and jobs: Evidence from US labor markets. NBER Working Paper No. 23285, National Bureau of Economic Research, Cambridge, MA.

Acemoglu, D., & Restrepo, P. (2017b). Secular stagnation? The effect of aging on economic growth in the age of automation. *American Economic Review, Papers & Proceedings, 107* (5), 174−179.

Acemoglu, D., & Restrepo, P. (2018). Demographics and automation. NBER Working Paper 24421, National Bureau of Economic Research, Cambridge, MA.

Acemoglu, D., & Restrepo, P. (2020). Robots and jobs: Evidence from US labor markets. *Journal of Political Economy.* (forthcoming).

Acemoglu, D., & Robinson, J. A. (2012). *Why nations fail: The origins of power, prosperity, and poverty.* London: Profile Books.

Aghion, P., & Howitt, P. (1992). A model of growth through creative destruction. *Econometrica: Journal of the Econometric Society, 60*(2), 323−351.

Ahituv, A. (2001). Be fruitful or multiply: On the interplay between fertility and economic development. *Journal of Population Economics, 14*(1), 51−71.

Arntz, M., Gregory, T., & Zierahn, U. (2017). Revisiting the risk of automation. *Economics Letters, 159*(C), 157−160.

Ashraf, Q., Weil, D., & Wilde, J. (2013). The effect of fertility reduction on economic growth. *Population and Development Review, 39*(1), 97−130.

Baldanzi, A., Bucci, A., & Prettner, K. (2019). Children's health, human capital accumulation, and R&D-based economic growth. *Macroeconomic Dynamics.* (forthcoming).

Baldanzi, A., Prettner, K., & Tscheuschner, P. (2019). Longevity-induced vertical innovation and the tradeoff between life and growth. *Journal of Population Economics, 32*(4), 1293−1313.

Becker, G. S. (1960). An economic analysis of fertility. In G. B. Roberts (Ed.), *Demographic and economic change in developed countries.* Cambridge, MA: National Bureau of Economic Research.

Becker, G. S. (1965). A theory of the allocation of time. *The Economic Journal, 75*(299), 493−517.

Becker, G. S. (1993). *A treatise on the family*. Cambridge, MA: Harvard University Press.

Becker, G. S., & Lewis, H. G. (1973). On the interaction between the quantity and quality of children. *Journal of Political Economy, 81*(2), 279−288.

Becker, G. S., & Tomes, N. (1976). Child endowments and the quantity and quality of children. *The Journal of Political Economy, 84*(4), 143−162.

Becker, S., & Woessmann, L. (2009). Was Weber wrong? A human capital theory of protestant economic history. *The Quarterly Journal of Economics, 124*(2), 531−596.

Ben-Porath, Y. (1967). The production of human capital and the life cycle of earnings. *Journal of Political Economy, 75*(4), 352−365.

Bloom, D. E. (2011). 7 Billion and counting. *Science, 333*(6042), 562−569.

Bloom, D. E. (2020). Population. *Finance & Development*, 4−9.

Bloom, D. E. (Ed.) (2019). *Live long and prosper? The economics of ageing populations*, London: CEPR Press. Available from https://voxeu.org/content/live-long-and-prosper-economics-ageing-populations. Accessed 31.12.2019.

Bloom, D. E., Cafiero, E. T., Jané-Llopis, E., Abrahams-Gessel, S., Bloom, L. R., Fathima, S., & Weinstein, C. (2011). *The global economic burden of non-communicable diseases*. Geneva: World Economic Forum.

Bloom, D. E., Cafiero-Fonseca, E. T., McGovern, M. E., Prettner, K., Stanciole, A., Weiss, J., & Rosenberg, L. (2014). The macroeconomic impact of non-communicable diseases in China and India: Estimates, projections, and comparisons. *The Journal of the Economics of Ageing, 4*(December 2014), 100−111.

Bloom, D. E., & Canning, D. (2000). The health and wealth of nations. *Science, 287*(5456), 1207−1209.

Bloom, D. E., & Canning, D. (2001). Demographic change and economic growth: The role of cumulative causality. In N. Birdsall, A. C. Kelley, & S. Sinding (Eds.), Population does matter: Demography, growth, and poverty in the developing world. New York, NY: Oxford University Press.

Bloom, D., & Canning, D. (2003). Contraception and the Celtic tiger. *Economic and Social Review, 34*(3), 229−247.

Bloom, D. E., Canning, D., & Fink, G. (2010). Implications of population ageing for economic growth. *Oxford Review of Economic Policy, 26*(4), 583−612.

Bloom, D. E., Canning, D., Fink, G., & Finlay, J. (2009). Fertility, female labor force participation, and the demographic dividend. *Journal of Economic Growth, 14*(2), 79−101.

Bloom, D., Canning, D., Kotschy, R., Prettner, K., & Schünemann, J. (2018). Health and economic growth: Reconciling the micro and macro evidence. IZA Discussion Paper No. 11940, Institute of Labor Economics, Bonn.

Bloom, D. E., Canning, D., Mansfield, R. K., & Moore, M. (2007). Demographic change, social security systems, and savings. *Journal of Monetary Economics, 54*(1), 92−114.

Bloom, D. E., Canning, D., & Moore, M. (2014). Optimal retirement with increasing longevity. *Scandinavian Journal of Economics, 116*(3), 838−858.

Bloom, D.E., Canning, D., & Sevilla, J. (2003). The demographic dividend: A new perspective on the economic consequences of population change. Population Matters Monograph MR-1274, RAND, Santa Monica, CA.

Bloom, D., & Canning, D. (2000). The health and wealth of nations. *Science (New York, N.Y.), 287*(February 18), 1207−1209.

Bloom, D., Chen, S., Kuhn, M., McGovern, M., Oxley, L., & Prettner, K. (2018). The economic burden of chronic diseases: Estimates and projections for China, Japan, and South Korea. *The Journal of the Economics of Ageing.* (forthcoming).

Bloom, D., & Finlay, J. (2009). Demographic change and economic growth in Asia. *Asian Economic Policy Review, 4*(1), 45−64.

Bloom, D. E., & Freeman, R. B. (1988). Economic development and the timing and components of population growth. *Journal of Policy Modelling, 10*(1), 57−81.

Bloom, D. E., Khoury, A., Kufenko, V., & Prettner, K. (2019). Spurring economic growth through human development: Research results and guidance for policymakers PGDA Working Paper 183.2020. Program on the Global Demography of Aging, Harvard University.

Bloom, D. E., Khoury, A., Algur, E., & Sevilla, J. P. (2020). Valuing Productive Non-market Activities of Older Adults in Europe and the US. *De Economist, 168*, 153−181.

Bloom, D. E., Kuhn, M., & Prettner, K. (2020). The contribution of female health to economic development. *The Economic Journal* (forthcoming).

Bloom, D., Kuhn, M., & Prettner, K. (2017). Africa's prospects for enjoying a demographic dividend. *Journal of Demographic Economics, 83*(1), 63−76.

Bloom, D., Kuhn, M., & Prettner, K. (2019). *Health and economic growth. Oxford Encyclopedia of Economics and Finance.* Oxford, UK: Oxford University Press.

Bloom, D., McKenna, M., & Prettner, K. (2018). Demography, unemployment, automation, and digitalization: Implications for the creation of (decent) jobs, 2010−2030. NBER Working Paper 24835, National Bureau of Economic Research, Cambridge, MA.

Bloom, D., McKenna, M., & Prettner, K. (2019). Global employment and decent jobs, 2010−2030: The forces of demography and automation. *International Social Security Review, 72*(3), 43−78.

Bloom, D., & Sousa-Poza, A. (2013). Aging and productivity: Introduction. *Labour Economics, 22*(June 2013), 1−4.

Bloom, D., & Williamson, J. (1998). Demographic transitions and economic miracles in emerging Asia. *World Bank Economic Review, 12*(3), 419−456.

Borghans, L., & ter Weel, B. (2002). Do older workers have more trouble using a computer than younger workers? *The Economics of Skills Obsolescence, 21*(September 2002), 139−173.

Börsch-Supan, A., & Weiss, M. (2016). Productivity and age: Evidence from work teams at the assembly line. *Journal of the Economics of Ageing, 7*(April 2016), 30−42.

Brander, J. A., & Dowrick, S. (1994). The role of fertility and population in economic growth. *Journal of Population Economics, 7*(1), 1−25.

Brussevich, M., Dabla-Norris, E., Kamunge, C., Karnane, P., Khalid, S., & Kochhar, K. (2018). Gender, technology, and the future of work. IMF Staff Discussion Note 18/07, International Monetary Fund, Washington, DC.

Canton, E., de Groot, H., & Hahuis, R. (2002). Vested interests, population ageing and technology adoption. *European Journal of Political Economy, 18*(4), 631−652.

Cervellati, M., & Sunde, U. (2005). Human capital formation, life expectancy, and the process of development. *American Economic Review, 95*(5), 1653−1672.

Cervellati, M., & Sunde, U. (2011). Life expectancy and economic growth: The role of the demographic transition. *Journal of Economic Growth, 16*(2), 99−133.

Cervellati, M., & Sunde, U. (2013). Life expectancy, schooling, and lifetime labor supply: Theory and evidence revisited. *Econometrica: Journal of the Econometric Society, 81*(5), 2055−2086.

Chen, S., Kuhn, M., Prettner, K., & Bloom, D. (2018). The macroeconomic burden of noncommunicable diseases in the United States: Estimates and projections. *PLoS One*, *13*(11), e0206702.

Cohen, D., & Soto, M. (2007). Growth and human capital: Good data, good results. *Journal of Economic Growth*, *12*(1), 51−76.

Dauth, W., Findeisen, S., Suedekum, J., & Woessner, N. (2017). German robots—The impact of industrial robots on workers. CEPR Discussion Paper 12306, Centre for Economic Policy Research, London.

Deaton, A. (2013). *The great escape: Health, wealth, and the origins of inequality*. Princeton, NJ: Princeton University Press.

de la Fuente, A., & Domenéch, R. (2006). Human capital in growth regressions: How much difference does data quality make? *Journal of the European Economic Association*, *4*(1), 1−36.

Diamond, P. A. (1965). National debt in a neoclassical growth model. *American Economic Review*, *55*(5), 1126−1150.

Doepke, M. (2005). Child mortality and fertility decline: Does the Barro-Becker model fit the facts? *Journal of Population Economics*, *18*(2), 337−366.

Edmonds, E. V. (2016). Economic growth and child labor in low income economies. GLM/LIC Synthesis Paper No. 3, Growth and Labour Markets in Low Income Countries Programme. Available from https://g2lm-lic.iza.org/wp-content/uploads/2017/06/glmlic_sp003.pdf. Accessed 20.12.2019.

Financial Times. (2019). Robots/ageing Japan: I, carebot. Available from https://www.ft.com/content/314c65a8-8829-11e9-a028-86cea8523dc2. Accessed 24.11.2019.

Ford, M. (2015). *Rise of the robots: Technology and the threat of a jobless future*. New York, NY: Basic Books.

Frey, C. B., & Osborne, M. A. (2017). The future of employment: How susceptible are jobs to computerisation? *Technological Forecasting and Social Change*, *114*(C), 254−280.

Galor, O. (2005). From stagnation to growth: Unified growth theory. In P. Aghion, & S. Durlauf (Eds.), *Handbook of economic growth* (Vol. 1, pp. 171−293). Amsterdam: Elsevier, chapter 4.

Galor, O. (2011). *Unified growth theory*. Princeton, NJ: Princeton University Press.

Galor, O., & Weil, D. (2000). Population, technology, and growth: From Malthusian stagnation to the demographic transition and beyond. *The American Economic Review*, *90*(4), 806−828.

Gehringer, A., & Prettner, K. (2019). Longevity and technological change. *Macroeconomic Dynamics*, *23*(4), 1471−1503.

Gertler, M. (1999). Government debt and social security in a life-cycle economy. *Carnegie-Rochester Conference Series on Public Policy*, *50*(June 1999), 61−110.

Green, D., & Riddell, W. (2013). Ageing and literacy skills: Evidence from Canada, Norway and the United States. *Labour Economics*, *22*(June 2013), 16−29.

Grossman, G. M., & Helpman, E. (1991). Quality ladders in the theory of economic growth. *Review of Economic Studies*, *58*(1), 43−61.

Gruber, J., & Wise, D. (1998). Social security and retirement: An international comparison. *American Economic Review*, *88*(2), 158−163.

Gruescu, S. (2007). *Population ageing and economic growth*. Heidelberg: Physica-Verlag.

Hanushek, E. A., & Woessmann, L. (2012). Do better schools lead to more growth? Cognitive skills, economic outcomes, and causation. *Journal of Economic Growth*, *17*(4), 267−321.

Hanushek, E. A., & Woessmann, L. (2015). *The knowledge capital of nations: Education and the economics of growth*. Cambridge, MA: MIT Press.

Hazan, M. (2009). Longevity and lifetime labor supply: Evidence and implications. *Econometrica: Journal of the Econometric Society, 77*(6), 1829–1863.

Heijdra, B. J., & Mierau, J. O. (2011). The individual life cycle and economic growth: An essay on demographic macroeconomics. *Economist (Leiden), 159*(1), 63–87.

Heijdra, B., & Romp, W. (2008). A life-cycle overlapping-generations model of the small open economy. *Oxford Economic Papers, 60*(1), 88–121.

Heijdra, B. J., & Romp, W. E. (2009). Retirement, pensions, and ageing. *Journal of Public Economics, 93*(3–4), 586–604.

International Federation of Robotics. (2018). World robotics industrial robots and service robots. Available from https://ifr.org/worldrobotics/. Accessed 7.03.2019.

Irmen, A. & Litina, A. (2016). Population aging and inventive activity. CESifo Working Paper No. 5841, Center for Economic Studies, Munich.

Jones, C. I. (1995). R&D-based models of economic growth. *Journal of Political Economy, 103* (4), 759–784.

Kalemli-Ozcan, S. (2003). A stochastic model of mortality, fertility, and human capital investment. *Journal of Development Economics, 70*(1), 103–118.

Kelley, A. C., & Schmidt, R. M. (1995). Aggregate population and economic growth correlations: The role of the components of demographic change. *Demography, 32*(4), 543–555.

Kortum, S. (1997). Research, patenting and technological change. *Econometrica: Journal of the Econometric Society, 65*(6), 1389–1419.

Krueger, A. B., & Lindahl, M. (2001). Education for growth: Why and for whom? *Journal of Economic Literature, 39*(4), 1101–1136.

Kuhn, M., & Prettner, K. (2016). Growth and welfare effects of health care in knowledge based economies. *Journal of Health Economics, 46*(March 2016), 100–119.

Kuhn, M. & Prettner, K. (2020). Automation in times of climate change. Mimeo.

Lee, R., & Mason, A. (2010). Fertility, human capital, and economic growth over the demographic transition. *European Journal of Population, 26*(2), 159–182.

Leitner, S. & Stehrer, R. (2019). The automatisation challenge meets the demographic challenge: In need of higher productivity growth. Fellowship Initiative Discussion Paper 117, European Commission, Brussels. Available from https://ec.europa.eu/info/sites/info/files/economy-finance/dp117_en.pdf. Accessed 21.12.2019.

Li, H., & Zhang, J. (2007). Do high birth rates hamper economic growth? *Review of Economics and Statistics, 89*(1), 110–117.

Lutz, W., Cuaresma, J. C., & Sanderson, W. (2008). The demography of educational attainment and economic growth. *Science, 319*(5866), 1047–1048.

Mahlberg, B., Freund, I., Crespo-Cuaresma, J., & Prskawetz, A. (2013). Ageing, productivity and wages in Austria. *Labour Economics, 22*(June 2013), 5–15.

Mankiw, G. N., & Weil, D. N. (1989). The baby-boom, the baby-bust and the housing market. *Regional Science and Urban Economics, 19*(2), 235–258.

McConnell, M., & Sunde, U. (2019). Ageing into risk aversion? Implications of population ageing for the willingness to take risks. In D. E. Bloom (Ed.), *Live long and prosper? The economics of ageing populations*. London: CEPR Press. Available from. Available from https://voxeu. org/content/live-long-and-prosper-economics-ageing-populations, Accessed 31.12.2019.

McKinsey Global Institute. (2017). Jobs lost, jobs gained: Workforce transitions in a time of automation. Available from https://www.mckinsey.com/~/media/mckinsey/featured% 20insights/future%20of%20organizations/what%20the%20future%20of%20work%20will%20 mean%20for%20jobs%20skills%20and%20wages/mgi-jobs-lost-jobs-gained-report-december-6-2017.ashx. Accessed 31.12.2019.

Nedelkoska, L. & Quintini, G. (2018). Automation, skill use and training. OECD Social, Employment and Migration Working Paper No. 202, Organisation for Economic Co-operation and Development Paris.

Preston, S. H., Heuveline, P., & Guillot, M. (2001). *Demography. Measuring and modeling population processes.* Hoboken, NJ: Blackwell Publishing.

Prettner, K. (2013). Population aging and endogenous economic growth. *Journal of Population Economics, 26*(2), 811−834.

Prettner, K. (2014). The non-monotonous impact of population growth on economic prosperity. *Economics Letters, 124*(1), 93−95.

Prettner, K., Bloom, D. E., & Strulik, H. (2013). Declining fertility and economic well-being: Do education and health ride to the rescue? *Labour Economics, 22*(June 2013), 70−79.

Prettner, K., & Canning, D. (2014). Increasing life expectancy and optimal retirement in general equilibrium. *Economic Theory, 56*(1), 191−217.

Prettner, K., & Strulik, H. (2016). Technology, trade, and growth: The role of education. *Macroeconomic Dynamics, 20*(5), 1381−1394.

Prettner, K., & Strulik, H. (2017a). Gender equity and the escape from poverty. *Oxford Economic Papers, 69*(1), 55−74.

Prettner, K., & Strulik, H. (2017b). It's a sin—Contraceptive use, religious beliefs, and long-run economic development. *Review of Development Economics, 21*(3), 543−566.

Prettner, K., & Strulik, H. (2018). Trade and productivity: The family connection redux. *Journal of Macroeconomics, 56*(June 2018), 276−291.

Prettner, K., & Trimborn, T. (2017). Demographic change and R&D-based economic growth. *Economica, 84*(336), 667−681.

Prettner, K., & Werner, K. (2016). Why it pays off to pay us well: The impact of basic research on economic growth and welfare. *Research Policy, 45*(5), 1075−1090.

Reher, D. S. (2004). The demographic transition revisited as a global process. *Population, Space and Place, 10*(1), 19−41.

Romer, P. (1990). Endogenous technological change. *Journal of Political Economy, 98*(5), 71−102.

Schich, S. (2008). Revisiting the asset-meltdown hypothesis. *OECD Journal: Financial Market Trends, 2008*(2), 209−222.

Segerström, P. S. (1998). Endogenous growth without scale effects. *American Economic Review, 88*(5), 1290−1310.

Shastry, G. K., & Weil, D. N. (2003). How much of cross-country income variation is explained by health? *Journal of the European Economic Association, 1*(2/3), 387−396.

Skirbekk, V. (2008). Age and productivity capacity: Descriptions, causes and policy. *Ageing Horizons, 8*, 4−12.

Solow, R. M. (1956). A contribution to the theory of economic growth. *The Quarterly Journal of Economics, 70*(1), 65−94.

Strulik, H., Prettner, K., & Prskawetz, A. (2013). The past and future of knowledge-based growth. *Journal of Economic Growth, 18*(4), 411−437.

Strulik, H., & Werner, K. (2016). 50 is the new 30—Long-run trends of schooling and retirement explained by human aging. *Journal of Economic Growth, 21*(2), 165−187.

Sudharsanan, N., & Bloom, D. E. (2018). The demography of aging in low- and middle-income countries: Chronological versus functional perspectives. In M. K. Majmundar, & M. D. Hayward (Eds.), *Future directions for the demography of aging. Proceedings of a workshop.* Washington, DC: National Academies Press.

Suhrcke, M., & Urban, D. (2010). Are cardiovascular diseases bad for economic growth? *Health Economics*, *19*(12), 1478−1496.

The Economist. (2009, June 27). A special report on ageing populations.

The Economist. (2016, April 30). 3D printing is coming of age as a manufacturing technique. A Printed Smile.

The Economist. (2019, February 14). An ageing world needs more resourceful robots. Grandma's Little Helper.

United Nations. (2019). World population prospects. The 2019 revision. Department of Economic and Social Affairs. Population Division. Available from http://data.un.org/Data. aspx?d = PopDiv&f = variableID%3A52. Accessed 24.11.2019.

United Nations. (2019b). International migration. Department of Economic and Social Affairs. Population Division. Available from https://www.un.org/en/development/desa/population/ migration/data/estimates2/estimates19.asp. Accessed 24.11.2019.

Weil, D. N. (2007). Accounting for the effect of health on economic growth. *The Quarterly Journal of Economics*, *122*(3), 1265−1306.

Weil, D. N. (2014). Health and economic growth. In P. Aghion, & S. Durlauf (Eds.), *Handbook of economic growth* (Vol. 2B, pp. 623−682). Amsterdam: Elsevier, chapter 3.

Willis, R. J. (1980). The old-age security hypothesis of population growth. In T. K. Burch (Ed.), *Demographic behaviour. Interdisciplinary perspectives on decision making.* Boulder, CO: Westview Press.

World Bank. (2019). *World development indicators 1960−2019.* Washington, DC: World Bank.

Chapter 7

Policy challenges

7.1 The challenges

As discussed theoretically and empirically in the preceding chapters, the high degree of substitutability among industrial robots, 3D printers, and artificial intelligence (AI) on the one hand and human labor on the other could lead to dramatic economic shifts. In general, automation offers abundant opportunities for both productivity gains and the beneficial replacement by robots of aging societies' shrinking labor forces. However, automation also threatens workers with lower skills or those who perform repetitive tasks. Even if displaced workers find jobs in other economic sectors, those jobs tend to pay less, which may raise wage inequality in the wake of automation. In addition, if the production factor capital—in the form of industrial robots—substitutes for workers, while the income that these robots generate flows to capital owners, a falling labor income share and higher income inequality result. The falling labor income share, in turn, will make financing pay-as-you-go social security systems and governmental expenditures out of payroll and income taxes more difficult. Finally, even if all the adjustment mechanisms work to the extent that most individuals benefit from the technological advances wrought by automation (which is by no means guaranteed), severe problems might still occur during the transition— such as job losses in certain occupations and lower wages or reduced wage growth for workers for whom robots are good substitutes. Policymakers could try to address these adjustment problems and help individuals during the transition toward the age of automation. This chapter discusses potential policies ranging from taxation and subsidization to regulation to investments in education and, finally, to adjustments in the design of social security systems. Different policies are discussed in terms of potential advantages and disadvantages—and by no means in terms of a necessity to introduce them. Some of the policies might even do more harm than good, as will be evident. The aim here is modest: to describe potential channels by which policymakers could mitigate bumps associated with the transition to a future of automation and AI.

Automation and its Macroeconomic Consequences. DOI: https://doi.org/10.1016/B978-0-12-818028-0.00007-7

In summary, the positive effects of automation relate to increasing efficiency; the negative effects are mainly distributional in nature.[1] The extent to which these effects constitute a welfare loss can be assessed by means of social welfare functions as discussed in Chapter 4. However, Chapter 4 also argues that estimating a society's inequality aversion is difficult, and thus, for all practical matters, optimal policy measures are impossible to identify reliably. Ideally, taxes and transfers that do not distort allocations should counter the undesired distributional effects of automation. The facts that almost all taxes and transfers are distortionary in some way and that the progression of automation renders the traditional way of taxing the production factor labor ever more difficult imply that such abstract and general statements are not very helpful in practice. This chapter therefore focuses on concrete policy measures that might help counter the negative effects of automation without jeopardizing its benefits. In this discussion, we address advantages and disadvantages of the respective policies, particularly focusing on the effects of these policy measures on efficiency and inequality. In addition, we evaluate whether implementing these policies seems feasible from a practical perspective. The goal is to provide insights into some coherent strategies that policymakers might adopt to address the economic challenges of automation and to help inform corresponding public debates. Some of the measures examined have already been proposed in different contexts, either in the academic literature or by policymakers or business leaders (see, for example, Corneo, 2018; Delaney, 2017; Frank, 2008; Geiger, Prettner, & Schwarzer, 2018; Guerreiro, Rebelo, & Teles, 2018; Korinek & Stiglitz, 2017; Prettner, Geiger, & Schwarzer, 2018).

7.2 Education as a strategy to cope with the negative effects of automation

Education is frequently mentioned as an important measure to counter the negative effects of automation. From a private perspective, of course, skill upgrading is a desirable response to the automation of low-skill tasks—for those workers who are able to obtain higher skills and who have the financial means to do so (Prettner & Strulik, 2020). The substantial costs of education (especially for college and advanced degrees) present a financial barrier for some. In many countries, the direct education costs, in the form of tuition fees, are high and rising; in the United Kingdom and in the United States, for example, tuition fees have risen at rates far above the

---

1. Negative consequences might also occur that economic policies can only partly address. For example, job losses often come with negative psychological and social effects, and people could experience a loss of identity and self-esteem if they cease working and become dependent on transfer payments.

general inflation rates over the last 20 years (Bureau of Labor Statistics, 2016; *The Economist*, 2017). On top of these direct costs, housing costs in university cities tend to be significantly higher than in cities without higher education institutions (Egner & Grabietz, 2018). Finally, the opportunity costs of education—foregone wage income—affect the children of low-income parents more severely than the children of high-income parents. Thus, as a policy corrective, governmental investments in education that primarily benefit the less affluent—such as stipends and tuition-fee waivers for the deserving children of low-income households or means-based public housing for students—are often recommended. Such policies reduce inequality and tend to have positive side effects from an efficiency perspective because (1) efficiency losses occur if talented individuals cannot get adequate education when they are credit constrained (Galor & Moav, 2004; Galor & Zeira, 1993); (2) the education level of the workforce is a crucial determinant of the long-run growth potential of an economy (Bucci, 2008; Cohen & Soto, 2007; de la Fuente & Doménech, 2006; Hanushek & Woessmann, 2012, 2015; Lutz, Cuaresma, & Sanderson, 2008; Romer, 1990; Strulik, Prettner, & Prskawetz, 2013); (3) individual education can have positive social benefits due to spillover effects, for example, in team production (Battu, Belfield, & Sloane, 2003; Lucas, 1988); and (4) education has the potential to reduce inequality by lifting more people out of low-paid jobs (Acemoglu & Autor, 2012; Goldin & Katz, 2009; Prettner & Schaefer, 2020; Strulik et al., 2013).[2]

To be effective in the age of automation, education investments should ideally prioritize those skills that, in the foreseeable future, are difficult to automate or that will complement automation. Such skills plausibly include nonroutine tasks related to science, technology, and engineering, interpersonal communication, empathy, teaching, management, critical thinking, and computer skills. From today's perspective, it would therefore make sense to invest in the following areas of tertiary education: science, engineering (particularly with respect to advanced technologies), software development, management, and teaching; and in the following areas of secondary education: child care, care for seniors, and nursing.

Investing in retraining programs for people whose jobs are increasingly being automated could help to facilitate job transformation or—in cases in which they were already displaced by automation—assist people with their re-entry into the job market. In general, retraining programs could help to curb

---

2. As a counterargument, Bloom and Sevilla (2004) argue that three conditions must be fulfilled for an education subsidy to have an overall positive impact: (1) the social benefit of education investments needs to be positive, (2) private actors need to have insufficient incentive or ability to provide the necessary investments to internalize the social benefits, and (3) the investment itself must generate higher social benefits than alternative investments. While item (1) is usually fulfilled, item (2) might not be fulfilled and item (3) is often difficult to assess.

structural mismatch unemployment and thereby increase labor market efficiency. Of course, retraining every unemployed worker to become a quantum physicist or a care assistant for older adults is not possible, simply because these occupations require very different skills compared with those that are automated. In other words, and more generally, acquiring completely new skillsets is often too great a leap, and matching individual workers with the right set of new skills to acquire could also be very difficult. Thus, retraining must be seen as only one component of a successful skill-upgrading strategy.

As another component of the overall education strategy to cope with automation, preparing young students for the flexibility required in the modern labor market should be prioritized. Stable employment and enduring career paths are becoming increasingly rare; changing employers, jobs, and even careers has become increasingly common, and automation and AI will only hasten the process. Thus, preparing the next generation of workers for the task of lifelong learning is critically important. In this context, reforming curricula in primary and secondary schools to prioritize subjects that are either in demand in the age of automation (e.g., computer science, information technology, natural sciences) or that increase learning flexibility (e.g., acquiring proficient reading and writing skills as early as possible and developing critical thinking skills that bolster the ability to learn how to learn) might prove useful. In the information age, memorizing facts that can be easily looked up is obsolete, while the knowledge of how and where to access accurate information—and critically process and evaluate that information—is required.

To summarize, educational investments form a central pillar of any adequate policy response to automation. However, education policies are unlikely, by themselves, to mitigate all the negative effects of automation—in particular, not every person who loses a job can be retrained to easily find a new line of work. Thus, other policy measures are also required to comprehensively address the negative effects of automation.

7.3 Labor market policies

Because automation is purported to result in a lower aggregate demand for labor (which is, as we have seen, controversial), one frequently raised proposal is a policy measure to reduce the length of the statutory work week to distribute available work among more individuals. This change could prevent a situation in which some individuals have to bear the full burden of unemployment deriving from the transition to new technologies. In addition, according to the evidence in the study by Collewet and Sauermann (2017) for (mostly part-time) workers in call centers, reducing working hours could lead to increasing productivity due to reductions in fatigue, even if the number of hours worked is already comparatively low.

However, a reduction in working hours without a corresponding reduction of worker salaries implies higher unit labor costs. This, in turn, would hasten the transition to automated production and could thereby have negative medium- and long-run consequences for labor demand.[3] In addition, a legally binding regulation of statutory working hours does not necessarily correspond well with the individual preferences of workers. Corneo (1995) shows in this context that a reduction in statutory working times actually raises inequality in terms of individual well-being, as leisure can be conceptualized as a normal good whose demand increases with income. Thus, high-income individuals would benefit disproportionately from a reduction in working times.

A law compelling the reduction in working hours as a policy response to automation is therefore likely to be ineffective, at best, and might have detrimental effects in terms of employment and income inequality, at worst. That said, the trend since the Industrial Revolution has been a slow but gradual decrease in working hours per employee, such that part of the productivity increase that technological change brought materialized not in the form of higher wages but in more leisure time. A gradual reduction of working hours over time, together with wages that increase by less than productivity growth due to automation, could therefore be a practical and beneficial strategy to follow for future labor bargaining sessions between workers and firms.

Another possible policy response to the costly adjustments associated with automation would be to increase the efficiency of the search-and-matching process to reduce frictional unemployment. Cords and Prettner (2019) show that automation implies higher frictional unemployment for low-skilled workers and lower frictional unemployment for high-skilled workers. Increasing the efficiency of the search technology can help to mitigate the negative effects on low-skilled workers. One concrete policy example is the Hartz III reform in Germany[4] that revamped job centers by creating the "Federal Office for Labour" and led to a strong increase in the number of job center employees who try to match employers with vacancies to the unemployed searching for jobs. In the course of this reform, the number of unemployed persons per advisor—and thus waiting times to re-employment—decreased

---

3. See Lordan and Neumark (2018) and Lordan (2019) for similar effects of increases in the minimum wage.

4. The Hartz reforms (consisting of four reforms from Hartz I to Hartz IV) comprise a series of labor market reforms enacted in Germany by the government of Chancellor Gerhard Schröder from January 1, 2003, to January 1, 2005. The reforms aimed at reducing the German unemployment rate, which had reached historically high levels at the beginning of the 21st century. The reforms mainly reduced the time period in which unemployment benefits can be claimed, introduced new forms of employment with less protection against dismissal, and revamped job centers. The unemployment rate in Germany declined from more than 10% in 2003–2005 to slightly above 3% in 2019 according to the World Bank (2019). The extent to which the Hartz reforms contributed to the decline in the German unemployment rate remains subject to intensive debate, as are the social consequences of the reforms (see, e.g., Carrillo-Tudela, Launov, & Robin, 2018; Giannelli, Jaenichen, & Rothe, 2016).

substantially. This shift was plausibly associated with an increase in the number and quality of job matches and, thereby, could have contributed to the substantial decrease in unemployment in Germany since the implementation of the Hartz reforms in the mid-2000s.

7.4   Taxation in the age of automation

Most of the research on the macroeconomic effects of automation suggests that it causes the production factor labor to diminish in importance compared with the production factor capital. This effect implies that the base of labor income taxes (one of the two core taxes by which governments finance their expenditures, with the other being consumption taxes) is eroding in the wake of automation. Therefore, the crucial question is: What can be done to design a tax system that is fit for the future, given the technological changes lying ahead? A standard policy proposal to address concerns about a falling labor income share is to increase the taxes on capital or capital income. The specific details that are proposed differ with respect to the tax base, the value of tax allowances, and the timing of when the taxes are collected. For example, the *wealth tax* proposed by Piketty (2014) is based on the total value of an individual's assets (potentially after considering tax allowances) and amounts to a yearly payment of a small fraction of one's wealth as a tax.[5] The *capital gains tax* is based on the profits realized from buying an asset at a cheaper price in the past and selling the asset at a nominally higher price at some later date, with the tax paid after the sale. The *inheritance tax* is based on the total value of bequests or gifts to one or more heirs or to other recipients (potentially, again, after correcting for tax allowances). This tax is to be paid after the bequest or gift is executed.

The common, crucial problem with these types of taxes—as opposed to taxes on labor income—is that some types of assets are highly mobile and could easily be moved abroad to circumvent the tax. Thus, the introduction of a wealth tax by one country in isolation is often seen as ineffectual; an internationally coordinated strategy would be required. Yet Piketty (2014) acknowledges that inducing the world's leading economies to cooperate in such a manner is nearly impossible. The mobility of the tax base is a bit less problematic when it comes to inheritance taxes, but it nevertheless exists and might prompt some wealthy individuals to move to jurisdictions in which the tax is lower or nonexistent.

Apart from these rather conventional policy initiatives, one novel countermeasure to the economic effects of automation is a direct tax on the value of installed robots. The argument in favor of such a tax is briefly as follows: workers pay taxes and social security contributions, but they are replaced by robots, which do not pay them (apart from the taxes that the owners of the

---

5. In general, the wealth tax can be designed in a regressive, flat, or progressive way.

robots pay on the profits that are partly generated by the robots); therefore, to level the playing field between workers and robots and to broaden the tax base, some argue that a robot tax is necessary. Microsoft founder Bill Gates proposed this strategy for addressing automation in an interview in 2017, stating "taxation is certainly a better way to handle it [automation] than just banning some elements of it" (Delaney, 2017). Gates further discussed methods for recouping lost income taxes, saying "Some of it can come on the profits that are generated by the labor-saving efficiency there. Some of it can come directly in some type of robot tax" (Delaney, 2017). Indeed, some governments and the European Parliament are discussing the possibility of implementing robot taxes (see, for example, Barden, Tirone, & Groendahl, 2017; Prodhan, 2017).

For formal treatments of the effects of robot taxes within the automation-augmented neoclassical growth literature, see Gasteiger and Prettner (2020) and Guerreiro et al. (2018). These contributions argue that the production efficiency theorem—which states that the best possible allocation in the absence of nondistorting taxes does not involve taxes on capital (Diamond & Mirrlees, 1971a, 1971b)—might not apply to robots. Gasteiger and Prettner (2020) and Guerreiro et al. (2018) describe some pathways by which robot taxes could lead to static and dynamic income and welfare gains. In Gasteiger and Prettner's (2020) overlapping generations (OLG) framework, robots reduce the wages of workers. The structure of OLG models implies, however, that wage income is the only source of saving and investment. Thus, automation limits workers' ability to save and invest and thereby hampers capital accumulation. Because capital accumulation is the very source of medium-run income growth in the neoclassical growth model, automation is, in some sense, sowing the seeds of its eventual demise in this framework. A tax on automation in this setting shifts investment away from automation capital toward traditional physical capital in the form of machines, assembly lines, office buildings, etc. The complementarity between traditional physical capital and labor ensures that wages would increase with the robot tax at the long-run steady-state equilibrium (and during the transition toward this equilibrium). These results hold for low and moderate robot tax rates, but, from some point onward, the negative effects of further robot taxes on overall capital accumulation would dominate.

In contrast to these results, some researchers find that taxing robots reduces the incentives to invest in automation in models in which research and development (R&D) and automation are endogenous.[6] In such a setting, the robot tax might hamper productivity growth, a prospect shown by Prettner and Strulik (2020), who augment an R&D-based growth model along the lines of Romer (1990) and Jones (1995) to include automation and

---

6. These dynamic implications come on top of standard concerns regarding static deadweight losses due to taxation.

endogenous education decisions. Prettner and Strulik (2020) study the effects of two tax-transfer schemes to address the negative effects of automation: a labor income tax and a tax on the value of a new robot when it is installed. In both cases, the proceeds of taxes are redistributed to the low-skilled workers in the economy. The simulations show that a robot tax reduces growth and inequality by more than a labor income tax because it reduces incentives to invest in R&D, and therefore, it reduces productivity growth. Overall, and in contrast to the aforementioned results in an OLG economy without R&D-based growth the robot tax implies a similar equity-efficiency tradeoff as most other taxes, even for low rates of the robot tax. From a pure efficiency point of view, a robot tax rate of zero would therefore maximize economic growth in a setting in which R&D is endogenous.

Furthermore, a robot tax poses feasibility problems from a practical perspective. First, the market for the "wage" of a robot has not been established, nor how this wage could be taxed, such that a tax on the value of robots is the only feasible option to date.[7] Even if that problem can be solved, robots are a form of physical capital, which is a very mobile production factor. This implies that if one country in isolation introduces a robot tax, firms could simply move their production to another country that does not collect this tax such that a "race to the bottom" in terms of robot taxes might occur. For example, in an effort to avoid the sizable home country robot tax, firms would undertake to produce goods more cheaply in a foreign country with a low (or no) robot tax and export the goods that they produce with the help of robots to their home country. The negative redistributive effects of automation do not vanish in this case, but, additionally, production shifts abroad. Thus, the robot tax would face similar problems as the wealth tax proposed by Piketty (2014) and discussed previously: the introduction of a robot tax would be most effective if enacted globally, but the difficulties of international political and economic cooperation are well known.

The discussion thus far shows that the potential of taxing productive capital is low because of its mobility, while the taxation of labor reaches its limits as a result of automation. A remaining tax source with a high potential for raising revenues is a tax on consumption, i.e., the value-added tax (VAT). However, the VAT is regressive because people with low incomes consume a larger fraction of their income, and thus, they pay a higher share of their income in terms of the VAT. In isolation, this effect ensures that a switch from progressive income taxation to a VAT would lead to an increase in inequality of after-tax disposable incomes.

For this reason, measures to introduce a progressive element into the VAT have been proposed. For example, Frank (2008) suggests that savings,

---

7. Kuhn and Prettner (2020) show that another possibility is to tax inputs in robots such as electricity, which would also help to cope with some of the negative environmental implications of automation.

instead of deductible expenses, should be reported to the tax office at the end of the year. The difference between income and savings within the tax year could then be used as the base for a progressive consumption tax (the rate of the VAT would increase with consumption expenditures). The advantages of such a system would be that a progressive consumption tax (1) does not reduce the incentives to work or to save (as with income taxes and capital taxes, respectively), (2) could reduce inequality depending on the progressiveness of the tax rates, and (3) could lead to a reduction in tax evasion because savings reduce the tax burden at home only if they are reported. This contrasts the current situation in which channeling savings to tax havens *reduces* the tax burden.

While a complete restructuring of the tax system toward such a progressive consumption tax might be difficult to achieve in practice, some elements of a progressive consumption tax already exist and could be strengthened easily. For example, goods that high-income earners or wealthier groups primarily consume could be subjected to a higher VAT rate. For example, the European Union allows for different VAT rates on different goods (food, drinks, books, and drugs often qualify for a reduced rate in various member countries). Via widespread adoption of a cleverly designed system of reduced rates, the progressive element of the consumption tax could become more pronounced. Another example is a higher tax rate on larger and more polluting cars, which is used in some countries and mainly affects those who have a preference for, and can afford to buy, these types of cars. In the case of higher taxes on more polluting vehicles, incentivizing the purchase of more environmentally friendly cars would even have a desirable knock-on effect.[8]

Another promising type of tax that is very popular among economists is a tax on the value of land (see, for example, George, 1878; *The Economist*, 2018). Land value taxes are popular because undeveloped land is of almost fixed supply such that (1) distortions of the tax are almost nonexistent and (2) the tax cannot be easily passed on to tenants because the demand for development is more elastic than the supply of land; in this case, an analysis of the tax incidence suggests that landowners would effectively pay most of the tax burden. As a consequence of these tax characteristics, the land value tax is less distortionary than other taxes, and it is progressive because the rich own disproportionately more land than the poor. As a desirable side effect, a tax on the value of land could be used to siphon the rents that accrue to landowners because of an appreciation of their assets (due to a reclassification of their land or due to public infrastructure provisions/

---

8. Note that high-income persons are also the most likely to purchase electric vehicles and hybrids, which are claimed to be more environmentally friendly but are still more expensive than cars with conventional engines. However, a high tax on polluting cars could also shift demand toward less polluting vehicles within the high-income group.

improvements that raise the value of their land). In contrast to property taxes, a land value tax does not deter land development because the value of the buildings on the given parcel is not taxed. In addition, land cannot move abroad to escape taxation, such that the "high-mobility argument" against this form of wealth tax does not apply.

According to *The Economist* (2018), the total value of land in the United States was estimated to be 160% of gross domestic product (GDP) in 2009 such that, in principle, a land tax could be used to raise a significant amount of revenue. Yet property taxes as such seem to be unpopular among voters. In California, for example, a ballot measure that forbids property taxes of more than 1% of the property's value (known as Proposition 13) passed in 1978 and has been held sacrosanct by voters for the 40 years since.[9]

Another option for reforming the tax system is to increase the amount raised by means of Pigovian taxes (Baumol, 1972; Pigou, 1920). The aim of these taxes is to increase the price of market activities that cause negative economic externalities. Consequently, the distortionary effect of the tax could be employed to internalize negative externalities and thereby bring the economy closer to the efficient allocation. A classic example of a Pigovian tax is an environmental tax on carbon dioxide (CO_2) emissions. Because CO_2 emissions lead to global warming, but polluting companies do not pay for this negative side effect, a tax on CO_2 emissions could shift the costs toward those who cause them. This, in turn, would reduce harmful production. Some authors argue that Pigovian taxes create opportunities for a "double dividend" if their revenue is used to reduce other distortionary taxes on desirable activities. For example, the revenues of a tax on CO_2 emissions could be used to reduce labor income taxes and thereby make the use of human labor—versus the use of robots—more attractive. For debates on the validity of the arguments regarding the double dividend, see Bovenberg and de Mooij (1994), Fullerton and Metcalf (1997), and Tullock (1967). Because the wealthy are typically also those who are responsible for more pollution (see the following paragraph), environmental taxes are likely to be progressive.

In reality, however, polluting activities are often subsidized instead of taxed (IEA, 2016; *The Economist*, 2015). For example, high fuel subsidies in Iran, Indonesia, and many other countries of course incentivize polluting activities (*The Economist*, 2013). To justify fossil fuel subsidies, apologists often claim that fossil fuels help the poor by enabling them to drive and to heat their homes. However, to the extent that those with higher incomes drive more, own bigger cars (or own cars at all), and live in bigger houses that

---

9. However, Proposition 13 might be going back on the ballot in 2020. Because many younger voters—who do not own a large fraction of the available land but benefit substantially from the proceeds of the tax that help finance education—are against Proposition 13, it could be softened or abandoned soon (*San Francisco Chronicle*, 2018).

require more energy to heat, those with lower incomes tend to gain less from these types of subsidies than those with higher incomes (*The Economist*, 2015). Because the amount of subsidies is very high globally (USD500 billion in 2014, according to IEA, 2016), these funds could be redirected in various, much more beneficial ways for low-income groups. As such, abolishing/reducing fossil fuel subsidies could go a long way in raising efficiency, reducing inequality, and safeguarding the environment.

Related to the Pigovian tax are the so-called sin taxes, consisting of taxes on tobacco, alcohol, soft drinks, or salty and sugary products. These taxes aim to reduce the consumption of unhealthy goods or otherwise deter individuals from behaviors that are deemed imprudent or undesirable, either privately or socially. However, because the poor tend to spend a larger portion of their income on tobacco and alcohol, such taxes are typically regressive.

Finally, the European Commission has introduced an initiative to reform corporate taxation in the digital age (European Commission, 2018a, 2018b). The problem with the current system of taxing corporations is that it is based on the physical presence of a firm in a specific country and the net profits that the firm registers there. However, many large digital companies currently earn high revenues in places where they have no physical presence. In addition, companies often reduce their high corporate tax burden by transferring profits within multinationals to low-tax jurisdictions ("transfer pricing"). To be able to tax digital companies fairly, the European Commission aims at taxing these businesses based on whether they have a significant interaction with users in a country, not on the company's physical presence. However, this is a long-term solution that requires international coordination, time to implement, and time to resolve many legal issues. Therefore, the European Commission proposed an interim solution by which big digital companies would pay a certain fraction of the revenues (e.g., from selling advertisements and utilizing user-provided information and digital intermediary activities) that they generate within a country. The European Commission plans to impose this interim tax on companies with annual worldwide revenues in excess of 750 million Euros, of which at least 50 million Euros need to have accrued within the European Union. This threshold would ensure that smaller tech start-ups are exempted. While the European Commission (2018a, 2018b) estimates that such a tax could generate an annual revenue of about 5 billion Euros, the majorities required in the European Council to implement such a tax seem out of reach at the time of writing (May 2020).

7.5   Social security in the age of automation

Because the expected progress of automation will leave some workers behind (i.e., not everybody who loses a job due to automation can be retrained), revamping the social security system to make it responsive to future challenges might be necessary. Strengthening unemployment insurance for those displaced workers who cannot find new jobs and would stay unemployed in the long run is particularly helpful as it would diminish the social, economic, and political instabilities that might follow from automation. In addition, bolstering health insurance systems and making them universal—in the sense of disconnecting them from whether or not a person has a job—is advisable. Such strategies have the potential to (1) improve the health status of the disadvantaged significantly, (2) reduce the potential for health expenditure−related poverty traps (Bloom, Khoury, & Subbaraman, 2018), and (3) lead to overall positive economic effects because of a better health status of the population (Aghion, Howitt, & Murtin, 2011; Bloom & Canning, 2000; Bloom, Canning, & Fink, 2014; Bloom, Canning, Kotschy, Prettner, & Schünemann, 2019; Cervellati & Sunde, 2011; Lorentzen, McMillan, & Wacziarg, 2008; Shastry & Weil, 2003; Weil, 2007).

Another argument for helping those who suffer the most from technological changes is the recent phenomenon of "deaths of despair" (Case & Deaton, 2015), wherein the parts of the population that face economic hardship are prone to alcoholism, drug abuse, and suicide. In the United States, death rates due to these causes have been on the rise; historically, this was also the case in the former Soviet Union when it transitioned to a market economy in the 1990s. The disruptions at that time predominantly affected prime-age males and led to widespread anxiety and increased consumption of alcohol (Bennett, Bloom, & Ivanov, 1998). Fortifying those elements of the social security system that help these disadvantaged groups could alleviate the financial burden that many people face. Thus, ensuring a decent unemployment insurance system and access to a universal healthcare system independent from employment status has the potential not only to reduce inequality but also to reduce morbidity and mortality on a potentially grand scale.

In the context of reforming social security systems, some argue that an unconditional (universal) basic income should replace the traditional social security system in the age of automation. Usually such a system is conceived as a complete replacement of the traditional social security system such that the administrative costs would fall significantly because eligibility verification becomes unnecessary. Opponents of unconditional basic income usually argue that it is prohibitively expensive and distorts labor supply decisions in a monumental way. Apart from these two counterarguments, an unconditional basic income as a substitute for the social welfare system could generate individual hardship if someone needs more than these baseline funds to survive. This situation would apply, for example, to people in need of long-term care, the chronically ill, and those who had a severe accident that led to disability. Following the elimination of all targeted benefits for such groups provided by the traditional social security system, these groups might no longer have an adequate level of benefits for survival. Such a scenario stands in sharp contrast to the central idea of a social safety net, namely, to help those who are the most in need in a society.[10]

Furthermore, in the context of an unconditional basic income (and, more generally, in the context of unemployment insurance), another important aspect is often overlooked: employees might benefit substantially from their work in terms of intrinsic motivation, self-respect, and social interaction. For example, many people derive meaning through their work, utilize their jobs as a primary means of socializing, and even find their romantic partners at the workplace. A job loss due to automation would, in this case, not only be associated with financial losses but also with additional losses in terms of subjective well-being. Even with a complete replacement of the income loss, such a situation could have devastating effects from a social perspective and deprive people of an aspect of their self-esteem, an important component of individual health. In this case, subsidizing selected types of employment would probably be more beneficial than an unconditional basic income or enhanced unemployment benefits (see, for example, Korinek & Stiglitz, 2017, p. 33). Some elements of such subsidization are present in the form of the earned-income tax credit (EIT) in the United States, which is basically a negative income tax for workers with low income levels. Without the EIT, it might not be financially prudent for firms to offer some types of jobs that are currently subsidized through this system.

In considering the declining labor income share, one policy option to mitigate the negative distributional effects associated with automation is to ensure that larger parts of the population are able to share in the gains of capital income. One possibility is to subsidize individual ownership of stocks, with the aim to raise the incentive to save and to broaden capital ownership. In this case, more individuals would benefit from rising profits driven by automation. However, low-income households often have trouble paying for subsistence needs, such that an expansion of saving for this group might be infeasible—even with substantial subsidies. Overall, the saving rate is positively correlated with income and wealth such that high-income and high-wealth households would predominantly benefit from subsidies on saving. Thus, state support for the accumulation of equity is likely to fall short as a solution to distributional problems caused by automation.

Another option often recommended is to ensure that a part of labor income is paid in terms of equity on behalf of the firms for which employees work. While this approach could safeguard the accumulation of equity by more individuals, employees of nonprofit firms, governmental employees, and those who are currently not part of the labor force would be excluded

---

10. While, in principle, a basic income could be means tested and paid in addition to the standard social security benefits, such a strategy would not lead to lower administrative costs, and why it would be better than the current means-tested social security system is not clear.

from such programs. In addition, for smaller firms that are not listed on the stock exchange or for family firms, dividing the ownership of the company could be problematic. Even for employees of large corporations, problems with such a plan could occur. For example, owning shares of the same firm for which an employee works leads to a clustering of risks: the bankruptcy of the firm would then not only imply the loss of employment but also eradicate a substantial part of both current individual wealth and retirement funds. Finally, from a practical perspective, paying income in terms of assets is tantamount to forced saving and could therefore crowd out other types of individual savings. This crowding-out would undermine the very purpose of such an initiative.

Corneo (2018) proposes an interesting idea to circumvent these problems (in general and not necessarily related to automation). He argues that the government could set up a fund by issuing government debt and investing the money in international stock markets. With the difference between the financing costs of the government and the return on investing in the stock market, the fund could then pay a "social dividend" of the same absolute amount to all citizens. Corneo (2018) estimates that the optimal size of such a fund would be around 30−50% of GDP in Germany and that it could pay approximately 1000 Euro per person per year at that level. Because the redistribution to citizens is a lump sum, such a scheme would reduce inequality. Particularly at times in which the government can borrow at an interest rate far below the rate of return on the stock market, setting up such a fund could even constitute a Pareto improvement in terms of efficiency.[11] The amount that such a fund could pay out is hardly large enough to allow it to mitigate all the negative distributional effects of automation; however, in contrast to an unconditional basic income, the governmental fund is not intended to replace the social security system, and the payments that it could finance are intended to supplement, not substitute for, labor income.

One critical determinant of this idea's success is how many economies set up such a fund. If the plan proliferates, the difference between the financing costs of governments and the rate of return on the stock market would narrow such that the income generated would shrink substantially. The reasons are that stock markets would appreciate, which reduces future expected returns, and that governmental debt would rise, which puts upward pressure on the interest rates that investors demand on government bonds.

Other possible options are deploying the fund to finance meaningful infrastructure projects that are associated with a high return on

---

11. Recall that Pareto efficiency means that no economic agent can be made better off without making another agent worse off. Thus, a Pareto improvement requires that at least one person is made strictly better off, while nobody else is made worse off.

investment or to provide funding for innovative firms in the home country. Infrastructure projects typically require a large initial up-front investment but then deliver steady payoffs that can be redistributed over a long time horizon. For example, these infrastructure projects could be systems of toll highways, tunnels, or bridges, with the proceeds redistributed in a lump-sum manner over the entire life cycle of the infrastructure project. The projects could also comprise publicly owned ports and airports that are rented out to private companies. The corresponding rental income could, again, be used to finance payments to citizens. Other options include hydro, tidal, wind, or solar power plants, which all require a high initial investment. The electricity that they generate over decades could then be used to finance the lump-sum payments. Finally, pumped-storage power plants would be an attractive option because they are typically highly profitable, using cheap electricity during the night to pump water into high-altitude storage basins and releasing the water to power generators for electricity production during the day (during peak demand and, therefore, the peak cost for electricity). Investments in domestic infrastructure would, furthermore, help to close the gap in financing highly needed new infrastructure projects and refurbish existing outdated infrastructure (American Society of Civil Engineers, 2016).

7.6   Demand-side policies

As the discussion so far and the theoretical and empirical considerations of earlier chapters have already made clear, automation is likely to lead to higher average productivity and higher inequality in the long run. In addition, during the adjustment to the long-run equilibrium, substantial hardship might occur in terms of technological unemployment and sluggish wage growth for low-skilled workers. Whether the discussed endogenous adjustment mechanisms that are supposed to compensate for the adverse effects of automation on labor demand work quickly and strongly enough to cushion the transition costs appreciably is unclear. Also unclear is whether policymakers will be willing and able to follow the strategies that could encourage broader parts of the population to gain from automation. Devising appropriate governmental policies in this area is not easy because (1) identifying *a priori* who will benefit and who will lose from automation is difficult, (2) knowing how much is needed individually and collectively to compensate losers is difficult, and (3) redistributive policies are often strongly opposed by those who are negatively affected by them. If adjustment mechanisms work insufficiently well in the short to medium run such that automation adversely affects many people for a considerable amount of time, indiscriminate traditional demand-side policies such as expansionary monetary policy and expansionary fiscal policy could be used to promote a smoother transition. As a side effect, these policies might be useful in reducing the opposition to new technologies with the potential for benefiting all. In extreme cases, such opposition could even stifle technological progress (cf. Frey, 2019; Schwarzer, 2014) to an extent that a country's international competitiveness could be diminished.

At the same time, because automation likely leads to a higher potential growth rate, demand-side policies, such as expansionary fiscal policy, have some additional room for maneuver. Complementing the automation-driven adjustment processes on the supply side by corresponding demand-side policies seems to be feasible and sensible in this situation. However, these types of policies are often difficult to implement in a responsible way. For example, often mentioned is that the expansionary monetary policy of the U.S. Federal Reserve Bank after the bursting of the dotcom bubble paved the way for reckless lending and the subprime mortgage crisis (see Rajan, 2010). In addition, expansionary fiscal policy is often deployed to favor politically important groups or groups with strong lobbies (e.g., farmers or coal miners), which would reduce the effectiveness of such policies to help those who might be in greater need of support.

7.7 Summary

This chapter provides an overview of the most important policy measures proposed to counter some of the negative economic effects of automation. In particular, it emphasizes the following characteristics of different policy measures: (1) whether they have the potential to promote economic efficiency, (2) whether they have the potential to reduce wage/income inequality, and (3) whether their implementation is realistic.

In this regard, educational investments in three areas are promising. The first are scholarships, tuition-fee waivers, and student housing investments for children of low-income households. These policies have the potential to raise efficiency by offering a university education to talented children who might otherwise not have had the opportunity to obtain a quality tertiary education. At the same time, these policies reduce inequality by benefiting less affluent families. The second promising education strategy is to invest in job retraining and job relocation programs, focused on those workers who become unemployed or otherwise displaced due to automation.[12] This policy would *ceteris paribus* reduce unemployment associated with mismatches between worker skills and job requirements and, because the less well educated are particularly

---

12. In principle, that policy could also comprise workers who lose their jobs indirectly due to automation, for example, if there is mass technological unemployment in a factory town with negative repercussions on businesses that are not subject to automation. However, it may be more difficult to identify this form of unemployment.

susceptible to automation, help to reduce inequality. The third promising education strategy is investing in primary and secondary education, with the aim of designing curricula that emphasize critical thinking skills and modern fields of study to enable students to cope with the lifelong challenges of technological progress, in general, and the challenges of automation, in particular.

We argue that, although education investments are a promising policy response to the adverse effects of automation, they cannot solve all of the associated problems. Some people will lose their jobs and retraining them accordingly will be difficult or impossible. Thus, other strategies are required as well. First, strengthening elements in the social security system that ensure a proper safety net for those who become chronically unemployed because of automation could be useful; these elements are mainly unemployment insurance and health insurance. An unconditional basic income that substitutes for the social security system does not appear to be an adequate strategy, as it leaves those who are hit particularly hard without the necessary means to survive. However, other closely related ideas are more promising. These plans range from a governmentally-financed fund that pays a social dividend (without abolishing social security) to a negative income tax that subsidizes the employment of low-wage workers.

As far as financing governmental expenditures is concerned, labor taxes and wealth taxes are limited in their capacity to deal with automation. Labor taxes are limited insofar as labor is displaced by automation, and wealth taxes are limited due to international capital mobility. Potential additional taxes that could be used to finance a significant part of governmental expenditures in the age of automation are land taxes and consumption taxes. However, because consumption taxes are regressive in their current design, relying on them would exacerbate the problem of increasing inequality due to automation. This problem could be countered by strengthening progressive elements in consumption taxes. However, a complete switch to a progressive consumption tax along the lines as sketched out seems difficult to achieve from a practical perspective.

Some standard policy measures constitute adjustments of the system as it exists now. These measures comprise taxation (such as making the income tax more progressive), social security (strengthening elements like unemployment insurance and health insurance), and demand-side policies to cope with temporary increases in involuntary unemployment (expansionary fiscal and monetary policies). Table 7.1 assesses the different policy measures discussed in this chapter according to their effects on efficiency and inequality and whether the policy measure is feasible. In Table 7.1, " + " indicates a positive effect on the given variable or that a policy seems to be feasible, "−" indicates a negative effect on the given variable or that a policy seems to be infeasible, and " ~ " indicates that the effect/feasibility is unclear or difficult to assess.

TABLE 7.1 Policy strategies and their effects.

Strategy	Efficiency/ growth	Inequality	Feasibility
Stipends, tuition-fee waivers, and housing subsidies for talented students of low-income households	+	−	+
Investing in retraining programs	+	−	+
Reducing statutory working times without decreasing wages	−	~	~
Refurbishing school curricula with the aim of strengthening lifelong learning and subjects that complement automation	+	~	+
Introducing a universal basic income instead of the social security system	~	~	−
Expanding the earned-income tax credit	+	−	+
Providing public jobs for the long-term unemployed	+	−	~
Subsidizing saving in terms of the ownership of shares	+	+	+
Subsidizing saving in terms of the ownership of shares (means tested)	+	−	~
Introducing a government fund that pays a social dividend	+	−	−
Increasing land taxes and reducing other distortionary taxes in exchange	+	−	−
Raising sin taxes and reducing other distortionary taxes in exchange	+	+	+
Raising environmental taxes and reducing distortionary taxes in exchange	+	−	~
Abolishing/reducing fuel subsidies and reducing other distortionary taxes in exchange	+	−	−
Introducing a tax based on the digital presence of companies and reducing other distortionary taxes in exchange	+	−	~
Introducing a progressive consumption tax and reducing other distortionary taxes in exchange	+	−	−
Strengthening progressive elements of the consumption tax	+	−	+

Notes: " + " indicates a positive effect or that a policy seems to be feasible, "−" indicates a negative effect or that a policy seems to be infeasible, and " ~ " indicates that the effect/feasibility is not clear or difficult to assess.

References

Acemoglu, D., & Autor, D. (2012). What does human capital do? A review of Goldin and Katz's the race between education and technology. *Journal of Economic Literature*, *50*(2), 426–463.

Aghion, P., Howitt, P., & Murtin, F. (2011). The relationship between health and growth: When Lucas meets Nelson-Phelps. *Review of Economics and Institutions*, *2*(1), 1–24.

American Society of Civil Engineers. (2016). Failure to act. Closing the infrastructure investment gap for America's economic future. Retrieved from https://www.infrastructurereportcard.org/wp-content/uploads/2016/05/2016-FTA-Report-Close-the-Gap.pdf. Accessed on 25.11.2019.

Barden, A., Tirone, J., & Groendahl, B. (2017). Austria's Kern targets robots' rise to blunt populist surge. February 24th 2017. Retrieved from https://www.bloomberg.com/news/articles/2017-02-23/austria-s-kern-targets-rise-of-robots-to-blunt-populist-surge. Accessed 01.01.2020.

Battu, H., Belfield, C., & Sloane, P. (2003). Human capital spillovers within the workplace: Evidence for Great Britain. *Oxford Bulletin of Economics and Statistics*, *65*(5), 575–594.

Baumol, W. (1972). On taxation and the control of externalities. *American Economic Review*, *62* (3), 307–322.

Bennett, N. G., Bloom, D. E., & Ivanov, S. F. (1998). Demographic implications of the Russian mortality crisis. *World Development*, *26*(11), 1921–1937.

Bloom, D. E., & Canning, D. (2000). The health and wealth of nations. *Science (New York, N.Y.)*, *287*(5456), 1207–1209.

Bloom, D. E., Canning, D., & Fink, G. (2014). Disease and development revisited. *The Journal of Political Economy*, *122*(6), 1355–1366.

Bloom, D. E., Canning D., Kotschy, R., Prettner, K., & Schünemann, J. (2019). Health and economic growth: Reconciling the micro and macro evidence. NBER Working Paper 26003, National Bureau of Economic Research, Cambridge, MA.

Bloom, D. E., Khoury, A., & Subbaraman, R. (2018). The promise and peril of universal health care. *Science*, *361*(6404), 1–8.

Bloom, D. E., & Sevilla, J. (2004). Should there be a general subsidy for higher education in developing countries? *Journal of Higher Education in Africa*, *2*(1), 137–150.

Bovenberg, A., & de Mooij, R. (1994). Environmental levies and distortionary taxation. *The American Economic Review*, *84*(4), 1085–1089.

Bucci, A. (2008). Population growth in a model of economic growth with human capital accumulation and horizontal R&D. *Journal of Macroeconomics*, *30*(3), 1124–1147.

Bureau of Labor Statistics. (2016). College tuition and fees increase 63 percent since January 2006. Retrieved from https://www.bls.gov/opub/ted/2016/college-tuition-and-fees-increase-63-percent-since-january-2006.htm. Accessed 23.08.2018.

Carrillo-Tudela, C., Launov, A., & Robin, J.-M. (2018). The fall in German unemployment: A flow analysis. IZA Discussion Paper No. 11442, Institute of Labor Economics (IZA), Bonn.

Case, A., & Deaton, A. (2015). Rising morbidity and mortality in midlife among white non-Hispanic Americans in the 21st century. *PNAS*, *112*(49), 15078–15083.

Cervellati, M., & Sunde, U. (2011). Life expectancy and economic growth: The role of the demographic transition. *Journal of Economic Growth*, *16*(2), 99–133.

Cohen, D., & Soto, M. (2007). Growth and human capital: Good data, good results. *Journal of Economic Growth*, *12*(1), 51–76.

Collewet, M., & Sauermann, J. (2017). Working hours and productivity. IZA Discussion Paper No. 10722, Institute of Labor Economics (IZA), Bonn.

Cords, D., & Prettner, K. (2019). *Technological unemployment revisited: Automation in a search and matching framework. GLO Discussion Paper Series 308.* Essen, Germany: Global Labor Organization (GLO).

Corneo, G. (1995). Distributional implications of a shorter working week: An unpleasant note. *Journal of Economics, 62*(1), 25−31.

Corneo, G. (2018). Ein Staatsfonds, der eine soziale Dividende finanziert. *Perspektiven der Wirtschaftspolitik, 19*(2), 94−109.

de la Fuente, A., & Domenéch, R. (2006). Human capital in growth regressions: How much difference does data quality make? *Journal of the European Economic Association, 4*(1), 1−36.

Delaney, K. J. (2017). Droid duties: The robot that takes your job should pay taxes, says Bill Gates. Retrieved from https://qz.com/911968/bill-gates-the-robot-that-takes-your-job-should-pay-taxes/. Accessed 01.06.2017.

Diamond, P., & Mirrlees, J. (1971a). Optimal taxation and public production I: Production efficiency. *American Economic Review, 61*(1), 8−27.

Diamond, P., & Mirrlees, J. (1971b). Optimal taxation and public production II: Tax rules. *American Economic Review, 61*(1), 261−278.

Egner, B., & Grabietz, K. J. (2018). In search of determinants for quoted housing rents: Empirical evidence from major German cities. *Urban Research & Practice, 11*(4), 460−477.

European Commission. (2018a). Fair taxation of the digital economy. Retrieved from https://ec.europa.eu/taxation_customs/business/company-tax/fair-taxation-digital-economy_en. Accessed 29.08.2018.

European Commission. (2018b). Proposal for a council directive laying down rules relating to the corporate taxation of a significant digital presence. Retrieved from https://ec.europa.eu/taxation_customs/sites/taxation/files/proposal_significant_digital_presence_21032018_en.pdf. Accessed 29.08.2018.

Frank, R. (2008). Progressive consumption tax. *Democracy: A Journal of Ideas, 8,* Retrieved from. Available from https://democracyjournal.org/magazine/8/progressive-consumption-tax/ Accessed 12.12.2019.

Frey, C. B. (2019). *The technology trap: Capital, labor, and power in the age of automation.* Princeton, NJ: Princeton University Press.

Fullerton, D., & Metcalf, G. (1997). *Environmental taxes and the double-dividend hypothesis: Did you really expect something for nothing?* Cambridge, MA: NBER Working Paper No. 6199, National Bureau of Economic Research.

Galor, O., & Moav, O. (2004). From physical to human capital accumulation: Inequality and the process of development. *The Review of Economic Studies, 71*(4), 1001−1026.

Galor, O., & Zeira, J. (1993). Income distribution and macroeconomics. *The Review of Economic Studies, 60*(1), 35−52.

Gasteiger, E., & Prettner, K. (2020). A note on automation, stagnation, and the implications of a robot tax. Discussion Paper 17/2017, Free University of Berlin, School of Business & Economics, Berlin.

Geiger, N., Prettner, K., & Schwarzer, J. (2018). Die Auswirkungen der Automatisierung, auf Wachstum, Beschäftigung und Ungleichheit. *Perspektiven der Wirtschaftspolitik, 19*(2), 59−77.

George, H. (1878). *Progress and poverty: An inquiry into the cause of industrial depressions and of increase of want with increase of wealth: the remedy.* New York, NY: Appleton and Company.

Giannelli, G. C., Jaenichen, U., & Rothe, T. (2016). The evolution of job stability and wages after the implementation of the Hartz reforms. *Journal for Labour Market Research*, *49*(3), 269–294.

Goldin, C., & Katz, L. (2009). *The race between education and technology*. Boston, MA: Harvard University Press.

Guerreiro, J., Rebelo, S., & Teles, P. (2018). *Should robots be taxed?* Cambridge, MA: NBER Working Paper 23806, National Bureau of Economic Research.

Hanushek, E. A., & Woessmann, L. (2012). Do better schools lead to more growth? Cognitive skills, economic outcomes, and causation. *Journal of Economic Growth*, *17*(4), 267–321.

Hanushek, E. A., & Woessmann, L. (2015). *The knowledge capital of nations: Education and the economics of growth*. Cambridge, MA: MIT Press.

IEA (International Energy Agency). (2016). World energy outlook 2016. Energy snapshots. Retrieved from https://www.iea.org/newsroom/energysnapshots/estimates-for-global-fossil-fuel-consumption-subsidies.html. Accessed 10.08.2018.

Jones, C. I. (1995). R&D-based models of economic growth. *Journal of Political Economy*, *103* (4), 759–783.

Korinek, A., & Stiglitz, J. (2017). *Artificial intelligence and its implications for income distribution and unemployment*. Cambridge, MA: National Bureau of Economic Research, NBER Working Paper 24174.

Kuhn, M., & Prettner, K. (2020). Automation in times of climate change. Mimeo: Vienna Institute of Demography.

Lordan, G. (2019). People versus machines in the UK: Minimum wages, labor reallocation and automatable jobs., IZA Discussion Paper No. 12716, Institute of Labor Economics (IZA), Bonn.

Lordan, G., & Neumark, D. (2018). People versus machines: The impact of minimum wages on automatable jobs. *Labour Economics*, *52*(2018), 40–53.

Lorentzen, P., McMillan, J., & Wacziarg, R. (2008). Death and development. *Journal of Economic Growth*, *13*(2), 81–124.

Lucas, R. E. (1988). On the mechanics of economic development. *Journal of Monetary Economics*, *22*(1), 3–42.

Lutz, W., Cuaresma, J. C., & Sanderson, W. (2008). The demography of educational attainment and economic growth. *Science*, *319*(5866), 1047–1048.

Pigou, A. (1920). *The economics of welfare*. London: McMillan.

Piketty, T. (2014). *Capital in the twenty-first century*. Cambridge, MA: Belknap Press of Harvard University Press.

Prettner, K., Geiger, N., & Schwarzer, J. (2018). Die wirtschaftlichen Folgen der Automatisierung. In C. Spiel, & R. Neck (Eds.), Automatisierung: Wechselwirkung mit Kunst, Wissenschaft und Gesellschaft. *Vienna, Austria*. Verlag: Böhlau.

Prettner, K., & Schaefer, A. (2020). The U-shape of income inequality over the 20th century: The role of education, *The Scandinavian Journal of Economics* (forthcoming).

Prettner, K., & Strulik, H. (2020). Innovation, automation, and inequality: policy challenges in the race against the machine. *Journal of Monetary Economics*. (forthcoming).

Prodhan, G. (2017). European parliament calls for robot law, rejects robot tax. Retrieved from http://www.reuters.com/article/us-europe-robots-lawmaking-idUSKBN15V2KM. Accessed 06.01.2017.

Rajan, R. (2010). *Fault lines: How hidden fractures still threaten the world economy*. Princeton, NJ: Princeton University Press.

Romer, P. (1990). Endogenous technological change. *Journal of Political Economy*, *98*(5), 71–102.

San Francisco Chronicle. (2018). Proposition 13 is no longer off-limits in California. Retrieved from https://www.sfchronicle.com/politics/article/Proposition-13-is-no-longer-off-limits-in-13492400.php. Accessed 25.11.2019.

Schwarzer, J. (2014). Growth as an objective of economic policy in the early 1960s: The role of aggregate demand. *Cahiers d'Économie Politique/Papers in Political Economy, 67*(2), 175–206.

Shastry, G. K., & Weil, D. N. (2003). How much of cross-country income variation is explained by health? *Journal of the European Economic Association, 1*(2/3), 387–396.

Strulik, H., Prettner, K., & Prskawetz, A. (2013). The past and future of knowledge-based growth. *Journal of Economic Growth, 18*(4), 411–437.

The Economist. (2013). Fuel subsidies in Indonesia: unpriming the pump. June 22, 2013.

The Economist. (2015). The Economist explains: The global addiction to energy subsidies. July 27, 2015.

The Economist. (2017). Fees high, foes fume: Two decades since their debut, tuition fees still spark arguments. July 6, 2017.

The Economist. (2018). On firmer ground: The time may be right for land-value taxes. August 9, 2018.

Tullock, G. (1967). Excess benefit. *Water Resources Research, 3*(2), 643–644.

Weil, D. (2007). Accounting for the effect of health on economic growth. *The Quarterly Journal of Economics, 122*(3), 1265–1306.

World Bank. (2019). *World development indicators 1960–2019*. Washington, DC: World Bank.

Chapter 8

Peering into the future: long-run economic and social consequences of automation; with an epilogue on COVID-19

This final chapter reviews and considers speculations on economic and social development in the context of further automation and progress in artificial intelligence (AI).[1] The treatment is naturally less theoretically and empirically rigorous than that of previous chapters. The intent is mainly to create awareness of these possibilities and to stimulate corresponding discussions—not to describe how we think the future will unfold. Thus, these discussions are more in the nature of conjectures and speculations than forecasts and predictions.

The main reason for this exercise is to raise important questions that society needs to address to prepare for and enable a desirable future in the age of automation and AI. The good news is that many of the potential developments will depend strongly on our own choices and policy responses, such that technology-driven scenarios of the future are not predestined but can be influenced to a substantial degree. Of course, technological progress itself is unlikely to reverse—provided that we manage to prevent catastrophic outcomes associated with, for example, large-scale wars, pandemic diseases, a plethora of extreme weather episodes, and other low-probability but high-impact events (see, e.g., Taleb, 2007 for discussions). Therefore, we must make certain choices to prepare economic and legal systems to contend with the evolving technology and culture. We can shape these choices to try to distribute the benefits of automation and digitalization so that as many people as possible will benefit. If we fail to ensure that wide parts of the population benefit, we risk increasing inequality and that some parts of the population will become disconnected from economic development. These parts of the population might face economic misery, which, in turn, could lead to social, political, and economic instabilities. In addition to the looming

---

1. We thank an anonymous reviewer for suggesting that we delve deeper into many of these topics and for interesting literature suggestions.

Automation and its Macroeconomic Consequences. DOI: https://doi.org/10.1016/B978-0-12-818028-0.00008-9

economic developments, more fundamental and dramatic changes lie ahead: our daily interactions with personal robots could transform society as we currently understand it. These changes range from more standard applications that we have already grown used to, such as personal digital assistants, algorithms that help judges and probation officers form their decisions, robo advisors, and robo counselors; to the next step of personalized pricing of different items based on the analysis of big data; on to social credit scores (described in the following) and deployment of robots in the realms of old-age care and sexual interactions; and finally to human−machine interfaces.

8.1 Joblessness, misery, and deaths of despair or "the happy leisure society"?

Failure to address the problems associated with rising inequality in the course of automation raises a strong possibility of negative repercussions on economic and social outcomes. Plenty of evidence indicates that inequality has risen in many countries in the world and that technological progress plays a major role in explaining this growing divide (Acemoglu, 2002; Atkinson, 2015; Atkinson, Piketty, & Saez, 2011; Autor & Dorn, 2013; Chetty, Hendren, Kline, Saez, & Turner, 2014; OECD Organisation for Economic Co-operation & Development, 2011; Piketty, 2014). Rising inequality, in turn, tends to reduce intergenerational income mobility, a phenomenon known as the "Great Gatsby Curve" (Chetty et al., 2014; Corak, 2013). If this process continues because, for example, the parts of the population with lower incomes cannot invest in their own education or in the education of their children (Galor & Zeira, 1993; Prettner & Schaefer, 2020; Prettner & Strulik, 2020) or because low-income households often lack access to adequate health insurance such that catastrophic expenditures loom in case of illness, then poverty traps emerge from which escape is difficult. Because a decent education and good health are themselves important drivers of economic growth (Becker & Woessmann, 2009; Bloom, Canning, Kotschy, Prettner, & Schünemann, 2019; Cervellati & Sunde, 2011; Hanushek & Woessmann, 2012, 2015; Strulik, Prettner, & Prskawetz, 2013), a feedback loop would emerge between higher inequality and overall sluggish economic development (Eggertsson, Mehrotra, & Robbins, 2019; Galor & Zeira, 1993; OECD, 2015; Summers, 2014).

However, some effects of high inequality and low social mobility are arguably more worrying than negative repercussions on economic growth. For example, the economic hardship of certain parts of the population could contribute to the phenomenon of "deaths of despair" (The Commonwealth Fund, 2019). Case and Deaton (2015) show that the mortality rate among white, middle-aged U.S. men has been rising over the last two decades, mainly due to suicides, alcohol abuse, and drug addiction. The problem is already so severe that despite the falling mortality of other population groups, average life expectancy at birth in the United States is falling—a problem now spreading to other countries as well (*The Economist*, 2019c). The wide disparities between the health of low- and high-income groups in the United States are best illustrated by the differences in the probability of a 50-year-old person reaching age 85. Based on the predictions of the National Academies of Sciences, Engineering, and Medicine (2015), this probability is 29% for the lowest income quintile and 72% for the highest income quintile, which translates into a gap in life expectancy of 13 years between these two groups (Kufenko, Prettner, & Sousa-Poza, 2019). Deaths of despair might be one phenomenon explaining the rise in overall health-related inequality among different socioeconomic groups.

Rising inequality not only results in those with higher incomes affording ever more material goods and staying healthier longer than those with lower incomes, but it also implies advantages in terms of political influence. Page, Bartels, and Seawright (2013) and Gilens and Page (2014) analyze U.S. voter preferences by income group and compare the results to enacted laws. They find that laws are much more likely to pass when the top 10% of income earners prefer them because these "elite" persons are more likely to donate to political parties or to interact with their representatives than people from lower income groups. Thus, clear signs indicate that we are exacerbating cronyism in society, with high inequality, plenty of political influence of the elites, poverty traps and low social mobility, and widespread despair among the poor. This polarization can be reproduced in the political process, which risks becoming increasingly dysfunctional as the discontent of the masses is reflected in "anger votes" in favor of candidates with immoderate views, or in favor of measures that claim to restore national strength such as Brexit. Such extreme measures are, however, often not in the best interest of the disadvantaged themselves. Ford (2015) draws an even more dystopian scenario in which the rich use robots and AI to suppress the poor, keeping them in line while preventing them from sharing in the gains of economic prosperity.

Fortunately, another possibility exists. As Keynes (1930a, 1930b) imagined, technological progress could be beneficial to the population at large and might enable people to enjoy greater material well-being, more choices, and the luxury of spending more time doing things they are interested in and at which they excel. Widespread automation in its strict sense could indeed, for the first time, lead to a situation in which wealth is created purely with the input of the production factor physical capital and the role that humans play might be to lie in a hammock reading and reflecting on "Das Kapital." Less benign interpretations include projections that the masses would need to be contented with certain forms of "tittytainment" (Martin & Schumann, 1996) or pursue working in "bullshit jobs" (Graeber, 2018) from which deriving any meaning is difficult.

How can we ensure we are on a path to a bright future with widespread benefits of automation and digitalization? Chapter 7 discussed potential policy measures that could point us in this direction. While many of the ideas are controversial (to say the least), there are some policy measures on which many economists and policymakers might be able to agree. First and foremost among them is the proposal to invest massively in education in general and, more specifically, to ensure that disadvantaged parts of the population have access to quality education (e.g., via means-tested or merit-based stipends, tuition fee waivers, student housing) (see Cohen, Bloom, & Malin, 2006). Revamping curricula to ensure that future generations have the hard and soft skills needed to adapt to fast-changing technological environments as smoothly as possible is also important. High-quality education is a first and invaluable step to increase the share of the population that benefits from automation, though we have seen that education will not solve all potential challenges.

As a second and complementary measure, ensuring that those who lose the race against the machine do not end up without social protection is thus important. Of course, designing policies that help to reduce inequality and, at the same time, do not hinder economic development can be difficult (Prettner & Strulik, 2020). Therefore, devising nondistortionary ways of financing social security and wealth redistribution that benefit the disadvantaged but do not influence their choices *a priori* will become more important. We have discussed some innovative ways of doing this, such as an alternative tax system based on taxing harmful activities or taxing more heavily those groups and sectors with a more inelastic tax base.

Third, we have described different measures that help low-income parts of the population benefit from automation (e.g., by ensuring that employees have a stake in future earnings generated by highly profitable firms in the age of automation and digitalization). Overall, we hope to have contributed in providing the basis for more intensive discussions and debate in these areas and think that, however they might unfold, such deliberations are imperative. In the following, we discuss some more profound social changes that could occur in the wake of automation and to which it might be even more difficult to adjust. In this context, keeping in mind that institutional change is usually evolutionary—which is not well suited to adapting to technological change, which is often revolutionary—is important.

8.2 Spatial and regional implications: the future of cities

Fundamental social and economic changes could emerge via progress in autonomous driving or when fully automated factories, with physical locations that will be diminished in relevance, become operable. We have already reflected on the potential economic consequences of millions of taxi drivers and truck drivers being replaced by algorithms. However, autonomous driving might also fundamentally change the way we live and the way that our cities are designed. First, if the driving time that is required to commute to and from work could be put to alternative uses such as sleeping, preparing for meetings, reading and responding to emails, or simply watching movies, the opportunity costs of commuting decrease substantially. This could lead to a change in urbanization patterns such that living areas might move even farther from city centers into areas with—at least initially—a more beautiful landscape, less pollution, less noise, a better microclimate, etc. In this case, cities might become mainly business districts and centers for entertainment in which people meet to interact because of work or for social reasons. The convenience of autonomous driving and the prospect of not owning vehicles but just hailing them on demand could potentially substitute for public mass transport and, in conjunction with increasing traffic because of urban sprawl, also exert negative environmental and congestion effects. However, as the creator of the problem, technological progress also might offer a solution to the problem. First, better management of private transport could become possible by implementing congestion-dependent toll systems on roads (because every vehicle can be location-tracked accurately) and by incentivizing car sharing (e.g., by giving shared cars access to priority lanes) such that one car might not only transport more than a person or two, but also packages, which *ceteris paribus* would reduce the overall amount of traffic. The uniform speed with which autonomous cars operate could also plausibly benefit traffic flow, as compared with the current situation in which individual drivers are inclined to drive at variable speeds, which tends to be inefficient. Also, fewer accidents might result from autonomous driving, reducing not only the number of deaths and injuries on the road (Chen, Kuhn, Prettner, & Bloom, 2019), but also congestion, allowing the average speed of vehicles to increase.

Furthermore, a new mode of transport—in between the extreme cases of mass public transport systems and private cars—could conceivably emerge: small autonomous buses could connect popular places cheaply and at a relatively high frequency, or they could be used to transport people on demand between locations that only have occasional traffic spurts (e.g., in case of sporting events, concerts). This could be a much more convenient form of transport than mass public transit, but it would also be more environmentally friendly and safer, and create less congestion than private car use.

As far as the environmental impact of increased traffic is concerned, technology could facilitate a reduction in combustion engines in favor of electric cars and changes in the way that electricity is produced and distributed. This way, traffic could become so efficient and clean that the environmental impact of transportation is reduced despite the potential overall increase in traffic. Also, the need to produce cars at all might decrease because, currently, private cars tend to sit idle more than 95% of the time (*Fortune*, 2016; NRMA, 2017). Using shared autonomous cars could thus reduce the overall number of cars because of a more efficient use of already extant cars. The reduced need for car production, in turn, would have positive environmental repercussions. Finally, the need for designated parking areas that tend to be sealed by asphalt would decrease. These areas could partly be used for public parks and recreational areas, which might improve the microclimate in cities.

Even more radically and over a longer time horizon, the network effects of cities and their economic attractiveness in terms of economies of scale could change because it becomes ever more convenient and efficient to (1) work from home and nevertheless stay connected, (2) produce goods where land is cheap (e.g., by means of three-dimensional printing or by fully automated factories) instead of where numerous suitably trained workers are available, and (3) transport goods from different locations to customers who live far apart (e.g., by means of delivery robots and drones). If the network externalities are greatly reduced in such a way, the benefits of urbanization would shrink drastically and urbanization could reverse.

While many of the aforementioned forces could reverse urbanization and reduce land and property prices in cities, major forces would still pull in the opposite direction. For example, (1) living in cities has a social cachet and some people prefer to live near bars, pubs, restaurants, theaters, etc., and to enjoy more options for goods and services on which to spend their money;[2] (2) in many countries and areas, population growth remains positive, which raises demand for housing and infrastructure; (3) incomes are rising, which allows more people to afford second homes or to increase the size of their first home by moving into a larger apartment/house; (4) the need for space for some types of activities could still grow dramatically (e.g., office space for doctors and psychotherapists, sales areas of luxury stores that tend to be located in city centers, theaters, and amusement parks); (5) zoning restrictions might prevent residential development and constrain housing supply, contributing to rising property values and land prices; and (6) the creation of public parks and recreational areas as mentioned previously might also require additional amounts of space.

8.3 The question of how we care for each other

But even beyond these changes, more fundamental shifts and corresponding decisions to confront are to be expected. How will robots change the way we interact with and care for each other? As far as the adoption of robots as nurses and caregivers is concerned, Japan is a forerunner (Moro, Lin, Nejat, & Mihailidis, 2019; *The Economist*, 2017) and will thus act as a model. Robots that become ever better substitutes for assisting with the care of older people could revolutionize the way we spend the last years of our lives. Instead of institutionalized care away from home or close family members

---

2. In addition, social services and infrastructure spending are more efficient in cities due to economies of scale (Bloom, Canning, & Fink, 2008).

having to shoulder the burden of care, robot nurses could help with showering, going to the bathroom, preparing food, distributing medication, and promoting adherence to drug protocols. In addition, robots appear to help to alleviate loneliness in old age and may even help in combating diseases such as dementia (Costescu, Vanderborght, & David, 2014; Vitelli, 2014).

That sex robots will revolutionize the pornography industry and prostitution is easy to imagine. However, they might also change the nature of human interactions altogether, and the legal and ethical challenges of interacting with sex robots are nascently understood (Sharkey, van Wynsberghe, Robbins, & Hancock, 2017). Will sex robots be banned in some countries— or states—and allowed in others? How will the use of sex robots affect psychological well-being and loneliness? How will sex robots change actual and perceived gender roles in a society? Regarding these aspects, much will depend on the evolution of the legal system and whether it treats robots like property or more like independent entities that deserve protection. For example, the debate on whether to ban programming sex robots as nonconsenting victims, which simulates sexual assault, is ongoing (Danaher, 2014; Sharkey et al., 2017; Sparrow, 2017).

In the judicial system itself, algorithms already help judges and probation officers with their decisions. While a first glance might suggest that decisions made by algorithms would be fairer than those made by humans because they are deemed to be free of biases and preconceptions, algorithms often tend to have or develop racial and gender biases that are difficult to trace back (see, e.g., O'Neil, 2016). In addition, the line between employing algorithms to assist humans in judicial decisions and crime prevention and suppressing (parts of) the population is fine. Using AI and big data for public surveillance and to induce "good" behavior in people is easy.[3] This could be done, for example, by means of a social credit system, where a social credit score is calculated for citizens and points are deducted for behavior classified as detrimental, such as crimes, traffic violations, and the late payment of bills (see *The Economist*, 2019b). While some claim that such systems lead to socially desirable outcomes, one should keep in mind that autocratic governments can deploy such systems to impair free speech, for example, by deducting points for criticizing the government.

In addition, other potentially highly disturbing possibilities lie ahead related to the use of military robots. These could be used to outsource the decision of whom to attack to an algorithm (Hellström, 2013). Furthermore, of course, nothing would prevent the use of these robots against internal enemies, raising the question of how much autonomy the robots will have in deciding who qualifies as an "enemy." In this case, we would be close to the

---

3. This observation brings to mind the 2002 blockbuster movie Minority Report, in which individuals are (based on a psychic technology) arrested to prevent future crimes they would otherwise commit.

dystopian scenario mentioned previously that Ford (2015) describes, in which an elite relies on robots and AI to suppress the rest of the population.

8.4 The meaning of being human

Future technological progress could even shake the foundations of what it means to be human. While a rather conventional way of racing against the machine is to invest in education, another way is human enhancement. Enormous progress has taken place in transcranial direct current stimulation, transcranial magnetic stimulation, and neuropharmacology over the last decade (Bavelier, Levi, Li, Dan, & Hensch, 2010; Coffman, Clark, & Parasuraman, 2014; Luber & Lisanby, 2014; Sale, Berardi, & Maffei, 2014). For example, Chi and Snyder (2012) show that humans who struggle to solve very difficult problems are better able to solve them after stimulating the anterior temporal lobe—a part of the brain important for the knowledge of objects, people, words, and facts. According to the authors, none of the trial participants were able to solve the so-called nine-dot problem (to connect nine dots in three rows by means of four lines without raising the pen) before treatment, whereas after 10 minutes of temporal lobe stimulation, 40% of participants were. In another example, Nelson, McKinley, Golob, Warm, and Parasuraman (2014) used transcranial direct current stimulation in a simulated air traffic control exercise for which performance among participants tends to drop over time. As compared with a placebo treatment, those who received the real treatment exhibited improvement in the rate of detecting planes on a collision course and higher cerebral blood velocity and cerebral oxygenation, which are associated with higher levels of vigilance.

While some physical devices for human augmentation, such as smart sunglasses that take videos of the surroundings and place them in the view of the wearer or exoskeletons that strengthen body parts, make physical work easier, or allow the paralyzed to walk, are already quite common and rather uncontroversial, the question of what it means to be human will become somewhat more blurred with the feasibility of genetic engineering, neural implants, and brain−machine interfaces (Li, Walker, Nie, & Zhang, 2019; Ma, 2018; The Economist, 2019a; Velleste, Perel, Spalding, Whitford, & Schwartz, 2008; Young, 2017). Overall, the most radical prediction related to the interaction between humans and AI is that of the "Singularity" made by futurist Raymond Kurzweil (2005) as mentioned in the introductory chapter. According to this prediction, machine intelligence and human intelligence will merge at some point and become infinitely more powerful than what we understand as intelligence today. If and when this happens, it will transform human life in a way that is currently difficult to comprehend.

Most developments in human augmentation are currently in their infancy, and assessing their potential effects is very difficult as of 2020. Altogether, however, evidence and trends indicate that increasing the performance of the human brain—sometimes with little effort—and, thus, staying competitive with machines for longer will be medically possible. Furthermore, developments in the area of CRISPR/Cas tools (by which genes can be removed or added at specified locations in the genome of a cell) make genetic engineering as another form of human augmentation ever more feasible—one that has already been used based on very questionable ethical foundations (Li et al., 2019). That people would be willing to use these methods/devices is easy to imagine, such that increasing prevalence of human enhancement by more controversial methods might only be a matter of time. The moral and legal questions of whether human enhancement should be welcomed or treated like doping in sports will definitely provide food for thought for ethicists, philosophers, and lawmakers in the near future. How society evolves in these areas will depend on the laws and regulations that governments and citizens choose to enact to cope with the new technologies and their potential challenges. What will civilization accept as the new normal of an automated society? Much will depend on the choices we make and the answers we give. So we had better engage in a serious and inclusive process of social discourse on these matters.

8.5 Epilogue on COVID-19

This book was written, reviewed, and finalized in 2019 and early 2020, before the COVID-19 pandemic engulfed the world, claiming the lives of hundreds of thousands, infecting millions, and significantly constraining the mobility and the social and economic interactions of billions.

The COVID-19 pandemic (and the realistic prospects of other dangerous pathogens lurking in our future) confirms or sharpens many of the key messages this book covers and brings some others into focus.

In support of this point, we offer four observations.

First, automation, robotics, modern information and communication technologies, and artificial intelligence (AI) enabled many enterprises to continue to operate, many workers to continue to work, and many individuals to socially distance effectively. Generally speaking, more educated, more skilled, and higher-income individuals have been better positioned to take advantage of these opportunities. As such, automation and related technologies are channeling the COVID-19 shock into greater social and economic inequality. The disproportionate impact of COVID-19 infections on disadvantaged racial and ethnic minorities, those with poor nutrition and health care access, those reliant on public transportation, and those whose economic situations are relatively precarious further magnifies this effect.

Second, the COVID-19 pandemic is likely to accelerate the development and implementation of automation, robotic, and AI technologies. This acceleration reflects greater incentives to substitute capital for labor—incentives associated with the fact that machines are immune to the pathogens that infect humans (though they are vulnerable to digital pathogens, as demonstrated by disruptive and costly episodes running the gamut from worms and viruses to malware and ransomware). In addition, working from home—which smart technologies facilitate—is likely to become a significantly more prominent feature of economic activity.

Third, smart technologies have tremendous value in enabling social distancing, disease surveillance, and contact tracing. Indeed, apps have already been designed and implemented in various countries to cross-classify symptoms of COVID-19 infection (both self-reported and direct measures) with a continuous set of smart-phone-derived geographic information system coordinates to monitor patterns of movement and interaction. Such apps can minimize the inconvenience, unpleasantness, and cost of large-scale COVID-19 testing and allow policymakers to get a fix on the progression of COVID-19 (and other dangerous pathogens) and the appropriateness of different social and economic policies. Smart technologies can also facilitate the provision of health diagnoses and advice without face-to-face contact. However, they are limited by network coverage, access to devices, and willingness and ability to engage with the app.

Fourth, the supply chain, trade, and travel disruptions caused by the COVID-19 pandemic are likely to undermine the integration of national (and perhaps some local) economies and to increase the value of self-contained and self-reliant economic systems, possibly offsetting the impulse in favor of increased social and economic inequality in the process. Diminishing the opportunities to take advantage of efficiencies in the international division of labor will increase costs of production and prices, slowing the pace of economic growth and changing the incentives for developing new technologies.

The bottom line is that COVID-19 is seeding the future of automation with both opportunities and challenges. These are accentuated by the realization that humanity faces the prospect of other major outbreaks and epidemics. Whatever the mix of defensive and offensive economic postures adopted by the private and public sectors, we are confident that smart technologies will play an increasingly significant role.

References

Acemoglu, D. (2002). Directed technical change. *The Review of Economic Studies*, *69*(4), 781–809.

Atkinson, A. (2015). *Inequality: What can be done*. Cambridge, MA: Harvard University Press.

Atkinson, A., Piketty, T., & Saez, E. (2011). Top incomes in the long run of history. *Journal of Economic Literature*, *49*(1), 3–71.

Autor, D. H., & Dorn, D. (2013). The growth of low-skill service jobs and the polarization of the US labor market. *American Economic Review*, *103*(5), 1553–1597.

Bavelier, D., Levi, D., Li, R., Dan, Y., & Hensch, T. (2010). Removing brakes on adult brain plasticity: From molecular to behavioral interventions. *Journal of Neuroscience*, *30*(45), 14964–14971.

Becker, S., & Woessmann, L. (2009). Was Weber wrong? A human capital theory of protestant economic history. *The Quarterly Journal of Economics, 124*(2), 531–596.

Bloom, D. E., Canning, D., & Fink, G. (2008). Urbanization and the wealth of nations. *Science, 319*(5864), 772–775.

Bloom, D. E., Canning, D., Kotschy, R., Prettner, K., & Schünemann, J. (2019). Health and economic growth: Reconciling the micro and macro evidence. NBER Working Paper No. 26003, National Bureau of Economic Research, Cambridge, MA.

Case, A., & Deaton, A. (2015). Rising morbidity and mortality in midlife among white non-Hispanic Americans in the 21st century. *Proceedings of the National Academy of Sciences of the United States of America, 112*(49), 15078–15083.

Cervellati, M., & Sunde, U. (2011). Life expectancy and economic growth: The role of the demographic transition. *Journal of Economic Growth, 16*(2), 99–133.

Chen, S., Kuhn, M., Prettner, K., & Bloom, D. E. (2019). The global macroeconomic burden of road injuries: Estimates and projections for 166 countries. *The Lancet Planetary Health, 3*(9), 390–398.

Chetty, R., Hendren, N., Kline, P., Saez, E., & Turner, N. (2014). Is the United States still a land of opportunity? Recent trends in intergenerational mobility. *American Economic Review, 105*(5), 141–147.

Chi, R., & Snyder, A. (2012). Brain stimulation enables the solution of an inherently difficult problem. *Neuroscience Letters, 515*(2), 121–124.

Cohen, J. E., Bloom, D. E., & Malin, M. (Eds.), (2006). *Educating all children: A global agenda.* Cambridge, MA: American Academy of Arts and Sciences/MIT Press.

Coffman, B., Clark, V., & Parasuraman, R. (2014). Battery powered thought: Enhancement of attention, learning, and memory in healthy adults using transcranial direct current stimulation. *NeuroImage, 85*(3), 895–908.

Corak, M. (2013). Income inequality, equality of opportunity, and intergenerational mobility. *Journal of Economic Perspectives, 27*(3), 79–102.

Costescu, C., Vanderborght, B., & David, D. (2014). The effects of robot-enhanced psychotherapy: A meta-analysis. *Review of General Psychology, 18*(2), 127–136.

Danaher, J. (2014). Robotic rape and robotic child sexual abuse: Should they be criminalised? *Criminal Law and Philosophy, 11*(1), 71–95.

Eggertsson, G., Mehrotra, N., & Robbins, J. (2019). A model of secular stagnation: Theory and quantitative evaluation. *American Economic Journal: Macroeconomics, 11*(1), 1–48.

Ford, M. (2015). *Rise of the robots: Technology and the threat of a jobless future.* New York: Basic Books.

Fortune. (2016). Today's cars are parked 95% of the time. Available from https://fortune.com/2016/03/13/cars-parked-95-percent-of-time/. Accessed 25.11.2019.

Galor, O., & Zeira, J. (1993). Income distribution and macroeconomics. *The Review of Economic Studies, 60*(1), 35–52.

Gilens, M., & Page, B. (2014). Testing theories of American politics: Elites, interest groups, and average citizens. *Perspectives on Politics, 12*(3), 564–581.

Graeber, D. (2018). *Bullshit jobs: A theory.* New York: Simon & Schuster.

Hanushek, E. A., & Woessmann, L. (2012). Do better schools lead to more growth? Cognitive skills, economic outcomes, and causation. *Journal of Economic Growth, 17*(4), 267–321.

Hanushek, E. A., & Woessmann, L. (2015). *The knowledge capital of nations: Education and the economics of growth.* Cambridge, MA: MIT Press.

Hellström, T. (2013). On the moral responsibility of military robots. *Ethics and Information Technology, 15*(2), 99–107.

Keynes, J. (1930a). Economic possibilities for our grandchildren. *The Nation and Athenaeum*, *48*(2), 36−37.

Keynes, J. (1930b). Economic possibilities for our grandchildren. *The Nation and Athenaeum*, *48*(3), 96−98.

Kufenko, V., Prettner, K., & Sousa-Poza, A. (2019). The economics of ageing and inequality: Introduction to the special issue. *The Journal of the Economics of Ageing*, *14*, 1−14.

Kurzweil, R. (2005). *The singularity is near: When humans transcend biology*. London: Penguin Books.

Li, J.-R., Walker, S., Nie, J.-B., & Zhang, J.-G. (2019). Experiments that led to the first gene-edited babies: The ethical failings and the urgent need for better governance. *Journal of Zhejiang University*, *20*(1), 32−38.

Luber, B., & Lisanby, S. (2014). Enhancement of human cognitive performance using transcranial magnetic stimulation (TMS). *NeuroImage*, *85*(3), 961−970.

Ma, A. (2018). Thousands of people in Sweden are embedding microchips under their skin to replace ID cards. *The Business Insider*, May 2018. Available from https://www.businessinsider.com/swedish-people-embed-microchips-under-skin-to-replace-id-cards-2018-5? r = DE&IR = T?r = US&IR = T. Accessed 22.12.2019.

Martin, H.-P., & Schumann, H. (1996). *The global trap*. Berlin: Rowohlt Verlag.

Moro, C., Lin, S., Nejat, G., & Mihailidis, A. (2019). Social robots and seniors: A comparative study on the influence of dynamic social features on human−robot interaction. *International Journal of Social Robotics*, *11*(1), 5−24.

National Academies of Sciences, Engineering, and Medicine. (2015). *The growing gap in life expectancy by income: Implications for federal programs and policy responses*. Washington, DC: National Academies Press.

Nelson, J., McKinley, R., Golob, E., Warm, J., & Parasuraman, R. (2014). Enhancing vigilance in operators with prefrontal cortex transcranial direct current stimulation (tDCS). *NeuroImage*, *85* (3), 911−919.

NRMA (National Roads and Motorists' Association). (2017). The future of car ownership. Available from https://www.mynrma.com.au/-/media/documents/reports-and-subs/the-future-of-car-ownership.pdf?la = en. Accessed 25.11.2019.

OECD (Organisation for Economic Co-operation and Development). (2011). Divided we stand: Why inequality keeps rising. OECD Publishing, Paris. Available from https://doi.org/10.1787/9789264119536-en. Accessed 22.12.2019.

OECD (Organisation for Economic Co-operation and Development). (2015). In it together: Why less inequality benefits all. OECD Publishing, Paris. Available from https://doi.org/10.1787/9789264235120-en. Accessed 22.12.2019.

O'Neil, C. (2016). *Weapons of math destruction: How big data increases inequality and threatens democracy*. New York: Crown Publishing Group.

Page, B., Bartels, L., & Seawright, J. (2013). Democracy and the policy preferences of wealthy Americans. *Perspectives on Politics*, *11*(1), 51−73.

Piketty, T. (2014). *Capital in the twenty-first century*. Cambridge, MA: Belknap Press of Harvard University Press.

Prettner, K., & Schaefer, A. (2020). The U-shape of income inequality over the 20th century: The role of education, *The Scandinavian Journal of Economics* (forthcoming).

Prettner, K., & Strulik, H. (2020). Innovation, automation, and inequality: Policy challenges in the race against the machine. *Journal of Monetary Economics* (forthcoming).

Sale, A., Berardi, N., & Maffei, L. (2014). Environment and brain plasticity: Towards an endogenous pharmacotherapy. *Physiological Reviews*, *94*(1), 189−234.

Sharkey, N., van Wynsberghe, A., Robbins, S., & Hancock, E. (2017). Our sexual future with robots: A foundation for responsible robotics consultation report. Available from https://responsiblerobotics.org/2017/07/05/frr-report-our-sexual-future-with-robots/. Accessed 22.12.2019.

Sparrow, R. (2017). Robots, rape, and representation. *International Journal of Social Robotics, 9* (4), 465−477.

Strulik, H., Prettner, K., & Prskawetz, A. (2013). The past and future of knowledge based growth. *Journal of Economic Growth, 18*(4), 411−437.

Summers, L. (2014). US economic prospects: Secular stagnation, hysteresis, and the zero lower bound. *Business Economics, 49*(2), 65−73.

Taleb, N. N. (2007). *The black swan: The impact of the highly improbable.* New York: Random House Books.

The Commonwealth Fund (2019). 2019 Scorecard on state health system performance. Available from https://scorecard.commonwealthfund.org/files/Radley_State_Scorecard_2019.pdf. Accessed 22.12.2019.

The Economist (2017). Machine caring: Japan is embracing nursing-care robots. November 23, 2017.

The Economist (2019a). Brain-machine interfaces. Elon Musk wants to link brains directly to machines. July 18, 2019.

The Economist (2019b). Keeping tabs. China's "social credit" scheme involves cajolery and sanctions. March 28, 2019.

The Economist (2019c). The economics of death. Deaths of despair, once an American phenomenon, now haunt Britain. May 16, 2019.

Velleste, M., Perel, S., Spalding, M., Whitford, A., & Schwartz, A. (2008). Cortical control of a prosthetic arm for self-feeding. *Nature, 543*(June 2008), 1098−1101.

Vitelli, R. (2014). The rise of the robot therapist. *Psychology Today*, November 17, 2014. Available from https://www.psychologytoday.com/us/blog/media-spotlight/201411/the-rise-the-robot-therapist. Accessed 22.12.2019.

Young, L. (2017). A spectrum of human augmentation. *Strategic Business Insights*, April 2017. Available from http://www.strategicbusinessinsights.com/about/featured/2017/2017-04-spectrum-human-augmentation.shtml. Accessed 22.12.2019.

Index

Note: Page numbers followed by "*f*" and "*t*" refer to figures and tables, respectively.

A

Adoption of automation technology, 21–22
Advanced Chess, 12–13
Age of automation
  social security in, 197–201
  taxation in, 192–197
Age-related noncommunicable diseases,
  174–175
Aggregate demand, 3, 53
  for labor, 190
Aggregate investment, 76–78
Aggregate production function, 70–75, 149
Aggregate social welfare, 104–106
Aging, 173–174
Agricultural production, 3–4
Artificial intelligence (AI), 9, 47
  based strategic reasoning, 10
Automation-augmented OLG model, 148–149
Automation capital, 90–96, 138–139, 147,
  172–173
Autonomous AI-based weapons, 10
Autonomous driving, 8–9

B

Balanced growth path, 72, 75–76, 93–95,
  99–100
Bordered Hessian matrix, 119–120
Budget constraint, 117, 122, 142–143

C

Canonical overlapping generations (OLG)
  model, 113–114, 140–141, 141*f*,
  144–145
  with automation, 149
  without technological progress, 145*f*
Capital accumulation, 132, 193
Capital gains tax, 192
Capital stock, 76–78, 80–81, 129, 137–138
Capital-to-labor ratio of economy, 149–150
Carbon dioxide (CO_2) emissions, 196

CES production function. *See* Constant
  elasticity of substitution (CES)
  production function
Cobb–Douglas production function, 72–75,
  78–80, 83–84, 92, 132, 144, 146,
  172–173
Complementary slackness, 123
Computable OLG models, 140–141
Congestion-dependent toll systems, 8–9,
  212–213
Constant elasticity of substitution (CES)
  production function, 61
Constraints, 117
Consumption Euler equation, 126, 129–131,
  137–138, 143, 147
Consumption path, 127–128
Continuous time
  consumption Euler equation in, 129–130
  dynamic optimization in, 126–131
  growth rates in, 67–69
Control variable, 126–127
Convergence process, 75–76, 87–88, 93–95,
  107–108, 137–138, 145–146
Cookbook-procedures/recipes
  for dynamic optimization, 124–131
  for static optimization, 115–124
Corporate taxation, 197
Costate variable, 127–128
CRISPR/Cas tools, 216–217
Cross-country evidence, on economic
  consequences of automation, 51–62
Cross-country income inequality, 24–26

D

Deaths of despair, 198, 210–212
Declining child mortality, 165–166
Deep learning, 152
Demand-side policies, 201–202
Demographic change, 168–171
Demographic dividend, 169

Dependency ratio, 168–169
Derivative of variable, 67
Differential equations, two-dimensional
    system of, 133
Digitalization, 10–11
Direct brain–machine interfaces, 13
Direct education costs, 188–189
Direct tax, 192–193
Discount factor, 124–125, 127
Discrete time
    growth rates in, 67–69
    Solow model in, 75–83, 79f
Double dividend, 196
Dynamic optimization, cookbook procedures
    for, 114–131
    in continuous time, 126–131
    in discrete time, 124–126
Dynamic programming, 124–126

E

Earned income tax credit (EIT), 199
Economic aggregates, 67
Economic challenges of automation,
    11, 188
Economic consequences
    of automation, 5–7, 51
        cross-country evidence on, 51–62
    of declining fertility, 169–170
    of demographic developments, 168–171
Economic development, 34–35, 80
Economic growth and welfare, dynamics of,
    22–30
The Economic Miracle, 27–28, 138,
    145–146
Economic model, 68
Economics of superstars, 6, 40
Economists, 2, 7–8
Economy-wide aggregate variables, 69
Education, 11
    investing in children, 26–27
    investments, 176–177, 190
    as strategy to cope with the negative effects
        of automation, 188–190
    substantial costs of, 188–189
Effective labor, 86–87
EIT. See Earned income tax credit (EIT)
Elasticity, 143
    of substitution, 61
Employment, 53–56
Employment projections based on automation,
    175–176
Endogenous savings
    in OLG model, 140–147

in Ramsey–Cass–Koopmans model,
    131–138
Endogenous technological progress and
    automation, 150–152
Environmental impact of transportation,
    213–214
European Commission, 9, 197
Exoskeletons, 174–175
Expansionary fiscal policy, 201–202

F

Female labor force, 169
Fertility rates, 163–164
Fiscal policy, 201–202
Financing social security systems, 12, 187,
    212
First-order conditions (FOCs), 118–119, 128
Foreign direct investment (FDI), 154–156
Fossil fuel subsidies abolishing/reducing,
    196–197
Freestyle Chess, 12–13
Frictional unemployment, 191–192
Functional income distribution, 38–39

G

Gaussian process classifier, 47
GDP. See Gross domestic product (GDP)
General equilibrium adjustment mechanisms,
    59
General solution of differential equations, 83
Gini coefficient, 29–30, 35–37
Great Depression, 34–36
Great Gatsby Curve, 210
Great Recession, 21
Gross domestic product (GDP), 24–26,
    29–30, 67
    logarithm of, 28f, 29f
Gross market incomes, 37

H

Hartz reforms, 191–192
Health insurance systems, 197–198, 203
Heterogeneity, 69
Hicks-neutral technological progress, 72
High-quality education, 211–212
High-skilled workers, 101–102, 108, 153
Hours worked, 31–32, 31f, 32f, 41
Households, behavioral changes of, 169
Human, meaning of being, 216–217
Human augmentation, 13, 216–217
Human capital, 82, 171, 178
Human intelligence, 216
Human labor, 47–48, 61, 196

I

IFR. *See* International Federation of Robotics (IFR)
Inada conditions, 71
Inada-type conditions, 116–117
Income distribution, 38–39
Income effect, 141–142
Increasing life expectancy, 165–166, 171
Industrial Revolution, 1, 22–24, 26–27, 191
Industrial robots, 7, 21, 27–28, 51–56, 175–176, 187
   diffusion, 21–22
   effects of investment in, 53–56
Inequality, 210–211
Inequality aversion, 104–107
Inequality, evolution of, 34–41
Inheritance tax, 192
Inquiry into the Nature and Causes of the Wealth of Nations, An (Smith), 1–2
Instantaneous utility, 127
Institutionalized care services, 7–8
International Federation of Robotics (IFR), 21, 23*t*, 51–53, 173
International trade, 154–156
Internet, 6
Inverse demand functions, 74–75
Investment in education, 26–27
Investment vehicles, 92–93
Isoelastic functions, 104–106, 141

J

Joblessness, 210–212
Judicial system, 215

K

Kaldor–Hicks efficiency, 107
Kaldor's stylized facts, 38–39
Karush–Kuhn–Tucker method, 123–124
Kuznets Curve relationship, 34–35

L

Labor-augmenting technological progress, 72–74
Labor demand, 59–60
Labor force, 172–173
   dynamics, 30–34
Labor income share, 7, 38–39, 60–61, 75, 96–97
   declining, 199
Labor income tax, 192
Labor-intensive services, 3–4
Labor market, 56–58

policies, 190–192
Labor-saving machines, 2
Labor taxes, 203
Lagrange method, 115–126, 142–144
Lagrangian function, 118, 120–123
Land value tax, 195–196
L'Hospital's rule, 141–142
Life expectancy
   at birth, 164–165, 164*f*, 165*t*
   declining fertility and rising, 171
Linear budget constraint, 117
Logarithm
   of GDP per capita, 29*f*, 88, 88*f*
Logarithmic utility function, 141–143, 147
Long-run economic growth, 24–27, 69–70, 78, 82
   elaborated models of, 131
Low-skilled workers, 33–34, 61, 101–102, 108, 152–153, 191–192
   wage rates for, 156

M

Machine intelligence, 216
Machine-learning algorithm, 47
Machine production argument, 59
Macroeconomic effects of automation, 63
Macroeconomic framework, for automation, 101
   aggregate production function, 70–75
   discrete and continuous time, growth rates in, 67–69
   representative individuals and representative firms, 69–70
   Solow model. *See* Solow model
   tradeoff between growth and inequality, 104–107
   traditional physical capital, share of investment in, 98–101
   wage inequality, 101–104
Macroeconomic models, 27–28, 72
Malthusian force, 26–27
Manufacturing sector, 58–59
Mean probability of automation, 51, 55*t*
   by industry, 57*t*, 58*t*
   by occupation, 55*t*
Medical robots, 174–175
Migration, 163–164, 166–168
Military robots, 10, 215–216
Minimum wage, 50
Misery, 210–212
Mixed market economy, 80–81
Modeling economic growth, 68

Modern dynamic macroeconomics, 113–114
Monetary policy, 201–202

N

Nascent capitalism, 80–81
Negative effects of automation, 188–190
Neoclassical growth model, 114–115, 193
Neoclassical production function, 70–74
Net disposable incomes, 37
Nine-dot problem, 216
No-Ponzi game condition, 136–137
North American Free Trade Agreement
(NAFTA), 173

O

Objective function, 115
Occupations, 47–51, 52t, 54t
mean probability of automation by, 51, 55t
OECD. *See* Organization for Economic Co-
operation and Development (OECD)
Older adults, 7–8
OLG models. *See* Overlapping generations
(OLG) models
*On the Principles of Political Economy and
Taxation* (Ricardo), 2
Operative industrial robots, worldwide stock
of, 22f
Opportunity costs, 176–177
Organization for Economic Co-operation and
Development (OECD), 48–50, 49t,
163–164
Overlapping generations (OLG) models,
69–70, 113–114, 124–126, 131, 193
automation in, 147–150
endogenous savings in, 140–147

P

Partial derivatives of function, 115
Particular solutions of differential equations,
82–83
Per-capita gross domestic product (GDP),
29–30, 67, 72, 168–169
logarithm of, 88, 88f
Phase diagram, 107–108, 130–131, 133f,
136f
Physical capital, 155, 194
Pigovian tax, 196–197
Polarization, 211
Policy challenges, 187–188
age of automation
social security in, 197–201
taxation in, 192–197

demand-side policies, 201–202
education as strategy to cope with the
negative effects of automation,
188–190, 204t
labor market policies, 190–192
Policymakers, 187
Polluting activities, 196–197
Population aging, 21–22, 166, 174
Present-value Hamiltonian, 127–129
Production function, 92–93
aggregate, 70–75
Cobb–Douglas, 72–74, 78–80, 83–84,
92, 132, 146, 172–173
neoclassical, 70–74
Production possibility frontier, 70–71
Progressive consumption tax, 194–195, 203
Proposition 13, 196
Public transport systems, 213
Pumped-storage power plants,
200–201

R

Race against the machine, 11–13
Ramsey–Cass–Koopmans model, 113–114,
126–131, 137–138, 143
automation in, 138–140
endogenous savings in, 131–138
phase diagram in, 133f, 136f
Solow model and, 146–147
Rawlsian social welfare function, 106–109
R&D-based growth model, 151–152,
193–194
Replacement rate of TFR, 163–164
Representative firms, 69–70
Representative individuals, 69–70
Research-and-development-based growth
models, 93–95
Retirement funds, and social security systems,
170–171
Retraining programs, 189–190
Risk of automation, 48–50
Robot(s), 6
and capital taxes, 12
demographic changes affect,
176–177
largest markets for, 25t
production, 175–176
Robot density, 47, 53–58, 173, 174f
Robot-enhanced therapy, 10
Robot tax, 193–194
Routine-replacing technical change,
59–60

S

Saddle path, 136–138
Science, technology, engineering, and
    mathematics (STEM), 11
Search-and-matching process, 191–192
    of labor market, 153–154
Secondary education, 189
Second-order conditions (SOCs), 126–127
Self-regulating management practices, 8–9
Sex robots, 9–10, 176–177, 215
Simple economic growth model, 60–61
Singularity, 13, 216
Sin taxes, 197
Skill-biased technological change, 40
Skyrocketing economic growth, 22–24
Social and economic changes, spatial and
    regional implications, 212–214
Social challenges of automation, 11
Social credit system, 215
Social dividend, 200
Social impact of automation, 7–11
Social security systems, 2, 12, 37, 152–153,
    187
    in age of automation, 197–201
    reforming, 198–199
    retirement funds and, 170–171
Social welfare function, 29–30, 104–106,
    198–199
Society's inequality aversion, 188
SOCs. *See* Second-order conditions (SOCs)
Solow model, 75, 137–138, 145
    augmented by human capital, 82
    with automation, 75, 90–97, 108
    in continuous time with technological
        progress and with population growth,
        82–90
    in discrete time, 75–83, 79*f*
Solution path, 135
Spatial and regional implications, 212–214
Standard chess programs, 12–13
Standard Solow model, 96–97
State-costate space, 129–130
State variable, 126–127
Static optimization
    method of Karush–Kuhn–Tucker,
        123–124
    method of Lagrange, 115–122
Steady-state capital stock, 80–81, 83, 86–90
Steady-state equilibrium, 78, 133–134
STEM. *See* Science, technology, engineering,
    and mathematics (STEM)
Storage media, 6

Strictly concave Lagrangian function,
    119*f*
Strictly concave utility function, 116, 116*f*

T

Tax and transfer system, 35–37
Taxation, in age of automation, 192–197
Taxing corporations, 197
Tax reform, 188
Tax system, 196
Technological changes, 6
Technological progress, 1–5, 48
    capital augmenting, 72
    on long-run economic growth, 69–70
    and with population growth, Solow model
        in continuous time, 82–90
    positive effects of, 1–2
    post-Industrial Revolution, 27
Technological unemployment, 2–3, 31,
    152–154
Tertiary education, 189
TFR. *See* Total fertility rate (TFR)
Three-dimensional (3D) printers technology,
    5–6, 155
Tiger economies, 169
Time-dependent variable, 67–68
Total fertility rate (TFR), 163–164
    and life expectancy at birth, 165*t*
    per woman, 163*f*
Traditional physical capital, 90–96, 138–139,
    148, 172–173, 193
Traditional social security system, 12,
    198–199
Transcranial direct current stimulation,
    216
Translation programs, 9
Transport mode, 213
Transversality condition, 136–137
Two-dimensional system, of differential
    equations, 133
Two-period optimization problem, 124–126

U

Unconditional basic income, 12
Unemployment, 68
    dynamics of labor force and, 30–34
    technological, 152–154
Unemployment insurance system, 197–198
Unified Growth Theory, 26–27
Universal basic income, 198–199
Urbanization process, 8–9, 212–214
Utility functions, 116–117, 116*f*, 122, 141

V

Value-added tax (VAT), 194
Variable, 67
    derivative of, 67
    growth rate of, 69
VAT. *See* Value-added tax (VAT)
Vivaldi, 6
Voice recognition software, 9

W

Wage bargaining process, 50

Wage inequality, automation and, 101−104
Wages, 2, 32, 41, 176−177
    of high-skilled workers, 102−103
    income, 193
    of low-skilled workers, 102−103, 156
Wealth inequality, 37−38, 37*f*, 38*f*
Wealth tax, 192, 194, 203
Welfare indicator, 29−30
Working-age population, 167−168
    vs. non-working-age population, 166

Printed in the United States
By Bookmasters